LEGAL NEGOTIATION AND SETTLEMENT

By

GERALD R. WILLIAMS

Associate Dean and Professor of Law
J. Reuben Clark Law School
Brigham Young University

ST. PAUL, MINN.
WEST PUBLISHING CO.
1983

COPYRIGHT © 1983 By WEST PUBLISHING CO.
50 West Kellogg Boulevard
P.O. Box 3526
St. Paul, Minnesota 55165

Library of Congress Cataloging in Publication Data

Williams, Gerald R.
    Legal negotiation and settlement.

    Bibliography: p.
    1. Compromise (Law)—United States. 2. Negotiation.
I. Title.
KF9084.W544   1983   347.73'77   82–19975
ISBN 0–314–68093–4   347.30777

        Williams Leg.Neg.and Settlement

        3rd Reprint—1987

DEDICATION

To my wife Claudia, and our children Colette, Jennifer,
Nicole, Michael, and Daniel

*

PREFACE

This book is written primarily for law students who are learning negotiating skills in clinical courses (live or simulated), but it will serve equally well for lawyers and others who are interested in the topic of negotiation. The materials are based upon empirical studies of the negotiating practices of lawyers, and they discuss negotiation in the context of lawyers' work. However, the principles of negotiation are equally valid for other settings, including business, labor, and government.

As recently as ten years ago, the concept of negotiation was not in vogue; it was interesting to a handful of scholars, but the scholarly literature was quite manageable. Lawyers negotiated as much then as now, but the topic was neglected by the profession and, with a few exceptions, by law teachers. Its importance for attorneys was recognized by a few whose names are now familiar: James J. White, Andrew Watson, Cornelius Peck, and Robert Mathews, who were teaching negotiation in law school seminars and were actively encouraging others to study and teach it. Harry T. Edwards and James J. White performed a major service with the publication of *The Lawyer as a Negotiator; Problems, Readings, and Materials* (West 1977), which presents some of the better literature on negotiation from several scholarly disciplines in a format usable to the legal practitioner, teacher, and student.

Within the past decade, however, there has been such a mushrooming of interest that we are faced with an embarrassment of popular literature on the topic. The current popular interest in negotiation is nourished by a sizable increase in scholarly attention to the topic, particularly among economic and behavioral scientists. In the space of ten or fifteen years, the published literature has grown to impressive proportions.

Lawyers face several difficulties in applying this literature. One problem is sheer numbers. The volume of scholarly literature is challenging even to keep up with. A recent book reviewing experimental studies of negotiation by social psychologists (representing a rather small subdivision of literature on bargaining) analyzed over five hundred studies published in some 40 scholarly journals over the preceding 14 years. Lawyers face a second problem in assessing the reliability of the studies and their relevance to the lawyering task. Most social psychological studies of bargaining are based upon experiments using college students to "negotiate" solutions in highly structured, narrowly limited simulation games. Lawyers must naturally be concerned about applying conclusions from these studies to bargaining between professionals in the legal system.

Perhaps the greatest challenge presented by the current scholarly output on negotiation is the number of schools from which the studies derive. Experimenters and theoreticians in economics, political science, international relations, communications, sociology, psychology, and business management have contributed to the evolution of many different schools of thought regarding the study and practice of negotiation.

Each school has its own methods, assumptions, theories, and attitudes about negotiation, which means that the interested researcher or practitioner must spend most of his time reading literature from outside his own discipline. A few scholars, most notably Oran R. Young and I. William Zartman, have compiled cross-disciplinary sets of readings and commentary representing the major fields of the available literature. They have made this literature more accessible to others. But even with their assistance, the intellectual challenge is intimidating and likely to become more so over time, if only because there are more schools of thought with contributions to make than has been supposed. For example, current knowledge embodied in such domains as decision theory, conflict theory, behavior exchange theory, learning theory, argumentation and persuasion theory, nonverbal communication research, and kinesics research has not yet been adequately appreciated for its potential contribution to an understanding of negotiation. It is not merely the timid who shy away from embracing the whole of them as sources for work on negotiation. Yet such a multidisciplinary approach does hold tremendous promise.

While we look forward to future developments in bargaining theory and in our knowledge of dispute processing generally, lawyers face the immediate problem of performing competently as negotiators in the legal system. This book is addressed to this very practical problem.

The methods and theories of traditional legal research do not lend themselves to a study of the negotiating behavior of lawyers;

the methods and theoretical approaches of the behavioral sciences must be called upon. Behavioral studies of the legal profession require a joint effort between legal researchers and behavioral scientists. The field research reported in the first part of this volume is the result of such a joint effort. The behavioral expertise was provided by Larry C. Farmer and J. Lynn England of Brigham Young University and Murray Blumenthal of the University of Denver, who collaborated with me in the research project from which these findings are taken. With them I wish to thank the National Science Foundation for financial support of this research.

After our data collection was completed and I started using portions of the findings in a legal negotiation course, it became apparent that law students are unable to visualize the kinds of negotiating behavior being described. Because law students have done little or no work among professional negotiators, they cannot visualize the processes and dynamics described by the data. I am indebted to Roger Croft, then of BYU's David O. McKay Institute, for providing the encouragement and impetus for capturing on videotape some very intense and authentic negotiations between experienced lawyers. He made the technical arrangements for professionally videotaping the spontaneous negotiation of seven cases by 14 practicing lawyers from across the United States. I am indebted to the Brigham Young University Media Production Studio for producing the videotapes and to the Studio and J. Reuben Clark Law School at BYU for jointly providing the necessary funds. Special thanks are due the attorneys who so kindly and expertly undertook the task of preparing and negotiating these cases under the warm glare of the television lights. Their efforts have provided the crucial means by which the research findings can literally be brought to life.

The efforts of these 14 attorneys is representative of the quality and intensity of the assistance we received from several hundred attorneys in Denver and Grand Junction, Colorado, and Phoenix, Arizona over the two-and-a-half years of data collection, including approximately three hundred attorneys who provided detailed verbal reports of cases they were then handling. Officers of bar associations and ethics committees gave much valuable support and counsel, as did the members of our attorney advisory committee in Denver. To all of these men and women we extend our warmest thanks and our hope they will feel their efforts worthwhile.

PREFACE

A note about gender: there is no consensus today about how best to acknowledge the role and aspirations of women when literary conventions have established the use of *he* and *his* as universal or generic referents. For some women and men, this usage is objectionable as imposing masculine assumptions on the reader. Earlier drafts of this work employed "he or she" and "his or her" in place of the generic term. It became a question of judgment how often to use the gendered forms and how often the generic. I have ended in the belief that the exercise only drew attention to itself, and that the generic use of he and his should be maintained throughout. I hope this will not prove offensive to any reader.

GERALD R. WILLIAMS

Provo, Utah
November 1982

ACKNOWLEDGEMENTS

I wish to acknowledge some very substantial debts to people whose work and influence are reflected in this volume. Robert Mathews, Cornelius Peck, James J. White, Harry T. Edwards, and Andrew Watson have long been teaching and encouraging others to teach negotiation in law schools. Their writings and speeches have provided crucial encouragement to many; in particular their influence moved me to join with three social scientists and to undertake the empirical study of legal negotiation that provides the core of this book.

One reason the actual practice of negotiation by lawyers has been neglected by legal researchers is that it is behavioral. It cannot be studied through traditional methods of legal research, but requires the methods, experience, and interest of social scientists. I was privileged to undertake such research as a joint project with three exceptional people: Larry C. Farmer, a clinical psychologist and Professor of Law at Brigham Young University; J. Lynn England, Professor of Sociology at Brigham Young University; and Murray Blumenthal, a psychologist and Professor of Law at the University of Denver. With them I wish to thank the National Science Foundation for financial support of major portions of our research.

With them I also wish to thank the hundreds of attorneys in Denver, Colorado and Phoenix, Arizona who contributed from one to six hours each responding to taped interviews, filling in questionnaires, and providing detailed tape-recorded reports of cases they were then handling. We also thank the officers of bar associations, members of lawyers' ethics committees, and members of our lawyers' advisory committee, all of whom gave valuable support and counsel.

I am indebted to Roger Croft, formerly of BYU's David O. McKay Institute, for assistance with instructional design; to law students Wilford Anderson, Jon Anderson, Janeen Jacobs, Rick Winder (now all practicing attorneys), Roy Johnson, Samuel Fuller and David Olsen for research and editorial assistance; and to successive generations of law students who have taken seminars and courses based on portions of these materials. As many of them will readily see, this current work would not have been possible without their substantial patience and interest.

ix

ACKNOWLEDGEMENTS

The descriptions and interpretations of legal negotiation presented here developed over several years. Often it was in response to the stimulus of presentations to groups of practicing attorneys in numerous locations around the country. I wish to thank all those whose questions and observations have contributed to this process. Significant portions of these materials were first introduced in various continuing legal education publications, all of them under my own copyright. The most important of these are *The Lawyer's Guide to Effective Legal Negotiation* (draft, reproduced by photocopying for use in continuing legal education seminars, 1980), and *A Lawyer's Handbook for Effective Negotiation and Settlement* (National Practice Institute, 1981).

SUMMARY OF CONTENTS

Page

PREFACE -- v

ACKNOWLEDGEMENTS ------------------------------------- ix

CHAPTER ONE. INTRODUCTION TO LEGAL NEGO-
TIATION --------------------------------- 1
   I. Overview -- 1
  II. Lawyer Competency: Are Lawyers Adequately
     Trained in Negotiation Skills? ----------------- 5
 III. Effectiveness in Legal Negotiation --------------- 7
 IV. What Cases Should Be Settled and What Cases
     Should Go to Trial? ----------------------------- 10
   Chapter Notes --- 13

CHAPTER TWO. THE NEGOTIATING PATTERNS OF
PRACTICING LAWYERS ------------ 15
   I. Introduction --------------------------------------- 15
  II. Description of the Legal Negotiation Research
     Project --- 15
 III. How Lawyers Negotiate: Lessons from Attorneys 18
 IV. Which Approach Is More Effective: Cooperative or
     Competitive? ------------------------------------- 41
  V. Which Type of Negotiator Are You? ------------- 41
   Chapter Notes --- 45

CHAPTER THREE. THE DYNAMICS OF COOPERATIVE
AND COMPETITIVE NEGOTIATING 47
   I. Introduction --------------------------------------- 47
  II. The Competitive Strategy ---------------------- 48
 III. The Cooperative Strategy ---------------------- 53
 IV. Further Applications of Bargaining Literature to
     Legal Negotiation ------------------------------- 54
  V. Client Relations and Negotiation --------------- 59
 VI. Conflicts Between Attorney and Client ---------- 62
   Chapter Notes --- 65

CHAPTER FOUR. STAGES OF THE NEGOTIATION
PROCESS ---------------------------- 70
   I. Introduction --------------------------------------- 70
  II. Discussion of the Stages ---------------------- 72

CHAPTER FOUR. STAGES OF THE NEGOTIATION
PROCESS—Continued   **Page**

  III. The Interplay Between Legal Proceedings and the
Negotiation Process ------------------------------ 85

  IV. Pre-Bargaining Dynamics ---------------------- 87

Chapter Note ------------------------------------- 90

CHAPTER FIVE. THE LAW OF NEGOTIATION AND
SETTLEMENT ------------------- 90

  I. Introduction: Is There a Law of Negotiation and
Settlement ----------------------------------- 90

  II. The General Policy of the Law Toward Compromise
and Settlement ------------------------------- 90

  III. Contract Law as a Source of Negotiation Law ---- 91

  IV. Formation, Interpretation and Enforcement of Settlement Agreements -------------------------- 95

  V. Defects in Compromise and Settlement Agreements 102

  VI. Special Rules Applicable to Insurers ------------ 105

  VII. Rules of Evidence ---------------------------- 106

CHAPTER SIX. THE ECONOMICS OF LITIGATION AND
SETTLEMENT --------------- 110

  I. Introduction --------------------------------- 110

  II. Economic Analysis of Cases: The Missing Lawyer
Skill --- 110

  III. Methods for Economic Evaluation of Cases ------- 115

  IV. An Objective Economic Method for Case Evaluation 119

Chapter Notes ------------------------------------ 133

Appendices

App.

  I. Research Methodology: The BYU Legal Negotiation
Project ------------------------------------- 137

  II. Tables -- 141

  III. Transcript of the Personal Injury Negotiation -------- 149

  IV. Transcript of the Divorce Negotiation --------------- 169

Bibliography -- 193

TABLE OF CONTENTS

Page

PREFACE --- v

ACKNOWLEDGEMENTS -------------------------------- ix

CHAPTER ONE. INTRODUCTION TO LEGAL NEGOTIATION

I. Overview --- 1
    A. Transactions ---------------------------------- 2
    B. Civil Disputes -------------------------------- 3
    C. Labor/Management Negotiations --------------- 3
    D. Criminal Cases ------------------------------- 4

II. Lawyer Competency: Are Lawyers Adequately Trained
     in Negotiation Skills? --------------------------- 5

III. Effectiveness in Legal Negotiation ----------------- 7

IV. What Cases Should Be Settled and What Cases Should
     Go to Trial? ------------------------------------- 10
Chapter Notes -------------------------------------- 13

CHAPTER TWO. THE NEGOTIATING PATTERNS OF
PRACTICING LAWYERS

I. Introduction ------------------------------------- 15

II. Description of the Legal Negotiation Research Project 15

III. How Lawyers Negotiate: Lessons from Attorneys ----- 18
     A. Characteristics of Effective Negotiators --------- 20
         1. Effective/Cooperative Negotiators ----------- 20
         2. Effective/Competitive Negotiators ---------- 23
         3. Similarities Between the Two Effective Types 25
     B. Characteristics of Average Negotiators ---------- 30
         1. Average/Cooperative Negotiators ----------- 30
         2. Average Competitive Negotiators ----------- 32
         3. Similarities Between the Two Average Types 33
     C. Characteristics of Ineffective Negotiators -------- 33
         1. Ineffective/Cooperative Negotiators --------- 34
         2. Ineffective/Competitive Negotiators --------- 37

IV. Which Approach Is More Effective: Cooperative or
     Competitive? ------------------------------------ 41

V. Which Type of Negotiator Are You? ----------------- 41
Chapter Notes -------------------------------------- 45

TABLE OF CONTENTS

CHAPTER THREE. THE DYNAMICS OF COOPERATIVE
AND COMPETITIVE NEGOTIATING

Page

I.   Introduction _____ 47

II. The Competitive Strategy _____ 48

III. The Cooperative Strategy _____ 53

IV. Further Applications of Bargaining Literature to Legal
     Negotiation _____ 54

V.   Client Relations and Negotiation _____ 59

VI. Conflicts Between Attorney and Client _____ 62

Chapter Notes _____ 65

CHAPTER FOUR. STAGES OF THE NEGOTIATION PROCESS

I.   Introduction _____ 70
     A.   Stage One: Orientation and Positioning _____ 70
     B.   Stage Two: Argumentation _____ 71
     C.   Stage Three: Emergence and Crisis _____ 71
     D.   Stage Four: Agreement or Final Breakdown _____ 72

II. Discussion of the Stages _____ 72
     A.   Stage One: Orientation and Positioning _____ 72
          1.   Orientation _____ 72
          2.   Positioning _____ 73
          3.   Inalterable Commitment to an Opening Position 77
          4.   Duration of Stage One _____ 78
     B.   Stage Two: Argumentation _____ 79
          1.   Overview _____ 79
          2.   The Problem of Making Concessions _____ 80
     C.   Stage Three: Emergence and Crisis _____ 81
          1.   Effect of a Deadline _____ 81
          2.   The Client, the Opposing Party, and the Nego-
               tiation Process _____ 82
     D.   Stage Four: Agreement or Final Breakdown _____ 84
          1.   Agreement _____ 84
          2.   Final Breakdown _____ 84

III. The Interplay Between Legal Proceedings and the Nego-
     tiation Process _____ 85

IV. Pre-Bargaining Dynamics _____ 87

Chapter Note _____ 90

CHAPTER FIVE. THE LAW OF NEGOTIATION AND SETTLEMENT

Page

I. Introduction: Is There a Law of Negotiation and Settlement 90
II. The General Policy of the Law Toward Compromise and Settlement 90
III. Contract Law as a Source of Negotiation Law 91
    A. The Notion of Good Faith in Bargaining 91
    B. The Use of Threats in Bargaining 92
IV. Formation, Interpretation and Enforcement of Settlement Agreements 95
    A. Offer and Acceptance 95
    B. Consideration 95
    C. Writings and Formalities 96
    D. Interpretation of the Agreement 97
    E. Conflict of Laws—Governing Law 99
    F. Federal Rules of Civil Procedure: Rule 68 Offers of Compromise 99
    G. Court Supervision and Approval of Settlements ... 101
    H. Effect of Negotiations on Statutes of Limitations . 102
V. Defects in Compromise and Settlement Agreements ... 102
    A. Introduction 102
    B. Fraud, Misrepresentation, and Mistake 102
    C. Mary Carter Agreements 103
VI. Special Rules Applicable to Insurers 105
VII. Rules of Evidence 106

CHAPTER SIX. THE ECONOMICS OF LITIGATION AND SETTLEMENT

I. Introduction 110
II. Economic Analysis of Cases: The Missing Lawyer Skill 110
III. Methods for Economic Evaluation of Cases 115
    A. Combined Formula Components 117
IV. An Objective Economic Method for Case Evaluation ... 119
    A. Introduction 119
    B. Time Value of Money 120
    C. The Appropriate Rate of Interest for Time-Value Calculation Use 127
    D. The Tax Aspects of Settlement 128
Chapter Notes 133

TABLE OF CONTENTS

Appendices

App.   Page

I. Research Methodology: The BYU Legal Negotiation
   Project --- 137
II. Tables -- 141
III. Transcript of the Personal Injury Negotiation --------- 149
IV. Transcript of the Divorce Negotiation --------------- 169

Bibliography -- 193

TABLE OF CASES

References are to Pages

Ace Heating & Plumbing Co. v. Crane Co., 101
August v. Delta Air Lines, Inc., 100

Balling v. Finch, 94
Booth v. Mary Carter Paint Co., 104

City of (see name of party)
City Street Improvement Co. v. Pearson, 95
Crisci v. Security Ins. Co., 105

Davies v. Canco Enterprises, 96
Dumont v. Dinallo, 107

Fidelity and Cas. Co. of New York v. Robb, 105

General Freight Transport Co. v. Riss & Co., 95
General Motors Corp. v. Lahocki, 103
Glicken v. Bradford, 101, 102
Gregg v. Weathersfield, 95

In re (see name of party)

Jamestown Farmers Elevator, Inc. v. General Mills, 94
Johnson v. Hardware Mutual Cas. Co., 105

Kricar, Inc. v. General Acc. Fire and Life Assur. Corp. Ltd., 105

Laemmar v. J. Walter Thompson Co., 94

Little Rock Packing Co. v. Massachusetts Bonding & Ins. Co., 95

Masterson v. Pergament, 101
Mayerson v. Washington Mfg. Co., 94
Middlesex Concrete Products & Excavating Corp. v. Carteret Indus. Ass'n, 91
Moore v. Gunning, 96
Morrow v. American Bank and Trust Co., 96

Peerless Weighing & Vending Machine Corp. v. International Ticket Scale Corp., 99
Percodani v. Riker-Maxson Corp., 101
Posey v. Lambert-Grisham Hardware Co., 95
Preine v. Freeman, 99
Protective Committee for Independent Stockholders v. Anderson, 101
Prudence Co., In re, 101

Stoddard v. Mix, 95

Thomas v. Hollowell, 90
Tucson, City of v. Gallagher, 104

Van Bronkhorst v. Safeco Corp., 90
Vernon Fire & Cas. Ins. Co. v. Sharp, 105

Wicker v. Board of Public Instruction of Dade County, 95

Young v. American Cas. Co. of Reading, Pennsylvania, 105

LEGAL NEGOTIATION AND SETTLEMENT

Chapter One

INTRODUCTION TO LEGAL NEGOTIATION

"The principal institution of the law in action is not trial; it is settlement out of court." [1]

I. OVERVIEW

Though we don't usually think of it in these terms, negotiating is a principal occupation of the lawyer. It is so much a part of the fabric of daily law practice that past generations did not identify it as a distinct skill or process. Today, this perception is changing. Judicial statistics inform us that only a small percentage of legal disputes are resolved by court trial. For example, of all cases filed in U. S. District Courts in 1980, only 6.5% reached trial; the remaining 93.5% were terminated without trial, in most cases by negotiated settlement agreement. Statistics are less precise for many state and local courts, but available figures indicate that for most jurisdictions, less than 10% of all cases filed with the courts are resolved by a trial verdict.[2]

To say that most cases are settled does not imply that trial is unimportant; trial provides the leverage or threat that pushes opposing parties into settlement discussions and agreements.

1. H. Laurence Ross, *Settled Out of Court* (Aldine, 2d ed. 1980) at 3.

2. In federal district courts, the average percentage of cases reaching trial verdict is 6.5%. The average for districts varies from a low of 2.0% to a high of 16.1% in the U. S. and 23.8% in the Canal Zone. By Circuits, the differences are less extreme, ranging from a low of 4.0% in the District of Columbia Circuit to a high of 8.4% in the Eighth Circuit. 1980 Annual Report of the Director—Administrative Office of the U. S. Courts, Washington, D.C. (1980) at page A–28 and A–29. The percentage of cases going to trial in federal courts also varies significantly according to the subject-matter or jurisdictional posture of the case, ranging from a low of 0.2% for actions by the United States to recover overpayments and to enforce judgments to a high of 50% for domestic relations cases and 54% for insanity proceedings. *Id.* at A–26 and A–27. Figures for particular state and local court systems vary considerably more. Statistics are also available for certain kinds of legal practice, the most notable examples being personal injury claims and criminal law. A major study of personal injury/automobile insurance cases shows that, of claimants represented by attorneys who obtained some compensation, 72% filed suit, 6.5% started trial, and 2% reached a verdict. AUTOMOBILE PERSONAL INJURY CLAIMS (U.S. Department of Transportation, Automobile Insurance and Compensation Study, 1970), cited in H. Laurence Ross, *Settled Out of Court* (Aldine 1980 2d revised edition 1980) at 275.

Lawyers also use a prediction of probable trial outcome as a basis for assigning a dollar or other value to their cases. But as important as trial (and trial advocacy skills) may be in law practice, they are used in fewer than one case out of ten. The remaining nine cases depend more importantly upon the attorney's skill as a negotiator.

While settlement negotiations are an extremely important part of lawyering, negotiation is significant for lawyers in non-dispute settings as well. American lawyers spend a major portion of their time in another area including negotiation skills, which is in the formation and execution of contractual transactions and relationships. In his major study of negotiation, Professer Eisenberg characterizes transactional negotiations as similar to private legislation in which parties develop rules to govern future conduct between them. He calls this "rulemaking-negotiation." [3] This work frequently involves lawyers in discussions within a client corporation about matters of decision making, negotiation of various kinds of contractual undertakings with other parties, labor/management negotiations, and negotiation of agreements with representatives of various federal, state, and local governmental agencies.

Because negotiation settings vary so much, it is clear that general knowledge of negotiation skills must be supplemented by specialized knowledge of applicable law, customs, and practices. Negotiation settings can be roughly divided into four categories: transactions, civil disputes, criminal disputes, and labor/management negotiations. Each category has unique aspects and must be approached with these in mind.

A. TRANSACTIONS

As a general rule, transactions are exchanges voluntarily arrived at by the parties, whether for purchase of real property, sales of goods, buying or selling a business, or any other kind of contractual undertaking. Attorneys must remind themselves that contractual relations are normally based upon a voluntary decision by both parties to do business with one another, sometimes in exchanges of short duration (in which interpersonal relationships are not very important), and sometimes in coopera-

---

3. In his analysis, Eisenberg compares dispute resolution by negotiation to adjudication, and calls it dispute-negotiation. Eisenberg, "Private Ordering Through Negotiation: Dispute-Settlement and Rulemaking," 89 Harvard L. Rev. 637, 638 (1976).

tive ventures of substantial duration (in which there is considerable interdependence). Contractual relationships are expected to be mutually beneficial, and particularly the longer-range relationships are based on observance of customs and practices in the industry involved which help to prevent the kinds of manipulation and distrust that might undermine good faith performance of the agreement.

Lawyers trained in the socratic classroom tend to see contract negotiations as adversarial, and they go to them prepared for a fairly high level of tension. The adversarial approach is such a breach of etiquette in most transactional settings that lawyers are often seen as rude, nitpicking, and counterproductive. Obviously, lawyers face a dilemma in knowing how far to go in "protecting" a client in an unfamiliar business context.

Transactions have many features in common, but they occur in virtually all of life's important settings, from sales of property between family members to commercial transactions to joint venture agreements between large corporations. A lawyer's effectiveness in each of these negotiating settings is enhanced in proportion to his understanding of the business facts associated with each type of transaction involved.

B. CIVIL DISPUTES

These are distinguishable from transactions on several important grounds. In civil disputes, one party or the other has (or believes he has) legal rights against the other that are enforceable in court. If the parties cannot resolve the dispute, the complaining party can compel the reluctant party to defend against the charge. At this point, the defending side cannot walk away and find someone more pleasant to dispute with. Since the two sides are forced to deal with one another, one or both can get away with much higher levels of aggressiveness and unreasonableness than would be tolerated in transactional settings.

C. LABOR/MANAGEMENT NEGOTIATIONS

These are hybrids: they have characteristics of transactions and of civil disputes. They resemble transactions because they look to contractual agreements, they involve on-going relationships, and there is often no wrong for which there is a judicially cognizable remedy (at least not without exhaustion of administrative procedures mandated by labor laws). On the other hand, labor/management negotiations resemble civil disputes in the sense that the parties have a legal duty to bargain.

The mandatory duty to bargain locks both sides into their seats at the bargaining table and requires them to talk in good faith. The adversarial aspects of the relationship give rise to elaborate and sophisticated bargaining strategies that may begin with psychological warfare long before talks begin and extend clear through until the last issue is resolved.

D. CRIMINAL CASES

While criminal law often involves economic interests (theft, embezzlement, criminal destruction of property), it is primarily directed at the protection of society from criminal acts and the concurrent protection of accused persons from unjustified or overzealous prosecution or punishment.

Plea bargaining is a direct and explicit form of negotiation which has been singled out for attention on several counts. Approximately the same percentage of criminal cases settle as civil, but in the criminal context a person's life or liberty are at stake. Plea bargaining by-passes many, if not all, of the formal constitutional protections built into the criminal justice system, and its pervasive use raises practical as well as philosophical concerns. For example, it is generally accepted that criminal court dockets are dependent on having 80% or more of the cases disposed of by plea bargain and that trial courts would be overwhelmed and paralyzed if all criminal defendants insisted upon a constitutionally guaranteed speedy trial in lieu of a bargained plea.

Most of what we learn about negotiation in civil contexts applies equally well to the criminal setting. However, criminal cases raise issues of justice, fairness, constitutional law, and public policy that are beyond the scope of this book.[4]

4. For an introduction to the extensive literature on plea bargaining, see the Special Issue on Plea Bargaining, 13 *Law and Society Review* Number 2, pp. 199–687 (1979), which includes articles reviewing historical patterns of plea bargaining, comparing practice in the U.S. to practices elsewhere, describing results of empirical research on plea bargaining, examining philosophical implications, and reviewing current literature on plea bargaining. For a lawyers' reference manual covering existing substantive and procedural law governing plea bargaining, see James E. Bond *Plea Bargaining and Guilty Pleas* (New York: Clark Boardman Co. 1978) (with regular supplements). For a more anecdotal description of plea bargaining that conveys the flavor of the courthouse, see Arthur Rosett and Donald R. Cressey, *Justice by Consent: Plea Bargaining in the American Courthouse* (Philadelphia: J.B. Lippincott Co. 1976).

Despite their differences, these four contexts have one crucial element in common: they all involve the skill of negotiation. Most of the information and principles in this and the remaining chapters apply equally well to all four settings. However, negotiation of civil disputes offers the most fertile ground for the focus of this book, because it includes a broad range of permissible behavior but stops short of the human rights issues raised by criminal law and the group dynamics issues raised by labor negotiations. For this reason, unless otherwise noted, the discussions in this book assume a civil legal dispute.

II. LAWYER COMPETENCY: ARE LAWYERS ADEQUATELY TRAINED IN NEGOTIATION SKILLS?

There has been mounting concern within and without the legal profession about how lawyers perform skill-related functions such as negotiation. Chief Justice Burger has repeatedly warned that lawyers need better skills training; a task force of the ABA Section of Legal Education and Admissions to the Bar has recommended that law schools make training in negotiation and other skills available to all law students;[5] and bar examiners have begun to develop methods for testing legal skills such as negotiation in state bar exams.[6]

The reasons for this concern are not always apparent. Are lawyers deficient in their negotiating skills? If so, what problems does this cause and how can they be remedied? The most serious criticism of lawyer negotiating skills would be a finding that clients are receiving inadequate assistance of counsel as reflected in the dollar value of cases that settle. We can therefore pose the question: if a number of experienced lawyers were paired against each other and assigned to undertake settlement negotiations on identical cases, would the resulting settlements be substantially identical, or would there be considerable variation in the dollar value of the outcomes? This question is vitally

5. *Lawyer Competency: The Role of the Law Schools* (ABA Section of Legal Education and Admissions to the Bar 1979); see also Law Schools and Professional Education (Report and Recommendations of the Special Committee for a Study of Legal Education of the American Bar Association, 1980).

6. Scott Slonim, *"Bar Exam Experiment Could Blaze New Path,"* 66 ABA J. 139 (1980), referring to experimental skills testing as part of the California bar exam and to a statement by Arthur Karger, chairman of the New York State Board of Law Examiners that "[t]esting for so-called clinical skills is very important".

important. If results are about the same, we might conclude lawyers are already doing an adequate job at negotiation and there is little justification for concern about lawyer competency.

To test the question of lawyer negotiating outcomes, I obtained the cooperation of 40 practicing lawyers in Des Moines, Iowa, who agreed to be divided into 20 pairs and to prepare and undertake settlement negotiations in a personal injury case. Approximately two weeks in advance of the negotiations, the attorneys were randomly assigned to represent either the plaintiff or the defendant (as counsel for his insurance company). Attorneys assigned to represent the plaintiff were given identical case files, as were attorneys assigned to the defense. Under the facts it was assumed the case arose in Iowa, Iowa law applied, and if the case went to trial it would be tried to a jury in Des Moines, Iowa. To assure comparability of predicted jury awards, photocopies of comparable jury awards from the Des Moines area were included in the case files for both sides, participating lawyers were informed that results of the negotiations would be published, with attorney names attached, among the participants at the workship. This meant the attorneys had their professional reputations riding on their outcomes.

After two weeks preparation time, the attorneys came together and were given adequate time to reach a settlement. They were then asked to fill out a form giving their names, the opening offer or demand made by each side, and the final outcome (i.e. the dollar amount if a settlement figure was agreed to or, a notation of "impasse" if no agreement could be reached).

At the expiration of the time period, 14 of the 20 pairs were willing to submit their signed statement of results. The outcomes are shown in Table 1–1.

The results of this experiment were sobering to the participating attorneys. The outcomes ranged from a high of $95,000 to a low of $15,000; the average outcome was just over $47,000; and the remainder of the outcomes are scattered almost randomly between the two extremes. Whether or not these results are representative of the legal profession as a whole, they give cause for concern. It is apparent that there were dramatic differences not only in the perceptions these lawyers had about the "value" of the case, but in the persuasiveness or skill with which they pursued their objectives. The study raises questions about how well lawyers are able, under present methods, to serve their own clients and/or the public interest through negotiated settlements.

Table 1–1.

Results of Des Moines Negotiations

Attorney's Names	Plaintiff's Opening Demand	Defendant's Opening Demand	Settlement
1. [omitted here]	$ 32,000	$10,000	$18,000
2.	$ 50,000	$25,000	no settlement
3.	$675,000	$32,150	$95,000
4.	$110,000	$ 3,000	$25,120
5.	Not reported	Not reported	$15,000
6.	$100,000	$ 5,000	$25,000
7.	$475,000	$15,000	no settlement
8.	$180,000	$40,000	$80,000
9.	$210,000	$17,000	$57,000
10.	$350,000	$48,500	$61,000
11.	$ 87,500	$15,000	$30,000
12.	$175,000	$50,000	no settlement: narrowed to $137,000—$77,000
13.	$ 97,000	$10,000	$57,500
14.	$100,000		$56,875
		Average settlement	$47,318

III. EFFECTIVENESS IN LEGAL NEGOTIATION

What does it mean to be an effective negotiator? This question will be a major concern throughout the book. Is the effective negotiator the lawyer who obtained a $15,000 settlement on behalf of his client insurance company in the outcomes listed above? If so, what can be said of his opponent, who accepted on behalf of the injured plaintiff an amount $80,000 *below* the potential highest award and $32,000 below the *average* award? If the insurance company lawyer who obtained the $15,000 settlement is rated as an exceptionally skillful negotiator, what does that imply about the meaning of "effective"?

Or are the effective negotiators the attorneys who came closest to the average award in the experimental case? If they are the most effective negotiators, then what meaning is being given to the word "effective"? What criteria are being applied?

As the preceding questions illustrate, people have a wide variety of beliefs about what constitutes effectiveness in negotiation. Popular Psychology sections of bookstores suggest an interesting variety of definitions. Consider the following titles: Robert J. Ringer, *Winning Through Intimidation* (Fawcett Crest Paperback 1973, 1974); Michael Schatzki, *Negotiation: The Art of Getting What You Want* (Signet Paperback 1981); Herb Cohen, *You Can Negotiate Anything: How To Get What You Want* (Lyle Stuart, 1980); Mort Welsinger and Arthur Henley, *How To Be a Perfect Liar* (Pocket Books Paper 1971); John M. Striker and Andrew O. Shapiro, *Power Plays: How To Deal Like a Lawyer In Person-to-Person Confrontations and Get Your Rights* (Dell paperback 1979); and Tessa Albert Warschaw, *Winning By Negotiation: How To Get What You Want From Your Spouse, Lover, Parents, Children, Employer, Friends, Doctor, Lawyer, Landlord . . . and Make Them Love You in the Process* (Berkley Paperback 1980, 1981). Compare these titles with the following, which seem to have a somewhat different flavor: *Peacemaking: A Guide to Conflict Resolution for Individuals, Groups, and Nations* (Barbara Standford, ed. Bantam paperback 1976); I. William Zartman, *The 50% Solution: How to Bargain Successfully With Hijackers, Strikers, Bosses, Oil Magnates, Arabs, Russians, and Other Worthy Opponents in This Modern World*; (Anchor Press 1976); Roger Fisher and William Ury, *Getting to Yes: Negotiating Agreement Without Giving In* (Houghton Mifflin Co. 1981).

We have been examining negotiator effectiveness from a largely subjective point of view; attorneys and law students will naturally have their own opinions and values on this issue. But in arriving at an opinion, larger issues should be taken into account as well. For example, to what extent should a definition of negotiator effectiveness be reconcilable with one's view of justice and of the public interest? Clearly, any attempt to define "effectiveness" must consider the purposes and effects of the legal system as a whole and of lawyers working within that system. While individual attorneys may be justified in zealously pursuing the interests of their clients, even to the serious detriment of the opposing side, lawyers as members of the legal profession must adopt a wider perspective. The legitimate interests of each party, and of society at large, must be given full consideration.

[*8*]

Researchers studying negotiator effectiveness outside of the legal context have also wrestled with the problem of how to define it. Many researchers, for example, define negotiator effectiveness in terms of monetary units only. The effective negotiator is one who obtains the maximum amount of money from the other side. While not ignoring the relevance of a monetary measure of effectiveness, other researchers have argued that it fails to take account of other necessary considerations, such as the following:[7]

1. What were the costs (in time, money, and social psychological terms) of resolving the problem? How do these compare to other methods that might have been used to process the dispute?

2. Were all of the issues resolved, or were some of them reserved for future action?

3. Is the agreement stable, or will one party or the other soon become dissatisfied with it and seek to overturn or dishonor it?

4. Does the agreement minimize the damage and maximize the benefits to both parties, or does it embody unnecessary costs or damage to one or both parties? Is the agreement economically efficient and socially productive?

5. To what extent were applicable rules, customs, and etiquette observed? What types of tactics (threats, promises, etc.) were used? To what extent did tactics increase the costs to one or both parties? Would agreement have been possible through some other set of tactics?

6. Did the negotiators make efficient use of available resources (communication channels, cost reducing procedures, case management techniques, judicial resources)? Did they give proper consideration to alternative courses of action?

It should also be recognized that not all successful negotiations end in the settlement of a lawsuit or the signing of a business agreement. In business discussions, for example, talks may lead to the conclusion that neither party has what the other wants. If so, then the discussions have achieved their purpose. By the same token, in civil or criminal disputes, negotiation may

7. For further development of the question of negotiator effectiveness, see J. Rubin & B. Brown, *The Social Psychology of Bargaining and Negotiation* (Academic Press, 1975) at 33ff.

accomplish nothing more than clarifying the issues and preparing the case for a trial that both sides agree is necessary. Thus, the mark of a successful negotiation is not always a settlement or agreement; it may be nothing more than mutual recognition that trial (or some other approach, such as mediation or arbitration) is necessary.

IV. WHAT CASES SHOULD BE SETTLED AND WHAT CASES SHOULD GO TO TRIAL?

One of the major problems for lawyers is knowing which cases to settle and which cases to take to trial. As a national average, approximately 90% of cases settle. Using this norm as a guide, approximately 9 out of 10 of each attorney's cases are settled.

For strategic reasons, lawyers frequently pretend they have no interest in settling a case, thus implying to their opponent that they have absolute confidence they will prevail at trial. The opposing attorney, not wanting to appear weak in the face of this tactic, also adopts the position that he will take the case to trial, where he is certain of victory. Bluffing of this sort seriously distorts the real issues, because it precludes rational weighing of the decision whether to settle and puts an onus on the attorney who opens settlement negotiations. A later chapter will return to the strategic issues raised by bluffing. The objective in this chapter is to spell out considerations going to the question of whether to settle or try a case. Certainly bluffing is a weak reason for going to trial.

Advocates of settlement arrive at their positions from divergent points of view. Some dislike the adversarial combat of trial and see negotiated settlement as one of several superior alternatives. Others admit the importance of trial as a forum of last resort, but argue that relatively few cases require (or deserve) going to that extreme. The reasons advanced below on behalf of settlement do not belong to any one school of thought.

In general, settlement offers the following potential advantages:[8]

1. Avoids the delays associated with trial (whether the delay is occasioned by crowded court dockets or by delay of one or both parties);

---

8. In light of these asserted advantages, courts generally have adopted policies favoring the negotiated settlement of disputes, and as a matter of

2. Avoids the economic costs of trial (attorneys fees in preparation for and conduct of the trial, court fees, additional discovery, expert witnesses, time lost by parties and non-expert witnesses in preparing for and attending trial, etc.);

3. Avoids social and psychological costs of trial (embarrassment to parties, further damage to the relationship between the parties, anxiety and stress over the spectacle of a public trial);

4. Avoids the uncertainty or unpredictability of trial outcomes;

5. Avoids the "winner-take-all" nature of most legal remedies, providing an opportunity to fashion a package in the best interests of both parties;

6. Reduces the pressure on trial courts, allowing more considerate treatment of cases that require pretrial and, if necessary, trial procedures;

7. Increases the number of cases attorneys can process;

8. Protects one or both sides from the risk of unfavorable interpretations of law and prejudicial admissions or findings of fact.

When deciding whether to attempt settlement of a case, these factors should be explicitly reviewed with the client, so that the potential advantages of settlement can be explored and a sound decision made.

However, there are situations in which the presumption is against settlement. Certainly a case should be taken to trial when it is the client's interest to do so and there are no compelling reasons not to. The difficulty is knowing when it is in the client's best interest. For example, attorneys have personal in-

policy will decide contested issues in support of appropriate settlement agreements. However, it is not uncommon for courts and commentators to find countervailing considerations as well. Blumberg, in "The Practice of Law as Confidence Game: Organizational Cooptation of a Profession," 1 Law and Society Rev. 15 (1967), argues that criminal defense lawyers become so caught up in the courthouse culture that their primary loyalties are to courthouse personnel rather than to their clients. Adopting a different perspective, Stephan Landsman, in "The Decline of the Adversary System: How the Rhetoric of Swift and Certain Justice has Affected Adjudication in American Courts," 29 Buffalo L. Rev. 487–530 (1980) worries that we are ignoring the inherent values of adversarial trial proceedings and are unwittingly undermining those values in our preoccupation with efficiency and settlement.

terests at stake too, particularly if they have a low volume of work and are dependent upon a small number of clients for their income. The temptation to pursue a case to trial for its fee creates a strong (if subtle) incentive to prolong the case. To continue a case (consciously or subconsciously) for the fees it generates is clearly improper.

In general, there is a presumption in favor of trying the case under the following circumstances:

1. Where the suit against your client is a frivolous or pure nuisance suit, brought only for its nuisance value;

2. Where your client is seeking new developments or clarifications in the law and prefers the potential gain of trial and appeal to whatever settlement might be negotiated;

3. Where your client feels very vindictive and the vindictiveness cannot be satisfied without letting the client have his "day in court";

4. Where the issue of liability or damages is so uncertain or difficult to evaluate that you want to shift the burden of evaluation to a judge or jury;

5. Where the opposing attorney is insufferably obnoxious and abusive, making meaningful dialogue impossible;

6. Where the other side is unwilling to compromise to an acceptable solution;

Items 3 through 6 involve factors the attorney has some power to control. For example, a vindictive client might receive more benefit from several hours of attorney time spent in counseling them than from one hundred hours invested in trial. In later chapters, we will devote considerable attention to these problems and suggest methods for dealing with them within the framework of a negotiated solution.

CHAPTER NOTES

1. *Alternatives to Settlement and Trial*

Discussion of negotiation and litigation as modes of dispute settlement is not meant to imply that all disputes cognizable in the legal system are resolved by these methods. Considering the numberless offenses to person and property that occur daily, only a tiny sampling actually develop into legal disputes. The process by which a comparatively few of these ripen into full-scale legal disputes is explored in Felstiner, Abel & Sarat, "The Emergence & Transformation of Disputes: Naming, Blaming, Claiming . . ." 15 Law & Society Rev. 531 (1980–81). Of those offenses that do occur, most are ignored; the injured or offended party absorbs the loss, or the offender volunteers some compensatory assistance. If the offended party seeks some redress, it may come in many forms, from a simple request for an apology to some act of retribution. Methods most frequently cited include self-help, avoidance, mediation, voting, arbitration, and various types of non-governmental courts (religious courts, neighborhood courts, private organizations). *See* Alvin Goldman, *Processes for Conflict Resolution: Self-Help, Voting, Negotiation, and Arbitration* (BNA Labor Relations and Social Problems Series, 1972); William F. L. Felstiner, "Influences of Social Organization on Dispute Processing" 9 Law & Society Rev. 63 (1974) and "Avoidance as Dispute Processing: An Elaboration", 9 Law and Society Rev. 695 (1975). It is not only the offended who are troubled by these daily kinds of problems; many people who commit offenses to persons or property feel a moral obligation to correct the wrong. This aspect of dispute resolution is explored by Stewart Macaulay and Elaine Walster in "Legal Structures and Restoring Equity", *in* June Lovin Tapp and Felice J. Levine, ed. *Law, Justice and The Individual in Society* (Holt, Rinehart and Winston: New York 1977).

2. Costs of Litigation and Problems of Court Congestion and Delay

An insightful essay on the costs of litigation is in Lawrence M. Friedman, "Legal Rules and the Process of Social Change", 19 Stanford L.Rev. 786, 799–802. There is a substantial literature treating the problems of court congestion and methods of solving it. A classic work is Hans Zeisel, Harry Kalven, Jr. and Bernard Buchholz, *Delay in The Courts* (Little, Brown & Co., 1959); for the subject of personal injury litigation, see Rosenberg and Sovern, "Delay and the Dynamics of Personal Injury Litigation," 59 Columbia L.Rev. 1115 (1959) and the recent work by H. Lawrence Ross, *Settled Out Of Court* (Aldine, 2d ed. 1980). For the problem of delay and waiting generally, see Barzel, "A Theory of Rationing by Waiting," 17 Journal of Law and Economics 73 (1974).

Expenses of trial are not the only costs. The theory of trial is that one party is right and one is wrong. To obtain a favorable verdict, it isn't necessary for one party to be absolutely right; it is sufficient to be slightly right—to have a mere preponderance of the evidence in the party's favor. Preponderance means slightly more than a draw. But when one party or the other establishes its position by a preponderance of the evidence, then the verdict goes entirely for him. Of course, there are mitigating doctrines like contributory negligence, comparative negligence, and various contract doctrines that may limit remedies to less than full damages. But the theory of remedies is that the person receiving the favorable verdict deserves his remedy; it is a theory of granting a whole remedy, or nothing at all. The idea of an all-or-nothing verdict (even when mitigated by various legal rules and by discretion of judge or jury) ignores what we know of human nature: that rarely in human affairs is one person absolutely blameless and the other entirely at fault. An all-or-nothing verdict gives the more blameworthy party an opportunity to gamble. By going to trial, he may avoid entirely the consequences of his conduct, but at the risk of being held entirely accountable for the wrong. This reality has led some commentators to propose that the concept of equality would be better served in cases of uncertainty by a different approach, such as fifty-fifty apportionments of responsibility in cases where there is genuine doubt. See J. Coons, "Approaches to Court Imposed Compromise—The Uses of Doubt and Reason," 58 Nw. U.L.Rev. 750 (1964) and J. Coons, "Compromise as Precise Justice" in *Compromise in Ethics, Law, and Politics* (J. Roland Pennock and John W. Chapman, eds., New York Univ. 1979).

The intensity of emotion and ill-will generated by litigation is frequently overlooked, particularly as regards the opposing attorneys. The level to which feelings rise is suggested in a report by co-counsel to the plaintiff in the Century City experimental mini-trial. He observed that: "Once an interparty decision has been made to pursue a mini-trial, *the transition is not easy from the contentiousness of pretrial discovery to a cooperative posture.*" He refers to hostility between the attorneys of each side, and notes that even within the protective confines of the non-binding mini-trial, if expressions of adversity should exceed the critical limit, "the rapport for settlement will be destroyed and the slugfest of full-scale litigation will resume." Byard B. Nilsson, "A Litigation Settling Experiment," 65 ABA J. 1818 (1979) at 1819–1820 (italics added).

Chapter Two

THE NEGOTIATING PATTERNS OF PRACTICING LAWYERS

I. INTRODUCTION

In his examination of clinical education, one law professor refers to "the major unstudied variable in the justice of the legal system—*the patterned behavior of individual lawyers*".[9] This chapter reports the results of a large-scale study of the negotiating patterns of practicing attorneys. The objective throughout the chapter is therefore very practical: to describe how lawyers negotiate.

II. DESCRIPTION OF THE LEGAL NEGOTIATION RESEARCH PROJECT [10]

The results of empirical research are no better than the methods used to collect them. For this reason, a brief outline of our research methods is presented in this chapter, followed by a discussion of the lawyer negotiating behavior described by the study. For those who are interested, a more detailed explanation of the research methodology is given in Appendix I.

Four basic research methods were used. The first was the survey questionnaire, a standard feature of social science. It was prepared, and sent with a cover letter by the president of the pertinent bar association, to approximately two thousand attorneys practicing in Denver, Colorado and Phoenix, Arizona. Conducting research in two cities allowed us to test for significant differences in attorney perceptions or behavior between two metropolitan areas.

After compiling the results of the mailed questionnaire, we returned to Denver, Colorado and conducted one-hour interviews with 45 attorneys. These were tape recorded and subsequently

---

9. Robert J. Condlin, "Socrates' New Clothes: Substituting Persuasion for Learning in Clinical Practice Instruction," 40 Maryland L.Rev. 223, 227 n. 10 (1981) (italics added).

10. For a report of the research leading to the project proposal, see Williams, England, Farmer, and Blumenthal, "Effectiveness in Legal Negotiation", in Harry T. Edwards and James J. White, *The Lawyers As A Negotiator* (West, 1977) (Hereinafter Williams et al. 1977).

transcribed for analysis. The purpose of these interviews was to build on the base of data accumulated by the questionnaires.

We next used an original technique developed to investigate the dynamics of negotiation over time as viewed by both sides to the negotiation. Up to this point in the project, our data consisted only of reports by attorneys on characteristics of other attorney-negotiators and the negotiation process among attorneys. The next step was to learn how attorneys actually carried out the negotiation or litigation of particular cases. This information needed to come from attorneys on both sides of each case, so the perceptions, expectations, and actions of the opposing attorneys could be compared. Therefore, we asked attorneys on both sides of selected cases to maintain an oral, tape-recorded account of their actions as they moved step by step through the cases. With the approval of the Ethics Committee of the Bar Association, we tested the technique using four attorneys from our advisory committee. They each selected a case that was scheduled to go to trial within the next three months, obtained the client's permission and gave us the name of opposing counsel (so we could contact him and ask him to keep a similar record of his dealings with the case). Using a tape recorder we provided, the attorneys then dictated an account of each significant step taken in handling the case (e.g., exchange of letters or telephone calls with opposing counsel, discovery, meeting with the client, legal research, pretrial procedures, etc.).[11]

After six months, the four cases were completed and we received the records from seven of the eight attorneys involved. These tape recordings were transcribed and analyzed. To our delight, the reports were rich in useful information about the perceptions and motives of both sides in the negotiating process. Encouraged by this result, we selected 50 more pairs of attorneys in Denver to conduct similar case studies. We also obtained additional funding and conducted approximately 100 similar case studies in Phoenix. The studies have been completed, collected, and transcribed, and we are in the process of analyzing them.

11. To maintain confidentiality and prevent improper transfer of information between the two sides of each case by the researchers, the actual names of the clients were kept out of the record, and attorneys kept the records until both sides were satisfied that the case had been terminated to their satisfaction. Only then was the information made available to the researchers.

After the research project was completed, it became apparent that we had overlooked a major source of information and understanding: videotape recordings of experienced attorneys engaging in negotiations. To meet this need, we prepared a total of seven cases (personal injury, breach of contract, products liability, divorce, criminal law, land-tenant, and business transactions) for negotiation by experienced lawyers.

Fourteen attorneys from across the United States agreed to participate. They were given ten days to prepare their cases and were then brought together in pairs to conduct their negotiations on videotape. The attorneys received no coaching on how to proceed; they were simply asked to negotiate the cases exactly as they would do in a real situation. These seven videotaped negotiating sessions add a crucial visual dimension to the data received through the other research techniques by illustrating what those data mean in behavioral terms.

As we began our research, the questions foremost in our minds were these: What are the characteristics of effective legal negotiators? Are there identifiable patterns to their negotiating behavior? What strategies do lawyers most commonly use? What objectives do lawyers have in mind when they negotiate? What attitudes? What combinations of traits are found in the most effective (and most ineffective) negotiators? What are their strong points, and what are their weak points?

The first phase of our research project was designed to answer these questions. The results are among the most dramatic and useful of the entire project.

In the Phoenix version of the survey questionnaire, which is reported here, attorneys were asked to think of their most recently completed case or transaction, to briefly describe the matter, to think of the attorney representing the other party in the matter, and to describe that attorney according to 137 characteristics listed in the questionnaire. When they had completed the descriptive ratings, they were asked to rate the negotiating effectiveness of the attorney they had described. This rating scale was divided into three categories: ineffective, average and effective.

The results were compiled and analyzed according to standard statistical routines, including the standard R-factor analysis, Q-factor analysis, multiple regression analysis, and discriminate analysis.[12] The results reported here were obtained by means of the Q-factor analysis.[13]

III. HOW LAWYERS NEGOTIATE:
LESSONS FROM ATTORNEYS

The Q-factor analysis was used to look for stable patterns in the negotiating behavior of attorneys. The results indicate that legal negotiation proceeds quite consistently within the parameters of two basic approaches. Both approaches are described in considerable detail by the analysis, providing exceptionally powerful insights into the nature of bargaining processes generally and the behavior of individual negotiators in particular. The pattern identified in a majority of the negotiators (65%) is best described as a *cooperative* approach to negotiation, while the second pattern (identified in 24% of attorneys) represents a *competitive* approach. These labels, *cooperative* and *competitive*, will be used to refer generally to attorneys of each type. Toward the end of the discussion it will become apparent that these labels are somewhat imprecise and that finer distinctions can be made. Knowledge of two basic patterns provides an exceptionally powerful tool for analyzing and understanding how individuals operate in the negotiation setting.

The strength of the two patterns was so pervasive that only 11% of the attorneys failed to identify with one or the other. The analysis failed to identify any consistent pattern in the characteristics of this latter (11%) group of attorneys, suggesting that they do not represent a third pattern of negotiation. A complete listing of results of the Q-factor analysis is given in Appendix II, while the most important findings are described in the text and tables below.

The distribution of attorneys among all categories is shown in Diagram 2–1. As indicated in the Diagram, neither pattern

12. A technical description of these analyses and their results is being prepared for publication in the periodical literature in collaboration with J. Lynn England, Professor of Sociology at Brigham Young University.

13. Steven R. Brown, *Political Subjectivity: Applications of Q Methodology in Political Science* (New Haven and London: Yale University Press 1980). Q-factor analysis is an exceptionally impartial method of analysis, because it avoids biases the researchers might have about what patterns will be found to exist. There is no attempt to tell the computer what kind of patterns to find, or to give special emphasis to one set of characteristics or another. The program merely looks for any identifiable patterns in the descriptions of attorneys. It ignores the pet theories and preferences of the researchers in favor of a more free form of analysis.

has an exclusive claim on effectiveness. Use of the cooperative pattern does not guarantee effectiveness, any more than does the use of the competitive pattern. An attorney can be very effective or very ineffective within the constraints of either. The higher proportion of cooperative attorneys who were rated effective does suggest it is more difficult to be an effective competitive negotiator than an effective cooperative.

Diagram 2-1
Approximate Number of
Each Negotiator Type Among the
Practicing Bar

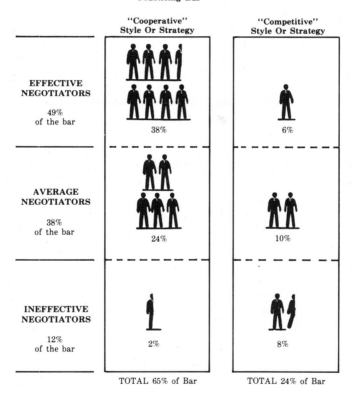

	"Cooperative" Style Or Strategy	"Competitive" Style Or Strategy
EFFECTIVE NEGOTIATORS 49% of the bar	38%	6%
AVERAGE NEGOTIATORS 38% of the bar	24%	10%
INEFFECTIVE NEGOTIATORS 12% of the bar	2%	8%
	TOTAL 65% of Bar	TOTAL 24% of Bar

 = Approximately 5% of the Bar

Note: Eleven percent of the rated attorneys fell outside these two categories.

Note: The silhouette figures are male because less than 3% of the sample was female. This percentage is too low to provide reliable statistics on distribution of women among these categories. None of the females in the sample were rated as ineffective, however.

[C5378]

Persons concerned about lawyer competency will be interested to observe that in our random sample of attorneys, 49% were rated as effective negotiators, 38% were rated as average negotiators, and 12% were rated ineffective.

The value of these findings comes in learning the major components of each strategy. What are the characteristics of the effective negotiators of each type? What do they do that differentiates them from the average and ineffective negotiators? How are the effective types different from each other, and how are they similar?

To answer these questions we selected the most strongly-rated descriptors of each group and sorted them into logical clusters to make their meaning more clear. The following analysis demonstrates this method. For more detailed information about the data, see Appendix II.

A. CHARACTERISTICS OF EFFECTIVE NEGOTIATORS

1. Effective/Cooperative Negotiators

The highest-rated characteristics of effective/cooperative negotiators fall into six informal clusters. The first cluster describes, in order of importance, their motivational objectives:

CLUSTER ONE

Conducting self ethically

Maximizing settlement for client

Getting a fair settlement

Meeting client's needs

Avoiding litigation

Maintaining or establishing a good personal relationship with opponent

It is surprising to find the predominant concern is with *ethical conduct.* This theme recurs among cooperative negotiators at all levels of effectiveness. The second concern is with *maximizing settlement for the client,* but this must be interpreted in light of item number 3, concern for *getting a fair settlement.* Attorneys of this type feel constrained in their conduct by a standard of fairness and ethical dealing. They want to know their clients' needs and, if possible, meet those needs without the necessity of litigation. They are also concerned with maintaining a good personal relationship with the opposing attorney.

Their strategy for meeting these goals is straightforward, as reflected in the following descriptors:

CLUSTER TWO

Accurately estimated the value of the case

Knew the needs of the client

Took a realistic opening position

Probed opponent's position

Knew the needs of opponent's client

Willing to share information

Forthright

Trustful

Willing to move from original position

Objective

Fair-minded

Reasonable

Logical (not emotional)

Did not use threats

CLUSTER THREE

Courteous

Personable

Friendly

Tactful

Sincere

CLUSTER FOUR

Organizing

Wise

Careful

Facilitating

Cooperative

The third cluster relates to personableness: effective/cooperative negotiators are seen as friendly, personable, courteous, and tactful. However, some degree of caution is called for in interpreting these words. A person unfamiliar with legal negotiation is likely to picture a "soft" negotiator who is, as a consequence of personableness, a pushover. This cannot be a correct interpretation, because the adjectives describe *effective* negotiators at work in the legal context. A richer sense of meaning will develop as additional adjective clusters are considered.

Effective/cooperative attorneys are also seen as fair, objective, reasonable, logical, and willing to move from their established positions. Interpretation of these adjectives is aided by the other Cluster two descriptors, which indicate these attorneys take realistic opening positions, support their position with facts, and are forthright.

While these traits are quite general, there are a number of descriptors that are focused on negotiating situations. For example, cooperative effectives seek to facilitate agreement, they avoid use of threats, they accurately estimate the value of cases they are working on, they are sensitive to the needs of their clients, and they are willing to share information with their opponent. It appears from these items that their strategy is to approach negotiation in an objective, fair, trustworthy way, and to seek agreement by the open exchange of information. They are apparently as concerned with getting a settlement that is fair to both sides as they are with maximizing the outcome for their own client.

The attitude of effective/cooperatives is reflected in attorney comments. For example, one attorney wrote: "The vital item in negotiation for me is trust in the other attorney. If an attorney has a good reputation and/or I have dealt with him before and found him honest, I can and will negotiate pragmatic settlements, hopefully to the long term benefit of both parties." In a similar vein, another attorney said, in speaking of his relationship with opposing counsel, "our relationship was constructive . . . we both tried to reach a fair settlement, which we did without trial." Finally, an attorney described his opponent (an effective/cooperative) in these words: "The attorney I negotiated with is highly ethical and [is] respected as a trial attorney. He has considerable experience as a prosecutor as well as for the defense."

2. Effective/Competitive Negotiators

The differences in approach between cooperative and competitive attorneys is most quickly illustrated by comparing motivational objectives. In order of their importance, competitive/effectives have as their goals:

CLUSTER ONE

Maximizing settlement for client

Obtaining profitable fee for self

Outdoing or outmaneuvering the opponent

Obviously, the goal of getting a maximum settlement value for the client means something different to a competitor than to a cooperater. To competitors, the goal includes a reward to self both in monetary terms and in satisfaction from outdoing an opponent. The difference in view between these two types becomes more apparent from examining other competitor traits. They are seen as:

CLUSTER TWO

Tough

Dominant

Forceful

Aggressive

Attacking

CLUSTER THREE

Ambitious

Egotist

Arrogant

Clever

CLUSTER FOUR

Made a high opening demand

Took unrealistic opening position

Used take-it-or-leave-it approach

Rigid

Disinterested in needs of opponent's client

Did not consider opponent's needs

Unconcerned about how opponent would look to his client

Willing to stretch the facts

Knew the needs of own client

Careful about timing and sequence of actions

Revealed information gradually

Used threats

Obstructed

Uncooperative

In contrast to the friendly, trustworthy approach of cooperative effectives, effective/competitives are seen as dominating, competitive, forceful, tough, arrogant, and uncooperative. They make high opening demands, they use threats, they are willing to stretch the facts in favor of their clients' positions, they stick to their positions, and they are parsimonious with information about the case. They are concerned not only with maximizing the outcome for their client but they appear to take a gamesmanship approach to negotiation, having a principle objective of outdoing or outmaneuvering their opponent. Thus, rather than seeking an outcome that is "fair" to both sides, they want to outdo the other side; to score a clear victory.

Fees are obviously important to this type of negotiator. Obtaining a profitable fee is rated as the second highest priority on their agenda, a priority that can lead to conflicts. One attorney, describing an effective competitive opponent, said the case would have settled if the other attorney had approached the matter "from a realistic standpoint, i.e., the welfare of the children and future relationships of the parties (the divorcing parents) instead of being primarily interested in increasing his fee."

Competitive/effectives are careful about the timing and sequence of their actions which underscores the gamesmanship element of competitive negotiating behavior. This reflects a high level of interest in tactical or strategic considerations, suggesting that they orchestrate the case for best effect. One ef-

[24]

fective/competitive attorney laughed when his cooperative opponent said the objective of negotiation was to accomplish a just
outcome. He said, "This is a poker game, and you do your best
to put the best front on your case and you try to make the other
fellow think that his weaknesses are bigger than he really ought
to consider them." Another attorney reported that the insurance defense attorney opposing him "could have appraised the
case more on injury to the plaintiff rather than on difficulty of
plaintiff in putting on a good case at trial." These comments
show the unbridgeable gap in perceptions and attitudes between
cooperative and competitive attorneys. Cooperatives feel that
cases should be evaluated objectively, on their merits, and that
both sides should seek to find the most fair outcome. Competitive attorneys view their work as a game in which they seek to
outwit and out-perform the other side. The tension between
these two styles raises major ethical, moral, and public policy
questions, many of which will be dealt with later in this book.

This description of effective/competitives makes them sound
somewhat machiavellian, in the "gunslinger" image of lawyers,
just as the description of effective/competitives makes them
sound surprisingly "soft". However, the descriptions in both instances are incomplete, because they give only the extreme differences between the two patterns without filling in the similarities. As indicated below, the additional information creates a
much more satisfactory picture of both types.

3. Similarities Between the Two Effective Types

While there are clear differences in approach between the
two types of effective negotiators, both types are, in fact, rated
as highly effective. Our interest is in what makes them effective, i.e., what traits they have in common. Common traits have
particular importance, since law students and attorneys can seek
to understand and emulate them irrespective of which pattern
they prefer to follow.

COMPARISON ONE: THE ADJECTIVE CHECKLIST

	Effective/ Cooperative Rankings	Effective/ Aggressive Rankings
Experienced	(1)	(2)
Realistic	(2)	(10)
Ethical	(3)	(15)
Rational	(4)	(4)
Perceptive	(5)	(3)
Trustworthy	(6)	(20)
Convincing	(7)	(1)
Analytical	(8)	(5)
Creative	(10)	(6)
Self-controlled	(11)	(12)
Versatile	(12)	(18)
Adaptable	(14)	(17)
Poised	(17)	(14)
Legally astute	(20)	(16)

COMPARISON TWO: THE BIPOLAR SCALES

	Effective/ Cooperative Rankings	Effective/ Competitive Rankings
Honest	(1)	(11)
Adhered to customs and courtesies of the bar	(2)	(14)
Intelligent	(3)	(4)
Thoroughly prepared on the facts of the case	(12)	(7)
Thoroughly prepared on the law of the case	(18)	(15)
Effective trial attorney	(22)	(3)
Skillful in reading opponent's cues	(23)	(18)
Active	(24)	(8)

COMPARISON THREE: OBJECTIVES

	Effective/ Cooperative Rankings	Effective/ Competitive Rankings
Conducting himself ethically	(1)	(4)
Maximizing settlement for client	(2)	(1)
Satisfaction in exercise of legal skills	(5)	(5)

These descriptors apply to effective negotiators regardless of which patterns of negotiation they follow. They may be considered a reliable statement of the characteristics of effective legal negotiators. Assuming that we all wish to improve our effectiveness as negotiators, it is important to learn the meaning of these terms.

Both types of effective negotiators are ranked as highly experienced. This comes as no surprise, since we normally assume that negotiating effectiveness improves with experience. Its meaning here is illuminated by the comment of a responding attorney, who wrote: "it is important to have enough experience in order that you have confidence in yourself and be able to convey that confidence."

More importantly, both types are seen as ethical, trustworthy and honest, thus dispelling any doubt about the ethical commitments of effective/competitives. However, the priority of these traits is ranked much higher for cooperatives (3rd, 6th and 1st in priority) than for competitives (15th, 20th and 11th in priority). Given the current interest and concern about professional responsibility in the Bar, the high ratings on ethical and trustworthy for both effective groups are worthy of notice. Although literature on professional responsibility generally argues that high ethical standards are a precondition to success in practice, many law students and some practicing attorneys continue to believe or suspect that they must compromise their ethical standards in order to effectively represent their clients and attain success in practice. The findings of this survey suggest such compromises may be not only unnecessary, but actually counterproductive to one's effectiveness in negotiation situations.

In the same vein, we see that both types are careful to observe the customs and courtesies of the bar. While some attorneys have argued that there are tactical advantages in deliberately departing from the etiquette of the profession, as a general rule effective negotiators observe it. The Model Code of Professional Responsibility indicates lawyers have an ethical duty to "follow local customs of courtesy or practice" unless they give timely notice to opposing counsel of their intention not to do so (EC 7–38).

Although effective/competitives were seen as taking unrealistic opening positions, in general they share with cooperatives the traits of being realistic, rational, and analytical. These three attributes become very important in interpreting negotiator behavior. They mean more than the idea of "thinking like a lawyer"; they impose limits on how far a negotiator may credibly go in such things as interpretation of facts, claims about damages and other economic demands, and levels of emotional involvement in the case.

Both effective types are seen as thoroughly prepared on the facts and the law of the case. They are also described as legally astute. This, again, is something to be expected. But it bears emphasis because, as we shall see, ineffective negotiators lack these qualities. One attorney had these traits in mind when he wrote, "In my experience, the most important part of negotiation is thorough preparation and a complete knowledge of the strengths and weaknesses of your position. . . .   I feel individual personality traits (e.g. loud, forceful, quiet, reserved) are unimportant."

Legal astuteness means they have not only done their homework by informing themselves about the legal and procedural ramifications of the case, but they also have acquired good judgment about how and when to act with respect to this information.

Both types of effective attorneys are rated as creative, versatile, and adaptable. This is true even though competitive effectives are also labelled rigid. Apparently there is a distinction between being tough (which competitive attorneys are) and being obstinate. An attorney should not be so rigid that he is unable to seek creative solutions to problems. The flavor of the terms is suggested in a comment by an attorney representing a party who was involved in a very acrimonious dispute with a neighbor over an irrigation ditch. He wrote, "Our problem was solved by a simple relocation agreement executed by the parties and recorded. The opposition attorney and myself, after great study and much effort, came up with the simple solution of simply relocating the ditch."

Both types are self-controlled. This is not a word all will welcome as an attribute of effectiveness; it somehow calls to mind the rigidity and tenseness we prefer to associate with engineers and accountants, not with lawyers. We will appreciate its meaning and importance after considering the characteristics of ineffective negotiators.

One of the more important marks of effective negotiators is skill in reading their opponent's cues. This refers not only to the ability to judge an opponent's reactions in negotiating situations, but to affirmatively learn from the opponent. The old saying is that experience is the best teacher. Experience is only a good teacher for those who are skillful at learning from it. In the course of interviews connected with Denver attorneys, they were routinely asked what they did when they were faced with an inexperienced opponent—an opponent fresh out of law school. Their responses were very informative. One group of attorneys would get a sly grin on their face, their eyes would light up, and they would say "I hammer them into the ground". By far the larger number of attorneys responded quite differently, however. They said that when they had a "green" opponent, they slowed the case way down, tried to spell everything out as they went, and tried generally to show the younger attorney the right way to go about handling a case.

Consider this problem from the perspective of law graduates recently admitted to the bar. During the first few months of practice, they encounter some attorneys who hammer them into the ground, exploiting and taking advantage of them at every turn, and others who are trying to teach them how to be good lawyers. The experience is not calculated to engender trust in fellow officers of the court. Rather, the tendency in young lawyers is to develop a mild paranoia and to distrust everyone. This is unfortunate, because *some* opponents are providing valuable information, albeit in subtle ways. The key, then, is to learn to observe and "read" the opposing attorney and know who can be trusted and who cannot and then learn from both types without being misled by either.

Competitive and cooperative effectives are rated as perceptive, a term that goes hand in hand with skill in reading cues. It relates in part to the ability to perceive an opponent's strategy and his subjective reaction to your strategy. It also has a larger connotation, referring to the accuracy of one's perception of the whole case. One attorney in our study gave a telling description of his perception of a recently completed case: "I lost the case. Though my opponent was ineffective in preparation and presentation—and was a drunk—the judge *disbelieved* my key witness, a fundamentalist Minister, and the plaintiff got every cent he had wrongly demanded from my client."

Finally, it must be stressed that both types of effective negotiators are also rated as effective trial attorneys. As mentioned earlier, the alternative to settlement is trial. If an attorney is known as a weak trial attorney, it will often be more profitable for his opponent to take him to trial than agree to a reasonable settlement. This creates an awkward and troublesome dynamic, because the weak trial attorney knows that his client would be poorly served by an inept trial of the case. The weak attorney discounts the case as an inducement to the other side to settle and avoid the costs (and benefits) of trial. The interplay between fear of trial and discounting of the case is not healthy. There appears to be only one solution: to be taken seriously, lawyers who negotiate legal disputes (as opposed to non-actionable matters) must either develop substantial expertise as trial attorneys, or must openly associate themselves (whether by partnership, a referral system, or some other way) with very effective trial counsel.

B. CHARACTERISTICS OF AVERAGE NEGOTIATORS

As we move down the effectiveness scale to the "average" negotiator level, we find that differences between the two negotiating patterns types are much more pronounced. They differed from each other on 13 of the 20 adjectives, in 25 of the 26 bipolar pairs, and all but 2 of the motivational objectives.

1. Average/Cooperative Negotiators

Selected characteristics from the adjective checklist that distinguish the average/cooperative negotiator from his competitive counterpart include the following:

SELECTED CHARACTERISTICS:
AVERAGE COOPERATIVES

Realistic

Self-controlled

Careful

Discrete

Objective

Analytical

Fair

Loyal

Perceptive

Helpful

Deliberate

Experienced

Organizing

Average/cooperative attorneys reflect many of the characteristics of effective/cooperative attorneys, such as trustworthy, experienced, ethical, and realistic, and their high ratings here raise the question of why they were seen as only average negotiators. Part of the answer may lie in their lower ratings on such characteristics as analytical, perceptive, convincing, and legally astute. In addition, they are noted for their caution, discretion, sociability, and obliging behavior, some of which may have a dampening effect on their effectiveness.

In describing an average/cooperative opponent, one attorney wrote, "The lawyer is a sincere, honest member of the bar with 15 years of practice; but [has only] moderate legal and intellectual ability."

2. Average Competitive Negotiators

In contrast, the average/competitive negotiator has the following characteristics:

SELECTED CHARACTERISTICS:
AVERAGE COMPETITIVES

Argumentative

Ambitious

Demanding

Bluffer

Egotist

Evasive

Suspicious

Greedy

Headstrong

Impatient

Complaining

Quarrelsome

Unpredictable

Average/competitive attorneys show a dramatic shift in the quality of the characteristics noted, since all the adjectives describing them have predominantly negative connotations: bluffer, demanding, headstrong, argumentative, and irritating. Interestingly, the behavior connoted by these adjectives has certain similarities to the style of advocacy sometimes associated with public interest advocacy and other "causes." The fact that these adjectives occur for the first time in the average groupings should not be taken as a demonstration of their effectiveness or ineffectiveness as styles in negotiating, since one's style or competitiveness may vary according to the demands of a particular situation. It is probable, for example, that strong and even irritating tactics are highly effective when selectively used. However, the preponderance of these characteristics in the average and ineffective range of competitive attorneys does suggest that as a matter of routine style or approach, they seriously detract from one's effectiveness.

In trying to understand the personality of average/competitive negotiators, it may be seen that greed, ambition, and egotism are associated with their style. None of these selfish or self-centered characteristics are seen as characterizing either of the effective groups, but rather were seen as decidedly *uncharacteristic* of effective attorneys.

One attorney described his average/competitive opponent in this way: "Obviously, this was an unpleasant and poor attorney, and I should say that he is in a minority; he just happened to be [my most recent opponent] . . . and unfortunately, there are still too many [like him]."

3. Similarities Between the Two Average Types

Of the 20 highest characteristics from the adjective checklist scales, only 7 are shared by both types. Since the most interesting comparisons come at the ineffective level, relatively little discussion will be given about average negotiators. The listing of characteristics, with their rank orderings, is sufficient.

	Average/ Cooperative Rankings	Average/ Competitive Rankings
Ethical	(1)	(7)
Trustworthy	(2)	(19)
Rational	(3)	(20)
Personable	(4)	(15)
Cautious	(5)	(12)
Sociable	(10)	(6)
Legally astute	(12)	(9)

There are substantial differences in the strength of these characteristics in the two average types, with cooperatives being rated more strongly on ethical, trustworthy, rational, personable, and cautious, while competitives were ranked as more sociable and more legally astute.

C. CHARACTERISTICS OF INEFFECTIVE NEGOTIATORS

The two ineffective types are a study in contrasts. We did not see this degree of difference between cooperatives and competitives at the effective level because they had a crucial similarity: they were *effective negotiators*. At the bottom level, the two types do not have that in common. What we have, then, is a description of the extremes of both styles, both of them ineffective, but in quite opposite ways. The ineffective extremes hold essential clues to the underlying dynamics of the cooperative and competitive strategies. Assuming that negotiators at the effective level have somehow discovered aspects of each strategy that are successful, we can assume that negotiators at the ineffective level are either omitting essential aspects of the strategies, or else they are defeating their own strategies by going too far with them or otherwise negating their effectiveness.

1. Ineffective/Cooperative Negotiators

Ineffective/cooperatives are characterized by many socially desirable traits.

SELECTED CHARACTERISTICS: INEFFECTIVE/COOPERATIVES

Honest

Forthright

Trustful

Willing to share information

Courteous

Adhered to customs and courtesies to the bar

Sincere

Friendly

Cooperative

Knew the needs of his client

Logical

Did not use threats

Facilitated

Tactful

Was willing to move from original position

Intelligent

Reasonable

Got to know my personality

Thoroughly prepared on the factual elements

Flexible

[*34*]

Informal

Emotionally detached

Probed my position

Revealed information early

Modest

Accurately estimated the value of the case

OBJECTIVES

Conducting himself ethically

Maximizing settlement for his client

Meeting his client's needs

Getting a fair settlement

Maintaining or establishing a good personal relationship
with opponent

Satisfaction in exercise of legal skills

The ineffective/cooperative does not have the skills or attitudes of an effective/cooperative, such as being perceptive, or convincing, or having the reasonableness cluster (realistic, rational, and analytical). Nor is he creative, self-controlled, versatile, objective, organizing, or legally astute. The ineffective is apparently unsure of himself or of the value of his case (conservative, staller, cautious, deliberate). He is torn between being gentle, obliging, patient, moderate, and forgiving, on the one hand, and demanding, "masculine", and argumentative on the other, and tends to be something of an idealist. The idealism may account for lack of versatility, adaptability, creativity, and wisdom.

a. **Similarities Between Effective and Ineffective Cooperative Negotiators**

Effective and ineffective cooperatives share five important characteristics. They are both seen as ethical, trustworthy, fair, personable, and experienced.

Selected Comparisons

	Effective/ Cooperative Rankings	Ineffective/ Cooperative Rankings
Ethical	(3)	(1)
Personable	(13)	(3)
Fair	(9)	(4)
Trustworthy	(6)	(7)
Experienced	(1)	(14)

Since these traits are shared by effective and ineffective cooperatives, they are apparently no guarantee of success as a negotiator. Rather, they should be interpreted as notable characteristics of the cooperative pattern of negotiation.

b.   Differences Between Effective and Ineffective Cooperative Negotiators

It is helpful to compare the differences between effective and ineffective cooperatives:

SELECTED DIFFERENCES

Effective/ Cooperative with Rankings		Ineffective/ Cooperative with Rankings	
Realistic	(2)	Complaining	(2)
Rational	(4)	Gentle	(5)
Perceptive	(5)	Conservative	(6)
Convincing	(7)	Masculine	(8)
Analytical	(8)	Staller	(9)
Creative	(10)	Obliging	(10)
Self-controlled	(11)	Demanding	(11)
Versatile	(12)	Cautious	(12)
Adaptable	(14)	Deliberate	(13)
Wise	(15)	Patient	(15)
Objective	(16)	Moderate	(16)
Poised	(17)	Forgiving	(17)
Careful	(18)	Argumentative	(18)
Organizing	(19)	Idealist	(19)
Legally astute	(20)	Sociable	(20)

2. Ineffective/Competitive Negotiators

Competitive/ineffective attorneys are characterized by negative traits, and can be generally described as *irritating*. The strength of this irritating characteristic (2.80 on a 3.00 scale) compares with the strength of the outstanding characteristics of effective attorneys: trustworthy for cooperative/effectives (2.82), and experienced for competitive/effectives (2.83).

The ineffective/competitive is also a case study, representing a type of person we have all met (perhaps trapped in some low-level bureaucratic position making life miserable for all around him) and have occasionally emulated. Like the ineffective/cooperative, he is complaining. He is also, in rank order:

CLUSTER ONE

Headstrong

Impatient

Intolerant

Rigid

Loud

CLUSTER TWO

Greedy

Demanding

Unreasonable

Uncooperative

Arrogant

Tactless

CLUSTER THREE

Complaining

Sarcastic

Insincere

CLUSTER FOUR

Devious

Conniving

[*37*]

Impulsive

Unpredictable

Evasive

CLUSTER FIVE

Suspicious

Distrustful

Unskillful in reading my cues

CLUSTER SIX

Unsure of value of the case

Took unrealistic opening position

Made a high opening demand

Used take-it-or-leave-it approach

Narrow range of bargaining stategies

Bluffer

Unwilling to share information

Disinterested in opponent's position

Took one position and refused to move from it

Used threats

Emotional

Quarrelsome

Rude

Hostile

Obstructive

CLUSTER SEVEN

Ineffective trial attorney

CLUSTER EIGHT

Disinterested in the needs of my client

Did not consider my needs

Disinterested in my personality

Unconcerned about how opponent would look in the eyes of his client

CLUSTER NINE

Maximizing settlement for client

Outdoing or outmaneuvering you

Obtaining profitable fee for self

The ineffective/competitive shares only *one* trait with his effective/competitive counterpart: egotist. The problem of the ineffective/competitive is relatively easy to define: he is obnoxious. This type of negotiator rates extremely low on such professionally-mandated standards as ethical and trustworthy. They are also rated extremely low in rational, perceptive, realistic, and convincing.

The reason ineffective/competitive attorneys are seen as highly irritating may be explained in part by the nature of their other notable characteristics: they were seen as hostile, intolerant, argumentative, demanding, bluffing, headstrong, egotistical, and quarrelsome. Because these adjectives typify socially undesirable behavior, a question arises as to whether there may be other elements lacking from their behavior which account for their ineffectiveness. This question is brought into better focus by considering the ratings of the ineffective/cooperative attorneys. Unlike competitives, they are seen as ethical, trustworthy, fair, personable, and self-controlled, which are traits they share in common with cooperative/effective attorneys. In addition, they are rated as being gentle, patient, obliging, adaptable, sociable, dignified, and forgiving. Since cooperative/ineffective attorneys appear to observe the social graces and yet are still seen as ineffective negotiators, it appears that it is not regard or disregard of the social graces which determines an attorney's negotiating effectiveness.

In describing an ineffective/competitive, one lawyer wrote, "My experience with this attorney was not typical of most. Other negotiations have been open and candid with generally favorable or reasonable results." Reflecting on his negotiations with an ineffective/competitive, another attorney said, "In my opinion, . . . negotiations break down or are fruitless and futile when the opposing attorney's attitude is arrogant, self-serving, unbending, and unrealistic." A similar view is reflected

[*39*]

by the attorney who wrote, in describing his opponent, "In his initial evaluation of the merits, the inept negotiator sells himself on the virtues of his position, sets unrealistic objectives, and falls in love irreversably with his position."

The adjectives we have been considering here suggest a possible hypothesis as to what makes ineffective/competitives ineffective. They lack such characteristics as perceptive, analytical, realistic, convincing, rational, experienced, and self-controlled, which both types of effective attorneys share in common. Indeed, it may be due to the positive effects of these attributes that competitive/effective attorneys are seen as ambitious, forceful, and dominant in their assertiveness rather than egotistical, argumentative, and bluffing. What is suggested here, then, is that a forceful person who has low regard for social amenities may function effectively as a legal negotiator *if* he can show himself to be perceptive, analytical, realistic, and self-controlled in negotiations. On the other hand, if the same forceful person does not demonstrate the skills of perceptiveness, analytical ability, and realistic evaluation of his position, yet tries to maximize his position by competitive tactics, he will be seen as argumentative, quarrelsome, and irritating, and as someone who, in lieu of skilled preparation, resorts to bluffing, bullying or evasive tactics in an effort to maximize his outcome.

Somehow, competitive/effective legal negotiators are able to apply their expertise without being seen as greedy or conniving, but rather as reasonable and realistic. Again, these comparisions seem to point to the quality of the legal work being performed, including the expertise with which an attorney has investigated the facts of his case, studied and understood the legal rules applicable to it, taken a realistic position with respect to the value of the case, and presented his position in ways that other attorneys accept as being rational, fair, and persuasive (convincing). It may follow that an attorney in this posture has little cause to be argumentative, quarrelsome, rude, and hostile, since he is prepared to effectively go forward on the merits of his position rather than to seek advantage by being personally offensive to the opposing attorney, or by stalling, bluffing, or quarreling.

IV.   WHICH APPROACH IS MORE EFFECTIVE: COOPERATIVE OR COMPETITIVE?

Individual negotiators may not have much choice about the basic approach they use, which may be determined largely by one's own personality and experience. Attorneys should probably be more concerned with improving effectiveness within their style of preference than with changing styles.

Still one wonders whether one approach or the other is more effective. The answer provided by our Phoenix data is that there is no difference in degree of effectiveness attributed to effective/cooperatives and effective/competitives. They received comparably high ratings for effectiveness. It does not appear, therefore, that either approach has the edge when it comes to obtaining the highest (as compared to greatest number) of effectiveness ratings. On the other hand, there are a substantially greater number of effective attorneys of the cooperative type than of the competitive type.

V.   WHICH TYPE OF NEGOTIATOR ARE YOU?

As you studied the various negotiating styles and levels of effectiveness, you probably began to ask yourself what type of negotiator you tend to be. This is an important question. For many people, the answer is clear. Some recognize (as the author did) a clear tendency to be a milquetoast, a classic cooperative/ineffective. Others see a clear pattern of successful gamesmanship, characteristic of an effective/competitive. But many people are not so sure; in one kind of situation they are likely to be very cooperative, but in other circumstances they can be highly competitive. In fact, the evidence suggests that we can all shift from one style to another or anywhere in between under sufficient encouragement or provocation.

Law students and attorneys often have strong feelings about the propriety of shifting "roles". Cooperatives are particularly prone to believe that it is dishonest to calculate which role to play; that the honest person must respond "naturally" to a situation, rather than plan in advance how to gain advantage. However, the data suggest that many effective attorneys have developed the capability to adopt either style convincingly. If this is true, then this kind of versatility is probably something to be desired. One attorney said, "Being a compromising person at

[*41*]

heart, I am becoming more impressed all the time how much more one can get by being mean and nasty (within bounds)." If some attorneys are learning to be "mean and nasty" to get their own way, then all attorneys need to learn to deal effectively with that strategy. It is not enough to rely on pure instincts. It is not enough to get mad and fight back with a vengeance. The effective negotiator needs to develop an approach that satisfies two conditions: (1) it should protect and be compatible with the interests of the client and society; and (2) it should provide adequate protection against the gamesmanship of others.

Versatility is more of an issue for lawyers than other professionals, because their primary function is to represent the legitimate interests of other people. If an attorney feels morally obligated to be irritating, hostile, and intolerant in all his dealings on behalf of clients, he will rarely serve their interests well because he is locking himself into a generally ineffective mode. Similarly, if an attorney feels morally obligated to be gentle, forgiving, patient, and unassertive in every situation (no matter how tough the opponent), he will by definition be unable to protect the client who is being pursued in an unscrupulous or overbearing way. This problem cannot be resolved here, but should be kept in mind for later discussion.

CHAPTER NOTES

1. Further Thoughts About Negotiator Effectiveness

The lack of consensus in the literature about the meaning of "effectiveness" in negotiation creates a problem for every researcher and practitioner. Anyone searching the authorities for definitions is forced to choose between inconsistent definitions and assumptions. In preparing our research, we developed a set of hypotheses about effectiveness, and where we found conflicting theories we opted for those favoring a cooperative model of effectiveness. These hypotheses are important *NOT* because they were correct (they were not correct), but because they led us to the classic error that virtually all researchers and commentators in the field of negotiation generally have made: The error of taking observations or hypotheses that are valid for *SOME* negotiators, and generalizing from them as if they were valid for all negotiators. Our hypotheses make this error in favor of "cooperative" behavior. Because they are fairly good statements of cooperative assumptions, they are worth reproducing here.

We hypothesized that among effective attorneys the following informal rules are observed:

A. *Dynamics.* Both sides will:

1. make serious attempts to reach agreement (will bargain in good faith);

2. when presenting a client's position, represent it accurately;

3. avoid emotionalism;

4. maintain trust, candor, confidentiality, and flexibility;

5. be prepared on the facts and on the applicable law;

6. avoid deception, insults, flagrant lies, rudeness, and impolite acts;

7. avoid interrupting or obstructing the routinized aspects of interpersonal relations; and

8. avoid causing the other attorney to lose face.

B. *Effectiveness Traits.* Effective legal negotiators can be distinguished from the less effective by superior ratings on traits such as:

1. legal acumen (skill in knowing and applying the law);

2. preparation;

3. reputation and ability as trial attorneys;

4. creativity (ability to invent or create new alternatives);

5. skillful use of tactics such as commitment, toughness, reciprocation, initial offers, and control of information flow; and

6. awareness of and skillful use of the strength of their position.

C. *Objectives.* In examining the objectives or end results lawyers try to achieve in negotiations, we hypothesized that, for effective negotiations, the dollar value of the out-

[*43*]

come for the client would be important, but that they would also take into account such concerns as:

1. the client's overall needs and desires;

2. the need for a favorable economic return to the negotiator; and

3. the need to maintain a favorable reputation within the bar.

D. *Variations Within the Bar.* We also hypothesized that there are more specific or technical expectations among practicing lawyers, and that these develop in unique ways within geographic areas and within legal specialties. For example, attorneys specializing in personal injury work in a particular city or region of the country develop a set of informal practices and assumptions different from the informal practices of lawyers within other specialties. This creates difficulties for attorneys who are not specialized, who are new to practice, or who come from other regions of the country, because failure to know and observe these unwritten rules reduces an attorney's negotiating effectiveness.

E. *Global Hypothesis.* We summarized these various concerns into a global hypothesis, which was stated as follows:

"the most effective legal negotiators will be characterized by positive social traits and attitudes and by the use of more open, cooperative, and friendly negotiating strategies." [14]

These projections were generally correct in describing the attitudes and skills of one type of effective legal negotiator, but they failed completely to anticipate the possibility of *two* major patterns, the competitive being left out.

2. Research on Negotiation in Other Disciplines

Outside of the legal context there has been an explosion of interest in the phenomenon of negotiation. Over the past thirty years the conception of negotiation has grown from that of an etherial art practiced discretely by diplomats to that of a fundamental decision-making process in democratic societies. In this short time span, the amount of scholarly attention paid to nego-

14. Williams, England, Farmer, and Blumenthal, "Effectiveness in Legal Negotiation", in Harry T. Edwards and James J. White, *The Lawyer As A Negotiator* (West, 1977).

tiation in such disciplines as economics, sociology, psychology, communications, political science, and international relations has increased significantly. Although this interest is still relatively recent and much of the literature is still somewhat removed from practical application, it has nevertheless produced a wealth of experimental and theoretical work that is of potential value to the lawyer. Equally important, this work has brought with it the development of research techniques that can be directly applied by legal scholars to the legal negotiating context.

Four particularly useful collections are:

O. Young, *Bargaining* (1975)

J. Rubin & B. Brown, *The Social Psychology of Bargaining* (1975)

I. W. Zartman, *The 50% Solution* (1976)

D. Druckman, *Negotiations* (1977)

For persons interested in labor negotiations, see:

I. Morley & G. Stephenson, *The Social Psychology of Bargaining* (1977) (published in Great Britain by George Allen & Unwin)

3. *Predictability of Negotiating Behavior*

All human beings have characteristic patterns of behavior. We see evidence of this in the habits and mannerisms of close friends and family members. We would see evidence of these patterns in others if we could observe them long enough and with sufficient attention to detail.

Coaches in college and professional football take advantage of this principle, and the better prepared among them apply it when preparing for each team they meet. The way they discover the patterns of an opposing coach is not necessarily by studying the coach, but by studying recent films of his games and charting the offensive and defensive plays executed by his team. Typically a coach will have a rather small number of basic plays, and his game is built around variations on those plays. One coach has referred to this set of plays as the "comfort zone", which consists of the plays a team does best and the coach feels most comfortable with.

Lawyers can apply this concept to negotiations, and begin to look for the patterns being followed by each opponent they face. These patterns generally represent a "comfort zone" for that negotiator, within which he or she is likely to want to keep the negotiation.

Chapter Three

THE DYNAMICS OF COOPERATIVE AND COMPETITIVE NEGOTIATING

"It is disgraceful, after much trouble, much display, and much talk, to do no good at all." Hippocrates

I. INTRODUCTION

The descriptions of cooperative and competitive negotiators provide a basis for evaluating our personal negotiating patterns and those of negotiators we may see in action. But the descriptions do not directly address the question of *how the cooperative and competitive strategies work: what are the dynamics of each strategy, and what determines the effectiveness or ineffectiveness of a negotiator's application of the strategy?* A negotiator's effectiveness is *NOT* determined by the pattern he follows, but rather by what he does with that pattern. The objective of this chapter is to describe the underlying dynamics of the cooperative and competitive patterns and determine, as well as possible, the principles that govern the effectiveness of each.

Until now, there has been no reliable way of knowing how to interpret and apply social scientific literature on bargaining to the negotiating tasks of lawyers. One interpretive difficulty has been the dichotomy between cooperative and "tough" (competitive) negotiating preferences in the literature.[15] No one has known which of these preferences was most applicable to the actual negotiation practices of lawyers. The finding that *both* patterns are routinely used by lawyers and that neither pattern has a monopoly on effectiveness helps shift the debate from the

---

15. Although we were unaware of it when we conducted our research, the existence of two patterns has been hypothesized and the moral and practical merits of each compared by able commentators in many disciplines. See, for example, discussions of administrators versus agitators by Lasswell (1930); shopkeepers versus warriors by Nicolson (1964); risk averse versus risk preferring by Posner (1972); co-active communicator versus actor orientation by Gamson (1968); cooperative orientation versus competitive orientation in social psychological literature as reviewed by Rubins and Brown (1975); and personality traits such as need for approval and trust as compared to machiavellianism discussed by London and Exner (1978). (For full citations to references, please see the bibliography). As these references suggest, the debate is extensive and enlightening.

question of which method is best to the more constructive question of *how each pattern works.*

II. THE COMPETITIVE STRATEGY

The experimental literature on negotiation contains a running debate between two opposing schools of thought: one arguing generally for a "cooperative" approach to negotiation and the other for a "tough" or "competitive" approach. The researchers who argue that tough negotiators are most effective are supported by a variety of interesting studies. Experiments conducted by Siegel & Fouraker (1960) on the process of making demands and counter-demands in bargaining indicated that tough negotiators obtain higher payoffs than negotiators who are not tough. These results have been duplicated in a large number of experimental settings. See, for example, Harnett, Cummings, and Hamner (1973).

What are the ingredients of a "tough" approach? As defined in social psychological literature, they include:[16]

1. making high initial demands;

2. maintaining a high level of demands in the course of the negotiation;

3. making few concessions;

4. making small concessions (when concessions are made); and

5. having a generally high level of aspiration.

These tactics are so consistent with the behavior patterns of competitive attorneys described in the preceding chapter that we can propose that most of the social literature on toughness and competitiveness in bargaining is relevant to understanding how competitive attorneys negotiate. The inverse should also be true: what we know about competitive attorneys will help answer questions presently unresolved in the literature.

What we have learned so far about competitive negotiators is brought to life by the insights of Herbert W. Simons. In *Persuasion: Understanding, Practice and Analysis*, pp. 133–134 (1976) he observes that the underlying dynamic of combative strategies is to move psychologically against the other person by

16. I. Morley and G. Stephenson,
The Social Psychology of Bargaining
(1977).

word or action. Videotapes of competitive lawyers engaged in negotiating do show a definite pattern of behavior of moving psychologically against the other (non-competitive) attorney. They make very high demands and few (if any) concessions. They use exaggeration, ridicule, threat, bluff, and accusation to create high levels of tension and pressure on the opponent.

What are the effects of these tactics? If used effectively, the tactics cause the opposing attorney to lose confidence in himself and his case, to reduce his expectations of what he will be able to obtain in the case, and to accept less than he otherwise would as a settlement outcome. As Simons observed, the combative approach is a manipulative approach, designed to intimidate the opponent into accepting the combative's demands.

Experimental studies of bargaining have shown that in many settings, use of toughness increases profits for the tough negotiator.[17] Our Q-factor analysis showed that maximizing settlement value is the primary concern of tough negotiators. But they are not only after money. They take satisfaction in winning—in outdoing or outmaneuvering their opponents.

Other researchers have tested the effectiveness of the tough or competitive strategy and have identified several limitations. These limitations are important for lawyers to know because the strategy will only be effective if its limitations are known and avoided.

Kahn and Kohls (1972) found that when negotiators lack sufficient information with which to negotiate they compensate by using increased toughness. However, use of toughness in these circumstances does not increase negotiator profits. This finding correlates very nicely with data from the last chapter. Ineffective competitive negotiators are rated as unprepared on the facts and the law, which means they lack sufficient information with which to negotiate. If the findings by Kahn and Kohls apply to lawyers, lack of preparation by ineffective competitive negotiators increases their toughness (pushing them into the hostile, strident category) and reduces their effectiveness.

17. The classic work is S. Siegel and L. Fouraker, *Bargaining and Group Decision Making* (McGraw-Hill, 1960). Many other experiments have confirmed this finding in selected negotiating situations. See, for example, Harnett, Cummings, & Hamner, "Personality, Bargaining Style and Payoff in Bilateral Monopoly Bargaining Among European Managers," 36 Sociometry 325 (1973).

Even when used by effective negotiators who are well prepared, toughness creates other problems as well. Osgood (1962)
found that the use of toughness and unilateral commitment in
negotiating generates a marked increase in tension and mistrust
between the negotiators. The tension and mistrust create a
whole series of additional effects, each of which may impact
negatively on the negotiations. One immediate effect is to distort the communications between the parties. Mellinger, as early as 1956, found that when people communicate under conditions of distrust, they tend to overstate the extent of agreement
or to overstate the extent of disagreement. Both have negative
consequences. In the first case, the tough negotiator is led to
believe that his opponent is closer to agreement than is in fact
the case, and therefore goes on to the next item on the agenda
or, if the agenda is completed, to seek closure on the case, only
to find ultimately that the opponent is in serious disagreement
and will not commit himself to the anticipated agreement. This
discovery often precipitates a breakdown in bargaining and, in
actionable cases, a resort to trial.

Misunderstanding can have other serious effects for the competitive negotiator and the opponent. When tough negotiators
begin (wrongly) to sense agreement in the opponent, they will
often increase their demands and expectations in the case.

Tension and mistrust can distort communication in the opposite direction as well, creating the appearance of more *disagreement* and being further apart than actually exists. The result
may be a complete breakdown in bargaining, or at best, it will
take substantial effort by both sides to overcome the misunderstandings that separate them. Since some of the distance between them is illusory, effort to reduce it is inefficient. Just the
same, unless some means is found to correct the misperceptions
through more accurate communication, the negotiation will end
in impasse and trial.

The effects of toughness on party perceptions are crucial to
the success of the strategy. In psychological terms, the toughness works on the emotions of the opposing party, causing them
to become preoccupied with emotional issues and lose sight of
the objective merits of the case, and even inducing them to accept less than the merits would dictate.

When emotions run high, the danger of impasse increases.
This conclusion has been established experimentally in non-legal
settings (Osgood, 1962). If the correlation between the experi-

mental literature on toughness and our empirical descriptions of competitive attorneys is as strong as we believe, we should find evidence of the same effects among competitive lawyers.

Data from the questionnaire research of several hundred Phoenix attorneys show the rate of impasse is significantly higher for effective competitive than for effective cooperative negotiators. Cooperative effectives obtained a settlement agreement in 84% of their cases and went to trial with the remaining 16%. By contrast, competitive effectives settled only 67% of their cases and faced breakdown and trial in 33%, just over double the trial rate of cooperative negotiators (16% vs. 33%). These statistics confirm the prediction of a higher rate of aborted negotiations as a consequence of the tough strategy.

There is nothing inherently improper with the higher rate of impasses and trials characteristic of the competitive strategy. It is obviously necessary to try some cases, and individual attorneys must make the decision whether to settle or try (with the informed consent of the client, to be sure). It may be that competitive attorneys obtain higher outcomes on settled cases as a result of their toughness, and that a higher trial rate is the price they pay. Assuming that clients are not disadvantaged by the higher rate of cases going to trial, then toughness is an efficient strategy. However, trial does impose high costs, and clients whose cases go to trial may be subsidizing clients whose cases settle.

The Phoenix data also allow comparison of trial percentages of average and ineffective negotiators of both types. Here the data are more subtle and complex. Average cooperative negotiators settled 62% and tried 38% of their cases (which is a higher trial rate than effective competitives), but their trial rate is better than their fellow average competitives, who settled 50% and went to trial with 50%. Thus, average competitives take a substantially higher proportion of their cases to trial than do average cooperatives.

The statistics on ineffective negotiators show a contrary tendency. Cooperative ineffectives, whom we suspected of giving their cases away, take an extraordinary 64% of their cases to trial (a settlement rate of only 36%), while their competitive counterparts go to trial only 33% of the time, a rate that compares favorably with the trial rate of competitive effectives. One explanation of this reversal is that cooperative ineffectives *know* they are too soft and, as a defense, they feel compelled to protect the client by trying the case (a dubious protection, however, given their low ratings on trial effectiveness). On the other hand, competitive ineffectives depend upon the bluff. They are (as we saw in the last chapter) not prepared on the facts or law, not legally astute, and not effective negotiators. They rely on extreme demands, quarrelsomeness, hostility, rudeness, and other ploys to coerce the other side into settlement. If the bluff does not work (as is generally the case) they face a particularly excruciating problem: as ineffective trial attorneys, if they try the case they will be publicly exposed as bluffers. Their safest bet is to bluff to the last minute then cave in. If ineffective competitives do follow this pattern, it helps to explain why so many cases settle during the last moments before trial.

When emotions run high and impasse occurs, the offended party is often filled with righteous indignation at what he considers unfair treatment. The angry opponent retaliates against the tough negotiator by working harder on the case and creating as many obstacles and costs as possible.

A fourth consequence of toughness is its damage to long-term relationships that depend upon mutual trust. Where attorneys are likely to encounter each other over the years, tension and mistrust generated in one case will influence the dynamics and outcomes of later cases against the same opponent. This effect is magnified as an attorney's reputation becomes known throughout the local bar.

The liabilities of the tough approach provide important clues to why so few attorneys use it effectively. Its effectiveness depends upon creating enough pressure and tension to induce an emotional reaction and a reduction in expectations in the opposing party. But if the pressure is excessive, or is maintained too long, the strategy backfires and trial against a vindictive opponent results.

Osgood's findings convinced him that toughness was not the optimal strategy. He proposed that negotiators instead develop a cooperative, trusting atmosphere in which to negotiate. With this proposal we join the issue in a longstanding debate of great interest to legal negotiators. Which is the best negotiating strategy: competition or cooperation? The fact that a Q-factor analysis of the attorney questionnaire data uncovered skillful (and unskillful) use of *both* strategies among legal negotiators is an empirical verification of their relevance.

III. THE COOPERATIVE STRATEGY

The elements of the cooperative approach also come from insights of Simons. The basic dynamic of the cooperative negotiator is to move psychologically *toward* the opposing attorney. Cooperative negotiators seek common ground. They communicate a sense of shared interests, values, and attitudes using rational, logical persuasion as a means of seeking cooperation. They promote a trusting atmosphere appearing to seek no special advantage for self or client. The explicit goal is to reach a fair resolution of the conflict based on an objective analysis of the facts and law.

Osgood observed a crucial dynamic here: the cooperative negotiator shows his own trust and good faith by making unilateral concessions. Making unilateral concessions is risky, but cooperative negotiators believe it creates a moral obligation in the other to reciprocate. The cooperative strategy is calculated (subconsciously) to induce the other party to reciprocate: to cooperate in openly and objectively resolving the problem; to forego aggression, and to make reciprocal concessions until a solution is reached.

Cooperative negotiators feel a high commitment to fairness, objecting to the competitive view of negotiation as a game. To a cooperative, the gamesmanship view is ethically suspect. They feel that to move psychologically *against* another person to promote one's own interest is manipulative and an affront to human dignity. On the other hand, cooperatives move psychologically *toward* other people to achieve their preferred outcome. Competitive negotiators have reason to ask whether this is any less manipulative. Their manipulation is designed to induce or permit the opponent to trust, cooperate with, and make concessions to the manipulator.

The strengths of the cooperative approach as identified in the literature are that cooperative strategies are often more effective than tough strategies for two primary reasons: they produce more favorable outcomes, and they result in fewer ultimate breakdowns in bargaining (in the legal context, resort to trial). (See, e.g., Bartos 1962 and Harnett, Cummings and Hamner 1973).

The cooperative strategy, like the competitive, has limitations. Its major disadvantage is its vulnerability to exploitation, a problem compounded by the apparent inability of some cooperative types to recognize it when it happens. When a cooperative negotiator attempts to establish a cooperative, trusting atmosphere, in a negotiation with a tough, non-cooperative opponent, the cooperative attorney has an alarming tendency to ignore the lack of cooperation and to pursue his cooperative strategy unilaterally. The strategy requires him to continue discussing the case fairly and objectively, to make concessions about the weaknesses of his case, and refrain from self-serving behavior. In this situation, the tough negotiator is free to accept all of the fairness and cooperation without giving anything in return. In fact, it would be irrational to do anything else. On these facts, the cooperative has placed himself at a serious disadvantage. He has foregone attacking the other's position, he has conceded the weaknesses of his own position, and he has received no reciprocal value in return.

The problem for cooperative negotiators does not end here. Competitive negotiators interpret cooperation as a sign of weakness. From their viewpoint, people who are strong and people with strong cases do not make concessions or admit to weakness. When an opponent acts cooperatively with them, they actually increase their level of demands and their expectations about what they will be able to obtain in the case.

Some attorneys argue that the cooperative attorney should not fear looking weak early in a negotiation, because it induces the tough opponent to overplay his hand and expose his strategy. However, reason suggests this is a poor strategy.

IV. FURTHER APPLICATIONS OF BARGAINING LITERATURE TO LEGAL NEGOTIATION

There are many valuable insights in the bargaining literature, many of them directly applicable to legal negotiation. In the past, it has been difficult to use this literature because there was no empirical frame of reference to guide its application to the legal context. The Phoenix data provide a framework for applying the literature on cooperative and competitive bargaining. This is only a small part of what can be done. Empirical studies of the legal system are becoming larger and more sophisticated and, at the same time, the non-legal bargaining literature is also coming into its own. The potential for productive interplay between these two bodies of knowledge is very real. The kinds of issues to be addressed are illustrated in the following brief suggestions from the bargaining literature:

1. The effect of time pressures or deadlines in negotiation: Bruno (1968) *

    a. The less time pressure felt by a negotiator, the better he tended to do in a particular case.

2. Effects of time pressures, cont'd: Bartos (1965)

    a. When both negotiators feel time pressure, there is a greater probability that making concessions (adopting a cooperative approach) will be a profitable strategy.

    b. Likewise, when time pressures are not at play, concession-making is less likely to be profitable.

3. Further effects of time pressures: Pruitt & Drews (1969)

    a. When experimental negotiations were conducted in stages, increased time pressure lowered negotiators' expectations, levels of demand, and their tendency to bluff at the first bargaining session. Note that it may have same effect on both negotiators.

4. When to introduce a bona fide settlement proposal: Bartos (1964)

    a. There appears to be a "recency effect" by which a proposal advanced later in a negotiating session tends to have a greater influence on the final outcome than proposals introduced earlier.

    b. This is particularly true when a mediator is present, with the study showing a mediator is likely to endorse the most recent proposal.

5. The effects of threats in bargaining: Borah (1963)

    a. Threats create stress in bargaining.

    b. Stress reduces a negotiator's ability to understand the opponent's ideas, plans, or wishes.

    c. Stress tends to reduce the effectiveness of interpersonal relationships.

* For a full citation, see the bibliography.

6. Effects of stress, cont'd: Deutsch & Krauss (1962)

   a. Threat is most likely to occur under the following conditions:

      — the threatener has no positive interest in the other person's welfare; and

      — the threatener believes that the opponent has no interest in the threatener's welfare.

   b. When these conditions are met, the threat is likely to be effective, or at least to do no harm to the threatener's position.

   c. In experimental negotiations, agreement was most easily reached when no threats were made by either side; agreement was more difficult to reach when a threat was made by one of the negotiators; and agreement was extremely difficult or impossible when threats were made by both negotiators.

   d. Just as with toughness, use of threats greatly increases the likelihood of impasse.

7. Use of frustration in bargaining: Berkowitz (1960)

   a. Frustration creates hostility, and

   b. Unexpected frustrations create more hostility than expected frustrations.

   c. However, if parties expect hostility but receive friendliness, they are more friendly and cooperative in return than those who expect friendliness.

8. Effects of magnitude of first offer: Liebert, Smith, Hill, and Keiffer (1968)

   a. Bargainers who were not sure of the value of the case tend to use the opponent's opening bid to set their own goals in the case.

   b. Bargainers who had a good idea of the value of the case used the opponent's opening offer "to assess the reasonableness of the opponent's goals."

9. Importance of understanding the opponent's position: Muench (1963)

   a. Many difficulties in negotiating arise from failure of the negotiators to listen to and to understand their opponent's proposals.

[*56*]

b. One good method for avoiding this difficulty is to first repeat to your opponent your understanding of his position before attacking the position. This often reveals misperceptions, and can help avoid further misunderstandings.

10. Flow of information as a fundamental dynamic of bargaining: Walton & McKersie model of three phases of information flow

   a. *Phase One.* Identification of the problem—maximum exchange of information by participants to identify issues. Effectiveness requires:

      1. Presenting the issues in a strategically favorable light;

      2. Selectively controlling the flow of information.

   b. *Phase Two.* Discovery and exploration of alternative solutions and their consequences. Effectiveness involves:

      1. Creativity in perceiving and exploring the fullest range of alternatives.

      2. Indicates that invention and creativity are valuable assets for the negotiator.

   c. *Phase Three.* Discovering best solution and agreeing to it. Effectiveness involves:

      1. Skill in evaluating the value to each party of the alternatives and combining them in the most profitable manner.

11. The importance of informal customs and practices within the profession: Ikle (1964) and Bartos (1967)

   a. Informal codes of bargaining behavior exist among professional negotiators.

   b. Codes are important because they specify what types of behavior are permissible.

   c. Effective negotiators are skilled in identifying the informal customs and practices which made up the code and in identifying the expectation of others.

   d. Negotiators who do not observe the informal code generate hostility and intransigence.

[57]

12. Legal ethical standards as part of the legal negotiator's required code of behavior: Carlin (1966)

    a. Carlin's study of ethical norms and behavior of New York City's attorneys showed levels of compliance with formal ethical standards as follows:

        1. Approximately 25% of attorneys were high conformers.

        2. Approximately 50% were "middle" conformers.

        3. Approximately 25% were "low" conformers (i.e. violators).

    b. Level of ethical behavior varied according to:

        1. Size of law firm.

        2. Type of clientele.

        3. Level of court or agency work.

        4. Work setting (location of office).

        5. Inner disposition.

    c. Ethical standards are enforced by formal and informal sanctions.

        1. Formal sanctions are imposed through the courts and bar associations.

        2. Informal sanctions within the profession serve to enforce ethical and courteous behavior.

13. Background and personality variables which influence bargaining effectiveness:

    a. Reputation as a negotiator.

    b. Level of personal ambition.

    c. Experience as a negotiator.

    d. Sex of the negotiator.

This listing represents only a fraction of the kinds of issues raised in bargaining and legal literature that are ripe for application to legal negotiation. The conditions for bringing these resources to bear on the practical problems of dispute resolution in the legal system have never been so good.

V. CLIENT RELATIONS AND NEGOTIATION

Two major issues in lawyer-to-lawyer negotiation recur with considerable force in the attorney-client relationship. One is the issue of negotiation as a decision-making process; the other is the issue of manipulation.

We have been assuming that the attorney and client on each side of a civil dispute were of one mind; that they were agreed on what course to pursue, and the value at which they would be willing to settle. In practice, attorney-client relationships with this degree of mutual understanding and harmony require a great deal of skill and patience on the part of the attorney. There are many potential sources of conflict and misunderstanding. Attorneys have specialized knowledge of the law, the legal system, and the dynamics of negotiation—areas not usually understood by the client. Clients have their own perceptions of the problem and motives for pursuing it, not all of which are communicated to the attorney representing them. Without pursuing these problems any further, it becomes apparent that there will be frequent occasions of misunderstanding between attorney and client.

In a sample of approximately 150 cases we studied in Phoenix, Arizona, the impact of attorney-client misunderstandings were the single largest factor in determining what cases went to trial rather than settling. This information came from attorneys whose cases actually went to trial. When asked to identify the reason why their case did not settle, over 50% of the attorneys said it was *due to the unwillingness of one or the other of the clients to accept a settlement figure recommended by their own attorney.*

This perspective on attorney-client relations is troubling. It suggests that attorneys are not good at communicating with their clients. We have already noted that negotiation is a decision-making process, and that the decisions are made over time as facts and other persuasive factors influence each attorney's view of the case. It is easy to see how the attorney might fail to keep his client informed not only of events occurring in the processing of the case, but of developments and changes in his own assessment of the case. If the client is left behind in this way, he will naturally resist a settlement offer based on case developments he has no knowledge of.

[*59*]

But there is a larger issue implicit in these findings: if attorneys are managing cases without fully informing the clients involved, then we must conclude these clients are not participating in any meaningful way in their own cases. Lack of client involvement in and ultimate control over their own cases may seriously reduce their level of satisfaction with the outcome [18], and there is convincing evidence that it may actually result in a lower dollar value of the outcomes.

The importance of client participation in the case is highlighted in a study of personal injury cases in New York City by Douglas Rosenthal. He found that the dollar outcomes of personal injury cases were consistently higher when the lawyer kept the client not only informed about the case, but actively participating in the case.[19]

Most clients have had little exposure to the legal system and they have no idea of what they can do to help move the case to a successful conclusion. Keeping the client informed and participating in his case requires extra effort by the attorney, and involves some risk. However, attorneys have been found to work more effectively on behalf of *informed* clients than uninformed ones. The attorney should take the time to reach mutual understanding with clients on fee arrangements, the scope of the attorney's undertaking (e.g. does the contingent fee cover the cost of taking the case on appeal), the factual and legal issues posed by the case, the probable time frame for processing the case, the potential for and difficulties likely to be encountered in negotiating an out-of-court settlement, the psychological difficulty in (and risk inherent in) signing a release from liability at the time of settlement (or, if the client is a defendant, of paying over the money or otherwise performing the settlement agreement), and the possibility of having the case go to trial with its attendant uncertainties and unpleasantness.

Once clients have some understanding of the legal process, the attorney should involve them in preparation of the case. A good attorney will explain what factual information will be needed in the case, and give clients given specific assignments to

18. The importance of a client's involvement in and control over the processing of his case is discussed in Spiegel, "Lawyering and Client Decisionmaking: Informed Consent and the Legal Profession," 128 U.Pa.L. Rev. 41 (1979) and Lehman, "The Pursuit of a Client's Interest," 77 Mich.L. Rev. 1078 (1979).

19. Rosenthal, Douglas E., *Lawyer and Client: Who's In Charge?* (New York: Russell Sage Foundation: 1974).

assist him in gathering the necessary documentation and other materials. Clients should be informed of the kind of records (medical records, expenses, lost earnings, etc.) they should be keeping, and how their actions may affect their claim. In plaintiff's personal injury cases, clients should be advised not to make any statements about the case without first informing the lawyer, and not to sign anything related to the case without the lawyer's advice.

Straightforward discussion of the case and of the client's responsibilities in the case helps prepare the client for what is to come. At the same time, it creates the opportunity to counsel the client not only on the legal aspects of the case, but if necessary on the medical, emotional, employment, family, and financial aspects as well. As Rosenthal noted for personal injury claims, these are all non-legal areas that may have a direct bearing on the claim—what doctor to see, when to return to work, when and how to pay medical bills, how to finance the period of recuperation, and how to adjust emotionally.

Finally, clients must be kept constantly informed of the progress on the case. There should be a steady stream of information flowing from the attorney to the client by way of letters, telephone calls, copies of documents, etc. to inform the client of each development. This helps the client and the attorney, because the client can often prevent costly mistakes such as forgotten aspects of the claim, misplaced information, incorrect assumptions about the facts, etc. As stated in Ethical Consideration 7–8:

> "A lawyer should exert his best efforts to insure that decisions of his client are made only after the client has been informed of relevant considerations. A lawyer ought to initiate this decision-making process if the client does not do so.
> . . . A lawyer should advise his client of the possible effect of each legal alternative. A lawyer should bring to bear upon this decision-making process the fullness of his experience as well as his objective viewpoint." [20]

---

20. Model Code of Professional Responsibility (ABA, as amended February 1980).

VI. CONFLICTS BETWEEN ATTORNEY AND CLIENT

Lawyers adopt either cooperative or aggressive styles. Our data do not reveal whether clients divide along similar lines, but other evidence suggests that they do. If these types are valid as applied to clients, it follows that cooperative clients will generally desire "fair" or equitable results openly and objectively obtained while aggressive clients will desire winning, maximizing outcomes which work as much havoc on the other side as possible. A client's personality type will have a crucial and potentially dominating influence on the negotiation. It can cause misunderstanding between attorney and client, conflicts in definition of objectives, conflicts in strategy, conflicts in interactions with the other side, and conflicts in expectations about ultimate outcome.

The aggressive client with a cooperative lawyer may feel that the lawyer is too mushy, naive, and uncertain. The cooperative client with an aggressive lawyer may feel that the lawyer is too pushy and demanding, and that the lawyer is running away with the case. By being alert to these differences between attorney and client, the attorney can establish and maintain more satisfactory client relationships.

CHAPTER NOTES

Individuals Differ in Their Definitions of Justice

A useful insight into your own bargaining objectives as well as those of your opponent comes with recognition that people (including lawyers) have different ideas about what constitutes "justice". A negotiator's view of the justice of a cause will be reflected in his approach to negotiation.

Consider the effect upon negotiations of each of the following four conceptions of justice:[21]

A. *Absolute Justice.* Under this conception of justice, a person believes that he represents "truth" and "justice", and

---

21. The ideas for these categories come from I. W. Zartman, *The 50% Solution* (Garden City, N. Y.: Anchor Press 1976) at 38 to 41, although the labels used here are new. Justice is referred to here in its common usage, which does considerable violence to the philosophical treatment of the concept. See materials under the heading of "Justice" in *Dictionary of The History of Ideas* (Vol. II) (New York: Charles Scribner's Sons 1973).

that compromise is therefore wrong because it represents a departure from undeviating enforcement of correct principles.

This is the position of a factory owner who would rather shut down the factory and go out of business (and risk being found in violation of national labor law) rather than be compelled to bargain with a newly-formed labor union representing his workers, not because the union's demands are inappropriate, but because he believes labor unions are evil and cannot be condoned.

While few law students or lawyers would adopt so extreme a position on an issue such as unionism, most people have sets of values they believe to be "true" and not available for compromise. In the legal setting, cases would rarely go to trial if one or both sides did not believe they were substantively "right".

B. *Conciliatory Justice.* Under this conception, a person assumes that in most disputes, the parties are acting in good faith and there is merit in the claims of both sides. Conciliatory justice points toward finding the good faith interests of both sides and then adopting the midpoint between them as the most "just" solution. The midpoint solution is the fair or just outcome.

C. *Compassionate Justice.* This concept of justice acknowledges merit in the good faith claims of both sides, but rather than arguing for the midpoint as a solution, it prefers an outcome divided according to need.

Compassionate justice allows the weaker side to use its weakness as an argument for better treatment. The moral force of the argument is evidenced in some affirmative action programs which give temporary preferential treatment to those traditionally denied equal treatment.

D. *Power Justice.* This conception of justice is the reverse-image of compassionate justice. It assumes that disputed goods or benefits should be distributed not according to need, but according to power.

Most people have not stopped to analyze which concepts of justice they apply in making decisions about distribution of scarce resources. This lack of insight into motives sometimes brings people up short when, after arguing in favor of a proposition, they are suddenly confronted with exposure of their underlying assumptions about justice.

How would you respond in the following situations?[22] Which concept of justice are you applying?

1.   Two friends, one rich and one poor, are walking, and the rich one finds some money lying on the sidewalk. What should they do?

    a. They should divided it equally.

    b. The finder should keep most or all of it.

    c. The finder should offer most or all of it to his friend.

2.   A teacher has been given some story books to give to the students in her class, but not quite enough for everyone. Should she:

    a. Give them to the children who don't have enough money to buy such books.

    b. Draw lots, so everyone has the same chance to get them.

    c. Give them to everyone except those who make a lot of noise and trouble.

3.   Two sisters are invited to a friend's party. One of them can't go because she is sick. The other goes, does very well in many games, and wins a large number of prizes. Their mother says that the two sisters should divide the prizes. How should they divide them?

    a. The sister who went should get most of them.

    b. The sister who didn't go should get most of them.

    c. They should divide them equally.

4.   A boy in a science club is working on a project, and wants to look at some things through a microscope and make drawings of them. He starts to sit down at the microscope just as another boy, who also wants to use it, comes over to it. What should he do?

    a. Tell the other boy to wait until he finishes.

    b. Talk it over with the other boy and decide together who should use it first.

5.   Two football teams have come out on the same field, both expecting to use it for practice. One of the teams got there five

---

22. Questions developed by Daniel Druckman, an active researcher on bargaining and editor of *Negotia-* *tions: Social-Psychological Perspectives* (SAGE, 1977).

minutes before the other.   What should the first team's captain do?

    a. Argue strongly; demand the field for his own team.

    b. Discuss it, try to work out an agreement with other team.

    6.   A school has been given a large box of candy.   Each class votes, and elects someone to enter a dart-throwing contest to see how much of the candy he can win for the class.   The winner of the contest gets 5 boxes for his class; all other classes get 2 boxes.   The winner comes back to his class with the 5 boxes.   Should he:

    a. Get the same as anyone else in the class.

    b. Get more than anyone else in the class.

    c. Get less than anyone else in the class.

In thinking about one's concept of justice, it is helpful to consider the meaning of the word "compromise".   For some, the word has a pejorative meaning; for others it embodies some of humankinds highest ideals.   In the legal context, compromise means a settlement of differences in which each side makes concessions.   Compromise is so important to the idea of settlements that legal encyclopedias and other reference works discuss legal rules governing settlement agreements under the heading of "compromise and settlement".

The requirement of compromise is consistent with each of the above definitions of justice except the first, which sees compromise (at best) as a necessary evil much to be avoided.   But the meaning of compromise is general enough to accommodate those who feel the division of interests ought to favor one side (whether the needier side or the stronger side) as well as those who believe it should be equal.

A fear of compromises or concessions is not irrational.   Everyone can recall occasions when they have made concessions only to find later that they were duped by the other side into giving up much more than they should have, or occasions where they have performed their side of a bargain only to have the other side accept the benefit then refuse to perform their part of the agreement.   In international relations there are continuing debates about whether it is safe to make concessions to an enemy, and when concessions are made there are always those who cry it was a "sell out".

[*65*]

The fear of being exploited, the fear of undiscovered facts, the uncertainty about credibility of evidence, all combine to make compromise an uncomfortable act. Much of the art of negotiation is learning when and how and why to compromise.

2.   *The Importance of Context and Objectives in Legal Negotiation*

Negotiations may arise in a wide range of settings, each requiring a somewhat different set of strategies. Effective negotiation is situation specific. There is no single approach or strategy that will serve in all negotiation settings. The simplest way to illustrate the relationship between strategy (or, if you prefer a milder term, "approach") and setting is to consider the dynamics called into play by representative negotiating tasks.

A.   You are counsel to the Salvation Army, which sends you from New York to Texas to work out the terms of (i.e. negotiate) a $5,000,000 charitable contribution by the 85-year old widow of a Texas oil millionaire. Her children are divided over the advisability of the contribution, and want to talk with you about it.

B.   You are counsel to Pan American Airways, which sends you to negotiate the terms of two-year contract for the purchase of flight fuel from Standard Oil Company of California.

C.   You are counsel to the Chicago Daily Express (an influential regional newspaper). The President of the corporation which publishes the *Express* retains you to represent him in a divorce. One of his major concerns is that there be *no* publicity.

D.   You are an attorney with a public interest law firm. You agree to represent the tenants of a decaying central city apartment house. The apartment house is in the pathway of an urban renewal project, and your first task is to represent the tenants in hearings before the City Council.

E.   You are representing the plaintiff (or, if you prefer, the insurance company defending the defendant) in a personal injury case. The judge calls you and opposing counsel in for a pretrial settlement conference.

F.   You are called in by a local trial judge and assigned to represent a man accused of rape.

G.   You are counsel to a major labor union and one of your duties is to participate (as a member of a team of five negotiators) in the negotiation of a new two-year contract with a hostile employer. When the current contract was negotiated, the two sides engaged in bitter, intense negotiations for over three months without ever reaching agreement. The union had been forced to strike and the workers were off the job for nearly four weeks before a federal mediator was able to help the parties come to agreement. In anticipation of expiration of the contract, both sides have started a propaganda campaign as they seek bargaining advantage for the upcoming talks.

WHAT USEFUL DISTINCTIONS CAN BE MADE BETWEEN THESE DIFFERENT TYPES OF SITUATIONS?

Some of the differences in the five situations are:

1. Transactions vs. disputes (planning relationships and preventing legal problems vs. resolving disputes or problems once they have arisen.)

2. Motives of principals involved may include:

   a. donative intent;

   b. economic exchange (profitable);

   c. avoid personal embarrassment;

   d. maximize/minimize dollar recovery;

   e. public good/political expediency;

   f. punish a wrongdoer.

3. Arena in which the negotiations will or might take place:

   a. Living room of wealthy donor;

   b. Business offices;

   c. Attorneys' offices;

   d. City Council or other administrative chambers;

   e. Judge's chambers;

   f. Trial court;

   g. Conference room of an office building or hotel.

4. Legal rules applicable to the transaction or dispute.

It should be clear that no single set of skills is going to carry an attorney safely through each of these situations. In fact, an attorney may be highly competent in two or three of the situations, but utterly ineffective in the others.

3. Some Questions About Choice of Strategy

The Phoenix data suggest that a negotiator will have a competitive opponent about 25% of the time. What strategies are available to the negotiator who wants to negotiate cooperatively (in the problem solving mode) for discovering, in the early stages of the negotiation, whether the opponent is dealing cooperatively or competitively?

Since the data suggest that some (perhaps most) attorneys have the ability to negotiate from either pattern, is there a possibility that a negotiator can, by his own conduct, influence the opponent's choice in favor of cooperation?

4. Use of Facts in Bargaining: Strategic Issues

A central issue in bargaining literature is the role of information in the process and outcome of bargaining. Most economic and game theoretic models of negotiation assume that both parties to a negotiation have "perfect" or "complete" information, which means that they have perfect knowledge of (1) the facts of the problem; (2) the rules governing the solution of the problem; (3) the range of alternatives or strategies available to each of them; and (4) the utility function of each of them (i.e. the importance or value to each party of each item in the payoff matrix). Most of these models further assume that neither side will change its utility functions over the course of the bargaining.

Economic and game theoretic models also assume that the negotiator and his opponent will both make decisions on the basis of rational choice, which is a formal concept meaning that "(1) the individual evaluates alternatives in his environment on the basis of his preferences among them, (2) his preference ordering is consistent and transitive, and (3) he always chooses the preferred alternative". *These assumptions define away the major problems of legal negotiation.*

The central problem for lawyers is the inverse of these two sets of assumptions: lack of information and lack of knowledge about how the opponent will act and react.

For lawyers, the problem of information becomes a problem of obtaining sufficient (or adequate) information and presenting it is a way which does justice to its truth (i.e. credibility). The skills involved in gathering, analyzing, and persuading with facts are complex and varied. Some relate to the insight and creativity required in knowing what to look for and where to look (e.g. in a products liability case, how do you prove negligent manufacture?) Other skills relate to the mechanics of discovery: knowing how, when, and why to use the various procedural devices available in a particular jurisdiction (indeed, sometimes the choice of jurisdiction may be dictated by the quality of discovery rules available—as between federal and state courts, for example). Additional, and more sophisticated, skills are required in making the strategic choices about when, where, and how to obtain information. On one hand, there is a danger of alienating the other side, polarizing the parties, and creating unnecessary delay, costs, and animosity by overly aggressive or burdensome discovery tactics. On the other hand, there is a constant danger of under-discovery; of overlooking or failing to effectively track down the crucial evidence or information upon which the case depends.

Finally, there is a strategic decision. When and how should you disclose facts to give them their best impact? Many trial attorneys recommend that you save your best facts (and your most persuasive arguments generally) so you can introduce them as surprises at trial. The difficulty of that position (however effective it may be if the case does go to trial) is that on the average, fewer than 2 cases in 10 go to trial. If attorneys reserve their best facts and arguments for use at trial *and* settle 8 out of 10 cases, then they are settling cases on *less than the best facts and arguments*, which strongly suggests they are getting less than full value for them in settlement.

Chapter Four

STAGES OF THE NEGOTIATION PROCESS

I. INTRODUCTION

Negotiation is a repetitive process that follows reasonably predictable patterns over time. Yet in legal disputes, so much of the attorneys' attention and energy are absorbed by pretrial procedure and the approach of trial that they fail to recognize the identifiable patterns and dynamics of the negotiation process.

A useful description of the dynamics of legal negotiation can be developed by selectively applying the insights and observations available in the existing non-legal literature to the dynamics of negotiation as observed in videotaped examples of legal negotiating. Based on such an analysis, four stages can be identified in legal negotiation.

A. STAGE ONE: ORIENTATION AND POSITIONING

1. Orientation

   a. Opposing attorneys begin dealing with each other.

   b. Relationships are defined and established.

2. Positioning

   a. Negotiators talk primarily about the strengths or merits of their side of the case (often in very general terms).

   b. Negotiators work to establish their opening positions. Possible positions include:

   (i) *Maximalist Position.* Asking more (sometimes much more) than you expect to obtain.

   (ii) *Equitable Position.* Taking a position you feel is fair to both sides.

   (iii) *Integrative Position.* Presenting or seeking to discover alternative solutions to the problem as a means of putting together the most attractive package for all concerned.

c. Each side creates the illusion of being inalterably committed to the opening position.

d. Time span of this phase is usually measured in months or years.

B. STAGE TWO: ARGUMENTATION

1. Each side seeks to present its case in the strategically most favorable light.

2. Each side seeks to discover the *real* position of the other, while trying to avoid disclosing its own real position:

   a. Issues become more clearly defined.

   b. Strengths and weaknesses of each side become more apparent.

3. Each side seeks to discover and reduce the real position of the other.

4. The expectations of each side about what can be obtained in the case undergo substantial changes.

5. Concessions are made by one or both sides.

C. STAGE THREE: EMERGENCE AND CRISIS

1. Negotiators come under pressure of approaching deadlines.

2. Each side realizes that one or both of them must make major concessions, present new alternatives, or admit deadlock and resort to trial.

3. Each side seeks and gives clues about areas in which concessions might be given.

4. New alternatives are proposed; concessions are made.

5. Crisis is reached:

   a. Neither side wants to give any more.

   b. Both sides are wary of being exploited or taken advantage of.

   c. Both sides have given up more than they would like.

   d. Both sides know they must stop somewhere.

e. The dealine is upon them; one of the parties must accept the other's final offer or there is a breakdown and impasse.

f. The client worries whether to accept the attorney's recommendation to settle.

D. STAGE FOUR: AGREEMENT OR FINAL BREAKDOWN

1. If the parties agree to a settlement, Stage Four includes:

a. Working out the final details of the agreement.

b. Justifying and reinforcing each other and the clients about the desirability of the agreement.

c. Formalizing the agreement.

2. *If the negotiations break down and are not revived, the case goes to trial.*

As simple as this outline is, it becomes a surprisingly powerful tool for the practicing lawyer. Inexperienced attorneys often misperceive which stage of the process the case is in and use tactics that are unnecessary or even harmful to the dynamics of the negotiation. One example is the tendency of cooperative attorneys to move psychologically through the stages more quickly than a tough opponent, then when no agreement is forthcoming, to assume that the final stage has been reached, and to precipitate a final breakdown in the negotiations.

II. DISCUSSION OF THE STAGES

A. STAGE ONE: ORIENTATION AND POSITIONING

1. Orientation

Stage One of the negotiation process involves two interrelated dynamics, described as orientation and positioning. Orientation is the less obvious of the two. In routine matters, it is the natural by-product of the interaction between the attorneys as they begin work on a case. Letters are exchanged, phone calls are made, and each lawyer becomes oriented to the basic approach and style of the other. In most cases the negotiator is not aware of the orientation dynamics. When the opposing attorney is a law student participating in a clinical course or a new law graduate, the operation of the orientation phase becomes obvious, and most attorneys become very aware of the nature of the relationship that is being established, occasionally guiding it in a benevolently paternalistic way. The importance of the orientation phase is not limited to such special situations, however. In every case, even between very experienced lawyers, the negotiating relationship that emerges will decide whether the negotiators will approach each other as competitive or cooperative negotiators, or a mix of the two, and will determine what strategies and tactics will be used by each attorney in the case. As in political campaigns, the heights or depths to which the opponents will go to gain advantage over each other is strongly influenced by impressions given and received at this stage.

2. Positioning

The second aspect of Stage One is closely related to the first, but also has a dynamic of its own. The lawyers come forward with an opening position. At this early stage in the dispute, that is not as simple as it appears. The facts are not all in, the legal questions are not fully researched, and unforeseen developments loom on the horizon. In the face of these uncertainties, the negotiators must leave themselves a certain amount of latitude, yet they must come up with something. What they come up with is an opening position.

As given in the outline, there are essentially three strategies that can be used in framing an opening position. A useful summary of these strategies as articulated in the non-legal literature is given by Ramberg (1978). According to Ramberg, the negotiator may adopt the maximalist strategy of asking for more than he expects to obtain, he may adopt the equitable strategy of taking a position that is fair to both sides, or he may adopt the integrative strategy of searching for alternative solutions in the hope of finding the most attractive combination for all concerned. Each strategy has its own strengths and weaknesses.

a. Maximalist Positioning

The arguments for maximalist positioning begin with the assumption that the opening position is a bargaining position, and that no matter how long the bargainer may deny it, he expects to come down from it to find agreement. Maximalist positioning has several advantages. It effectively hides the bargainer's real

[*73*]

or minimum expectations, it eliminates the danger of committing to an overly modest evaluation of the case, it provides a cover for him while he seeks to learn his opponent's real position, and it will very likely lead the opponent to reduce his later expectations in the case. It also provides the negotiator with something to give up, with concessions he can make, in order to come to terms with the opponent. This last factor may be especially important when the opponent also opened high, and the negotiator is required to trade concessions in order to arrive at mutually agreeable terms. These advantages lead Siegel and Fouraker (1960) to believe that the negotiator who makes high opening demands, has a high level of expectations, makes relatively small and infrequent concessions, and is perceptive and unyielding will fare better in the long run than his opponent.

The potential benefits of the maximalist position need to be weighed against its potential demerits, which are those of tough strategies generally as discussed at some length in Chapter Three. The most important weakness is the increased risk of breakdown and throwback to trial. The competent opponent will prefer the extra burden of trial to the unreasonable demands and supporting tactics of the maximalist negotiator unless the opponent himself is equipped with an effective strategy for dealing with them.

We observe in the data that competitive attorneys at all levels of effectiveness are rated as making high opening demands. Yet, by definition, effective/competitives use the strategy effectively, and ineffective/competitives do not. We are forced to conclude that in the legal context the maximalist strategy does not consistently bring high returns for those who use it; only for those who use it effectively. For ineffective/competitive attorneys, at least, it is unsuccessful.

How high a demand can be without losing its effectiveness undoubtedly depends on several considerations. One is the nature of the remedy being sought. By their nature, contract damages are less inflatable than personal injury damages, for example, and the negotiator who multiplies his contract damages as he does his personal injury claims will undermine his own credibility. Another consideration is local custom. Specialized groups within the bar develop norms and customs that provide measures against which the reasonableness or extremism of a demand can be evaluated. So we see that not all high demands are the same. Some demands lack credibility on their face by their inappropriateness and lack of congruity in the context in which they are made. But the level of demands is not the sole factor. The data suggest that effective/competitive negotiators are able to establish the credibility and plausibility of high demands by convincing legal argumentation. Ineffective/ competitives lack the skills to do so and in the absence of convincing support, their high demands suffer further losses of credibility.

Finally, it should be noted that how effective a high demand is will depend upon the opponent against whom the high demands are made. Experimental findings have demonstrated two possible effects (Liebert, Smith, Hill and Keiffer, 1968). In cases where the opponent is unsure of the actual value of the case, high opening demands by the maximizing negotiator have the desired effect. The opponent, unsure of the value of the case, uses the maximizer's high opening demands as a standard against which to set his own goals in the case. However, when the opponent had evaluated the case and arrived at a judgment of its value, the opponent interpreted the maximizer's high opening demands as evidence of unreasonableness. In this latter case, we expect that the maximizer's credibility is diminished and the likelihood of breakdown and trial increased.

b.   Equitable Positioning

The equitable position is one calculated to be fair to both sides. Its most notable proponent is Bartos (1978). Bartos challenges the assumption of maximalist theorists that both sides to a negotiation are trying to maximize their own payoffs or benefits. He argues that a competing value is also operative; that negotiators feel a cooperative desire to arrive at a fair solution for both. In support of this argument, he cites not only humanistic literature defending equality as an essential ingredient of justice, but also anthropological and sociological studies confirming the widespread existence and operation in society of an egalitarian norm of reciprocity. Bartos has conducted numerous theoretical and experimental studies of negotiation which lead him to believe that the human desire to deal fairly with others, the equitable position, is preferable to toughness as a strategy. This is seen as the most economical and efficient method of conflict resolution. It minimizes the risk of deadlock and avoids the costs of delay occasioned by extreme bargaining positions. Bartos recommends that negotiators be scrupulously fair and that they avoid the temptation to take advantage of the opponent. He cautions that the equitable positioning requires trust, which he views as a positive and necessary attitude, but not naivete. Trust must be tempered with realism. It is out of trust that a negotiator makes concessions, but if the trust is not rewarded or returned in fair fashion, further concessions should be withheld until the opponent reciprocates.

As conceived by Bartos, then, equitable negotiators do not as a matter of practice open the negotiations with a statement specifying their final view of the ultimate fair solution. Rather, they open with a position that shows they are serious about finding agreement, and they trustingly work toward a mid-point between their reasonable opening position and the reasonable opening position of their opponent. Until both sides come forward with reasonable opening positions, Bartos considers the case unready for serious negotiation. It is not ripe.

Referring back now to the data on cooperative and competitive negotiators, we intuitively suspect that Bartos' equitable negotiator is a cooperative type, or that cooperative types embody the equitable position. This observation is borne out by the extremely high ratings received by cooperative attorneys on characteristics such as trustworthy, ethical, honest, and fair. Just as with our analysis of maximalist positioning by competitive attorneys, it must be pointed out that the use of equitable positioning by cooperative attorneys does not always bring satisfactory results. It is obviously satisfactory as used by effective/cooperatives, but it is just as obviously deficient when used by ineffective/cooperatives. We must conclude that the positioning strategy, whether maximalist or equitable, does not guarantee success. Whichever one is used must be used with care and acumen or it will not be effective.

c.   Integrative Positioning

Integrative Positioning is more than an opening position. It describes an attitude or approach that carries through the other stages of the negotiation, and is an alternative to bargaining by positioning. The most effective advocates of this method for our purposes are Roger Fisher and William Ury, *GETTING TO YES*, (Boston: Houghton Mifflin Co. 1981). Among business people, the method is seen as the art of problem solving.

The integrative negotiator views the case as presenting a number of alternative solutions, and he believes that chances for reaching agreement are enhanced by discovering the various alternatives, evaluating them in light of the interests of the parties, and seeking to arrange the alternatives in a package that yields maximum benefit to both parties. This strategy is often identified with exchange transactions involving many variables, and is generally seen as having limited utility in a personal injury action, for example, where the fundamental issue is how much money the defendant is going to pay the plaintiff (a distributive problem). Further analysis will reveal, however, that cases such as this have important integrative elements that should not lightly be dismissed. In an era of double digit inflation, for example, a $10,000 payment today has the same value as a $15,000 payment three years from now based on prevailing interest rates alone. If savings in avoidance of discovery, motions, briefs, and other legal costs are calculated in, $10,000 paid today will resolve claims that will cost the defendant $30,000 or $40,000 three years from now. Additional utilities are introduced by examining the interests of the injured plaintiff in receiving something today to pay doctor and car repair bills compared to a larger amount three years from now.

We may conclude that even in the domain of actionable disputes, there is substantial opportunity for use of an integrative approach. In reference to the data on negotiator types in Part I, it appears likely that integrative bargaining is used by effective negotiators of both types, and perhaps ineffective/cooperatives are open to integrative suggestions as well.

Ineffective/competitives, however, appear more resistant to the approach.

3. Inalterable Commitment to an Opening Position

The next element of Stage One relating to positioning is that each side seeks to establish the illusion that he is inalterably committed to his opening position. The purposes served by this tactic are several. It lends credibility to the demand, and particularly in the case of high opening demands, it gives time for the demand to have its effect on the hopes or expectations of the other side. It gives each negotiator time to make further evaluations of the value of the case and to gain information about what the other side is willing to accept. When the negotiators are ready to begin more serious negotiation, they are better informed and better able to bargain than when the extreme demands were established. As with the other elements of the ne-

[77]

gotiation process, however, this strategy can easily be overdone. It must be used with judgment, perceptiveness, and flexibility.

4. Duration of Stage One

The final element in Stage One is the observation that it generally continues over a longer period of time than all of the other stages combined. At least one reason for this is that in many actionable cases the attorneys do not begin seriously considering settlement until trial deadlines make themselves felt.[23] However, court calendars are so crowded that these deadlines may not approach for two years or more. Few cases require this amount of time to become ripe for settlement, and so clients must endure long delays attributed to court congestion even though their cases will ultimately be settled.

The solution to this problem is also suggested in our Phoenix data. The major problem giving rise to congested trial courts is not inefficient administration of cases by judicial personnel; it is the disproportionately high percentage of cases brought to trial by a certain identifiable subsection of the practicing bar. We found in 300 cases studied that the percentage of cases brought to trial by attorneys was directly related to the negotiating skills of the attorneys. The less skilled they were at negotiation, the more cases they brought to the trial court for resolution by judge or jury. Effective negotiators as a group constitute half of the practicing bar (49%), yet with their high settlement rate they account for only 31% of the cases going to trial in Phoenix courts. Average negotiators constitute 37% of the bar, yet they account for fully 46% of the cases going to trial. Ineffective negotiators constitute 14% of the Bar, yet they account for 23% of the cases going to trial. Together, average and ineffective negotiators constitute roughly half of the bar (51%), yet they account for over two thirds (69%) of the cases that went to trial.[24]

---

23. The tendency to wait for trial deadlines to approach before seriously preparing a case for settlement discussions is well documented. In Phoenix, for example, we found that over 70% of all cases were settled within 30 days of the trial date. Of those a hefty 13% settled on the day of trial itself.

24. The actual figures were as follows: In cases where one of the attorneys was rated as an effective negotiator, only 2 out of 10 cases went to trial. Eight were settled. However, when the attorney was rated as a less effective (average) negotiator, the number of cases going to trial doubled, to 4 out of 10. Finally, when the attorney was rated as an ineffective negotiator, the percentage of cases going to trial increased again, to 5 out of 10. If we calculate the number of cases brought to trial by each group of attorneys and combine it with the above data, we can see the impact ineffective negotiators have on the court system.

The implications of these findings are further demonstrated by evaluating them in light of data on the trial effectiveness of the lawyers studied. Effective negotiators of both types were rated as highly effective *trial* attorneys. Unfortunately for the quality of trial court proceedings, these effective trial attorneys settle 80% of their cases and although they make up 49% of the bar they account for a disproportionately low 31% of all cases going to trial. By comparison, less effective negotiators (except the cooperative average group) were rated as decidedly ineffective trial attorneys, and although they make up only 51% of the bar, they account for 69% of the cases going to trial. The remarkable statistic is that if these less effective negotiators could improve their negotiating skills enough to bring their settlement rates into line with those of effective negotiators, their increased settlement rate would reduce the trial burden of Phoenix courts by a full 37%.

The suggestion that less effective negotiators can develop their negotiation skills and thereby significantly reduce the number of cases they must take to trial is not one to be dismissed. Our state of knowledge about negotiation has vastly increased in the past three or four years. Properly organized and taught, this knowledge will introduce dramatic increases in the negotiating effectiveness of lawyers, and less effective negotiators will benefit the most from these developments. To be sure, the objective is not a higher settlement rate, but improved procedures for the fair resolution of disputes. The emerging field of knowledge about legal negotiation and the concurrent development of innovative methods for delivering the new knowledge in usable form to the practicing bar hold a potential for major improvements in the administration of justice in the United States.

B. STAGE TWO: ARGUMENTATION

1. Overview

It is axiomatic that the opening positions established by negotiation in Stage One will be some distance apart. If not, there would be no controversy and the case would be resolved immediately. Given the distance between the opening positions, some method or procedure is necessary whereby it may be explored and evaluated. These dynamics come into play in Stage Two. Both sides begin to gather information about the real or hidden expectations of the other, while at the same time trying to avoid disclosing information about their own minimum expectations and utilities. A great deal of information may be exchanged, but it is presented in a favorable light. Through this process, the legal and factual issues become better defined and the strengths and weaknesses of each side become more apparent.

2.   The Problem of Making Concessions

It is usually in Stage Two that the first concessions are made. Concessions are important devices because they are the primary means by which agreement can be approached. They also have importance as instruments of strategy. The task of the cooperative attorney is to establish a cooperative, trusting atmosphere where a just or equitable outcome can be sought. One of the primary means for doing this is through the selective granting of concessions. By comparison, the task of the competitive or maximalist negotiator is to obtain the maximum number of concessions from his opponent while making the fewest and smallest concessions possible. This is consistent with his goal of obtaining the maximum possible outcome.

These conflicting approaches illustrate why the issue of concession-making assumes such importance in economic models of bargaining (see Young 1975 at 137–140) and why it calls for more respectful treatment within the legal context. Zartman (1978 at 81) gives a short synopsis of four sets of theories about concession rates that are relevant here. The theories are, in effect, predictions about what effect concessions will have on an opponent. The first prediction is that concession rates will be reciprocal, in the sense that concessions by one negotiator will be matched by concessions of comparable value by the opponent. A second and inconsistent prediction is that concession rates will be exploitive, meaning that concessions by one negotiator will be met by concessions of the opposite magnitude by the other. By this view, the negotiator who makes large concessions will find his opponent making small concessions in exchange, while the negotiator who makes small concessions will find his opponent making large concessions in return. The third prediction is that concession-making by one negotiator is unresponsive to the concession-making behavior of the other in the ways suggested above, but responds instead to the pressure of deadline. As the deadline approaches, both sides use the pressure to induce the other to make favorable final concessions. The fourth prediction is the projective view, which argues that parties mutually aim at a target point falling between their opening positions and they consciously or unconsciously adjust their concessions to arrive at that mid-point.

The crucial task for the effective negotiator is to determine which prediction accurately describes the way concessions will operate in each specific negotiating situation, and then to learn to adjust his own negotiating strategy according to that knowledge.   As we see in videotaped examples of attorney negotiations, not all attorneys take this task adequately into account.

C. STAGE THREE: EMERGENCE AND CRISIS

1. Effect of a Deadline

As the deadline approaches, a crisis is reached. Concessions have been made, neither side wishes to give anything more, both sides are wary of being exploited, and both sides know that they must stop somewhere. At this point, one party suggests a final offer and says, in effect, that's the best I can do. Take it or else we go to trial. It has been helpfully observed in non-legal literature that this kind of demand actually presents a threefold choice: take it, or leave it, or come up with something else (Ikle 1964). This acute observation suggests that the attorney who lacks imagination may see only a two-fold choice: take it or leave it. He may decide that since he cannot take it, impasse has been reached, and the negotiation is over. It is important to bear in mind the third alternative, to come up with something else. Furthermore, what the negotiator comes up with does not have to be a significant concession. It can be an integrative proposal, suggesting another alternative or new combinations of alternatives that increase the utility of settlement to the parties without decreasing their total payoffs.

However, there is economy in waiting until the trial is near before negotiating. It is necessary to prepare the case only once; if negotiations fail, the preparations can be used for trial.

The Phoenix data suggest that deadline pressures are perceived differently in each specialized area of law. In criminal law, deadline pressures are not extreme until a few days before trial; it is the same in personal injury cases. But in commercial and real property disputes, the mere threat of filing a case may be considered heavy handed, and if the case is filed, the deadline pressures begin to mount two months or more before trial. Attorneys should adjust their own expectations and sensitivities accordingly. The personal injury lawyer who feels an intense need to settle two months before trial is likely to be doing his client and himself a disservice if he overreacts to the closer approach of the trial date.[25]

2.   The Client, the Opposing Party, and the Negotiation Process

We have said little in our analysis of bargaining stages to suggest there is a client, preferring to focus exclusively on dynamics between the attorneys. We have been following, in the language of non-legal literature on bargaining, the Negotiator-as-Bargainer model (Druckman 1978). However, the attorneys are not negotiating on behalf of their own immediate interests but rather on behalf of clients. The clients come with their own sets of expectations about what the case outcome should be—expectations that derive from a wide variety of sources, many of which are outside the attorneys' cognizance and control. These include general expectations about how cases are processed through the American legal system, about the importance of trial as a standard of fairness and a forum for vindication of wrongs, about the anticipated monetary value of the case, and so on. The attorney has also had an input in creating client expectations. His greatest influence is probably during the first few consultations with the client, perhaps even before the client accepts the attorney as his representative. Attorneys may estimate for the client a probable value of the case, often based on an assumption of 100% liability or clear breach of contract. In

25. The most extreme example of this is in real property disputes and commercial disputes; fully 35% of the real property disputes and 29% of the commercial disputes were settled without filing. The actual invocation of the legal process was not necessary. This compares with only 7.5% of personal injury cases and 13.8% of divorce cases. At the other end of the scale are criminal cases; none were considered to have been settled without formal charges being made, and a telling 32.3% were not resolved until the day of trial. An additional 35.5% were settled from 2 to 20 days before trial, with the remainder settling from 11 to 90 days before trial. By contrast, in personal injury cases only 2.5% held out until the day of trial, with a surprisingly high 42.5% being settled from 2 to 10 days before trial. That is clearly the crucial period for personal injury attorneys and clients. Commercial and real property cases are more strung out, indicating that attorneys prefer not to allow the trial date to get so close as in criminal and personal injury cases. In commercial cases, for example, 4.5% settle the day of the trial, only 12.5% settle 2 to 10 days before trial, and the bulk of cases settle from 11 to 60 days before trial.

the attorney's mind, value is then subtracted to reflect the degree of factual weakness in the claim, while in the client's mind, the 100% figure is what he expects to obtain. For whatever reason, the expectations of clients are commonly some distance from those of the attorney, and it is in this context that the relationship of the client to the negotiation process becomes obvious and determinative. We see this, for example, in the Phoenix data, where attorneys judged that client refusal to accept the deal was the primary reason for failure to settle in over 50% of the cases that went to trial.

The lawyer, after all, is expressly commissioned to represent the interests of the client, and the task includes helping the client to form realistic expectations of how and on what terms his case should be resolved. However, because of the high level of uncertainty inherent in the valuation of cases and prediction of outcomes, the lawyer himself cannot make unfailingly accurate judgments in the early stages of the dispute. Arriving at these judgments is a process that can only occur over time. In the largest number of instances, the lawyer's own evaluation substantially changes during that process as the full dimensions of both sides of the case become revealed. The task for the lawyer, then, is to create realistic expectations in his client at the outset, and keep him abreast of the lawyer's own evolving evaluation of the case.

The attorney has a duty to develop a solution to the case that is acceptable not only to himself and his client, but also to the opposing attorney and his client. However, once a solution is made, psychological reinforcement may be required by all concerned. The effective negotiator will not only seek reinforcement for himself, but will take great pains to provide adequate reinforcement to the opposing party. If the negotiator fails to provide it, he may well be faced with a subsequent repudiation of the agreement by the disgruntled opponent.

For these reasons, the negotiator must make a point to include, as integral parts of Stages Three and Four, procedures that will reinforce the opposing party, as well as his own client, in accommodating themselves to the decision reached.

D. STAGE FOUR: AGREEMENT OR
FINAL BREAKDOWN

1. Agreement

If the parties come to an agreement, the work is not over. There are important steps yet to be taken. The first of these is to work out the details of the agreement. Some attorneys negotiate in a way that keeps the details alive and active in the ongoing discussion. This is a common feature of integrative bargaining, where alternative solutions to each sub-issue are explored and creative solutions sought.

By contrast, other attorneys prefer to negotiate only the most basic issues, such as money, while leaving the others to be wrapped up after general agreement has been reached. One variation of this strategy is to separate the issues according to how difficult they are to resolve, then to resolve them working from the easiest to the most difficult. Whatever variation or combination is used, the attorneys at some point have an agreement, yet important details may remain to be worked out. These are sometimes known as "Oh, by the way's." These details must be considered important to the overall quality and favorability of the agreement and should be given the attention they deserve.

The need for attention to detail becomes apparent as negotiators undertake the process of formalizing the agreement. This process is covered in Chapter 5, Section IV(c) below. Treatment may also be found under the somewhat obscure heading of "Compromise and Settlement" in *Am.Jur.2d* and *Corpus Juris Secundum*. Both encyclopedias also provide extensive forms and other supporting documents.

2. Final Breakdown

If the parties are unable to arrive at a settlement and the negotiations are not revived, a final breakdown has occurred and the case goes to trial for resolution. The term final breakdown is used because not all breakdowns in negotiation are final. Breakdowns occur as negotiating ploys designed to put pressure on the opponent. As a simple example, insurance defense counsel effectively use this tactic to bring increased pressure to bear on their opponents by refusing to enter into serious negotiations until a few days (sometimes a few hours) before trial. They would be robbed of this tactic if plaintiffs' counsel adopted a firm policy, and held to it, of never negotiating once the case is within a week of trial. The effect would be to move the operative deadline to a week before trial. It might yield advantages to one or both sides.

III. THE INTERPLAY BETWEEN LEGAL PROCEEDINGS AND THE NEGOTIATION PROCESS

To this point, we have been preoccupied with the dynamics of negotiation as a dispute resolution process. In the legal context, however, it cannot be analyzed independently. It is operating concurrently with a competing process having a force and dynamic of its own: litigation. In our discussion, we noted the pressures for settlement occasioned by trial deadlines. In reality, however, the arrival of the trial date is the culmination of a complex series of preparatory actions that begins before the case is filed and proceeds step by step through the complex procedures of choosing a forum, pleading, discovery, preparation of witnesses, preparation of evidence (documentary and demonstrative), pretrial conference, motions and all related work. These aspects of legal procedure are undertaken (or have the potential of being undertaken) by the attorneys concurrently as the case moves, psychologically, through stages one to four of the negotiation process. Some procedures, such as pleading, coincide with basis elements of the negotiation process, such as statement of (extreme) opening positions. The utilization and timing of other procedural steps is a matter open to the discretion of the attorneys and can be used either to help or to hinder the psychology and dynamics of each successive stage in the negotiation process.

The effective negotiator will take full cognizance of the relationship between pre-trial procedures and the stages identified in the negotiation process. He will calculate his moves within the legal sphere to further his objectives of arriving, if possible, at a settlement more favorable to his client than trial combat would be.

For example, in a contract dispute between two reputable businesses, it is commonly feasible and desirable to engage in the bargaining process and arrive at a suitable agreement without ever filing an action. On the other hand, if one or both par-

[*85*]

ties refuse to negotiate seriously, and other efforts fail, a forum is selected and complaint filed. In a business context, this is a serious step, and it may well be enough to engender serious attempts to resolve the case without trial. If it is not, then further pre-trial procedures are undertaken step by step, always in ways that have the greatest strategic value for an advantageous settlement as well as maximum value in the event of trial.

The example of a business dispute just mentioned suggests the essential tension that exists between negotiation and formal legal processes; the former requiring a conciliatory approach and the latter an adversarial approach. (For an illuminating sociological discussion of this conflict, see Aubert 1963). In Macaulay's pioneering study (1963), the typical sequence of escalation from conciliation to adversariness was as follows. First, the two businesses, usually production or purchasing people, would try to work out the differences informally. If this failed, the production or purchasing people would talk with house counsel or outside counsel concerning possible approaches to the other party, and they would then attempt again to arrive at a resolution with their counterparts in the other business. If this was not fruitful, legal counsel would be asked to write a letter to the other business on letterhead stationery, so that they could see lawyers were now being involved. If this level of legal involvement was not sufficient, then attorneys were authorized to file an action. This sequence represents a gradual shift from a conciliatory approach to an adversarial one, and it has important implications for the outcome of the dispute and the future relations between the parties involved. In an adversarial relationship, there are not only the publicity and expenses and delays of legal process, but positions are hardened, relationships strained, and ill feelings bred. These are obviously detrimental and even fatal to the on-going business relationships involved.

The importance of restrained, conciliatory approaches to dispute resolution in the business context is often overlooked by attorneys. They become accustomed to using the legal process as a means of putting direct and unmistakable pressure to bear on the opposing side. They come to accept this level of tension as normal and desirable. While this attitude is obviously highly functional in many kinds of cases, it does not fit them all, least of all the business context.

IV. PRE–BARGAINING DYNAMICS

Returning for a moment to a broad perspective of the negotiation process, it has been noted by Young (1975 at 405–406), negotiation may include as many as five different dynamics, all of which seem relevant to legal negotiation. First, a negotiator may consciously seek to develop his reputation as a negotiator, and, in view of what the data say about reputation as a trial attorney, as a litigator. An extreme example of this is Henry Kissinger, who at his zenith was assumed capable of achieving the impossible. More common examples are the attorneys in every bar who are known and feared for their prowess at the negotiating table and/or in the courtroom. In many instances, even judges stand in awe and reverence of these advocates.

Second, one may begin an inventory and collection of resources that may prove useful once negotiations are underway. Taking a course in negotiation in law school is an obvious example, as is the development of a negotiation notebook. A third dynamic is to exercise control over the timing of the bargaining; when it will begin, how long sessions will last, over how much time will the whole process be drawn, when will it finally terminate. It is likewise possible to have some influence over the location of the bargaining (my office, your office, a neutral third place) or the means of communication (telephone, letter, face to face meeting, etc.) Advantage here is to the plaintiff, who has the burden of moving forward and who should see it as an opportunity, not a curse.

Fourth, there is sometimes a possibility of influencing the rules under which bargaining will take place. While legal negotiation presupposes legal rules, there is, however, influence over the tenor and style of the negotiations; over the informal etiquette that will (or will not) prevail. And finally, there is nearly always the chance to influence, and perhaps unilaterally determine, the definition of the issues at stake in the bargaining. Advantage here, again, is to the plaintiff, who can move forward on terms defined by his own preferences and strategy.

CHAPTER NOTE

1. Effects of Pretrial Conference on Case Settlement

The pretrial conference was conceived in large part as a device for reducing court congestion by helping attorneys settle their cases without trial. It has been widely adopted, nearly always with the hope it would help relieve court congestion. Many commentators offer the opinion that pretrial conferences do improve the settlement prospects of cases (Van Alstyne and Grossman 1963 at 169–171; Baer and Broder 1973 at 147–150).

However, empirical studies of the pretrial conference have shown that the same percentage of cases will settle before trial, regardless of whether a pretrial conference is held. The pretrial conference does not increase the likelihood of settlement (although it does appear to clarify factual and legal issues and thus reduce the burden of trial to some degree) (M. Rosenberg, *The Pretrial Conference and Effective Justice* 1964). Negotiators should not be misled into assuming that, if negotiations break down, the pretrial conference will help bring the opponent around to a reasonable settlement. This is probably not the case.

The insertion of a judge into the negotiation process significantly complicates the dynamics. A judge is the symbol and embodiment of power in the legal system. He is expected to exercise this power. His function is to encourage stipulations of fact and law and to make express rulings regarding discovery and other matters basic to the interests of the attorneys. Attorneys face a genuine conflict between cooperative and adversarial demands made upon them in this context.

This conflict is compounded by the formality of many pretrial conference situations: a stenographer is often present, a record is being preserved, and the attorneys are naturally moved by this formality to adopt an adversarial approach for the record. This tendency to argumentation is encouraged by the fact that the pretrial judge offers an important testing ground on which the attorney can try the theories and arguments he has developed for the lawsuit. Inspection of videotapes of pretrial conferences demonstrates the validity of these observations. It can be seen that both attorneys become preoccupied with persuading the judge of the reasonableness and compelling nature of their positions and the unreasonableness of the opponent's attitude and position. Attorneys are also compelled to adversarial advocacy for influencing the judge to make favorable rulings and to apply pressure upon their opponent to settle.

Because of these factors, it is probably naive of attorneys to expect meaningful help from most judges in settling their cases. They must instead pay increased attention to their own skills and knowledge of negotiation in order to obtain favorable settlements.

On the other hand, in most jurisdictions there are "settling judges" who work more actively if not aggressively to draw the attorneys into a settlement. Some judicial training programs are encouraging judges to take more active approaches. When they do, they probably can induce settlements in cases that would otherwise go to trial. Such judges are known by reputation in each locality and it is only logical that an attorney assigned to such a judge should plan his case with this additional factor in mind.

Except when appearing before true "settling judges," however, the attorney is best advised to harbor no illusions about pretrial conferences. Since statistics show they do not measurably improve the probability of settlement, the wisest course is to rely on your own negotiating skills for settlement discussions and to use the pretrial conference as leverage toward this end. Objectives would obviously include: obtaining favorable rulings on discovery matters; obtaining stipulations to reduce the factual and legal issues to their simplest terms; showing the opponent the strength of your position and your ability to argue convincingly to the judge; obtaining the judge's and the opponent's off-hand reactions to your legal theories in the case. In addition, if the judge conducting the conference is a settling judge, one goal should be to develop skills in diplomatically fending off or avoiding unwarranted pressure on you to accept unfavorable terms in settlement.

Chapter Five

THE LAW OF NEGOTIATION AND SETTLEMENT

I. INTRODUCTION: IS THERE A LAW OF NEGOTIATION AND SETTLEMENT

It has been generally assumed that there was no body of law specifically applicable to the bargaining process. Negotiation has been perceived as an adjunct of the litigation process, which is governed by extensive collections of procedural, substantive, and ethical rules. The Code of Professional Responsibility has standards regulating trial conduct, trial publicity, communication with jurors, contact with witnesses and courtroom officials, relationship with clients, relationship with opposing counsel, and relationship to the judge. Civil and criminal procedure are major bodies of law in their own right. The law of evidence and of remedies govern substantive aspects of the litigation process. So long as negotiation was perceived as incidental to litigation, there was no apparent need for rules focusing specifically on the process of negotiation.

The legal profession has finally become aware, however, that negotiation is quantitatively more than an adjunct of litigation. It is the primary means of formal dispute resolution in the United States. It is time that attention should shift to a more serious consideration of the role of negotiation in the legal system.

II. THE GENERAL POLICY OF THE LAW TOWARD COMPROMISE AND SETTLEMENT

When the validity of settlement agreements is challenged, courts routinely assert a general policy in favor of negotiated settlements. Courts consistently affirm that there is "an overriding public interest in settling and quieting litigation",[26] and that, "it has always been the policy of the law to favor compromise and settlement." [27] In support of this policy, courts will often enforce settlement agreements despite minor errors in their formation and give broad interpretation to legal rules in

26. Van Bronkhorst v. Safeco Corp., 529 F.2d 943, 950 (9th Cir. 1976).

27. Thomas v. Hollowell, 20 Ill. App.2d 288, 291, 155 N.E.2d 827, 829 (1959).

order to preserve a settlement. The policy is based on the perceived benefits of settlement in comparison with litigation. Settlements reduce legal expenses, save time for the parties and the court, and are more conducive to amicable outcomes and future relations between the parties.

However, the judicial policy of favoring settlement agreements is weighed against other considerations of public policy as well. Courts will overturn settlement agreements found contrary to other public interests.[28]

III. CONTRACT LAW AS A SOURCE OF NEGOTIATION LAW

Settlement agreements are contracts, and are subject to the rules governing the formation, performance, and enforcement of contracts. Most of this law is unexceptional and need not be discussed here. This section discusses developments in contract law relating specifically (though not uniquely) to settlement agreements.

A. THE NOTION OF GOOD FAITH IN BARGAINING

Several developments in negotiation law are advanced in the recent *Restatement, Second, of Contracts* (1981). A new section, 205, articulates a duty of good faith and fair dealing in the performance and enforcement of contracts, defining good faith as, "honesty in fact in the conduct or transaction concerned." [29] *See also* UCC Section 1–201(10).

How is a contractual duty of good faith relevant to legal negotiators? The Restatement defines the duty of good faith and fair dealing to apply to the assertion, settlement, and litigation of contract claims and defenses, all of which lawyers are

---

28. *See, e.g.,* Middlesex Concrete Products & Excavating Corp. v. Carteret Industrial Association, 37 N.J. 507, 181 A.2d 774 (1962).

29. Professor Summers has observed that a good faith standard operates primarily as an "excluder" of "bad faith" conduct. Summers,

" 'Good Faith' in General Contract Law and the Sales Provisions of the Uniform Commercial Code", 54 Va. L.Rev. 195, 199–207 (1968). Section 205 adopts the excluding strategy by prescribing conduct that violates community standards of decency, fairness, or reasonableness.

frequently involved in.[30]   Comments to Section 205 specifically condemn such acts as:

1. Conjuring up a pretended dispute,

2. Asserting an interpretation contrary to one's own understanding,

3. Falsification of facts,

4. Taking unfair advantage of the necessitous circumstances of the other party to extort a modification of a contract,

5. Harassing demands for assurances of performance,

6. Rejection of performance for unstated reasons,

7. Willful failure to mitigate damages,

8. Abuse of a power to determine compliance or to terminate a contract.

B.   THE USE OF THREATS IN BARGAINING

Sections 175 and 176 of the *Restatement, Second, of Contracts* limit the use of threats as negotiating tactics.   Section 175 states:

"If a party's manifestation of assent is induced by an improper threat by the other party that leaves the victim no reasonable alternative, the contract is voidable by the victim."

The meaning of improper threat is elaborated in Section 176, which establishes two categories of improper threat:

"(1) A threat is improper if

"(a) what is threatened is a crime or a tort, or the threat itself would be a crime or a tort if it resulted in obtaining property,

"(b) what is threatened is a criminal prosecution,

"(c) what is threatened is the use of civil process and the threat is made in bad faith, or

---

30. See generally Summers, " 'Good Faith' in General Contract Law and the Sales Provisions of the Uniform Commercial Code", 54 Va. L.Rev. 195 (1968).   The good faith standard enunciated in the Restatement (Second) of Contract does not tell us whether remedies beyond rescission of the contract should be available.   At a minimum it appears that a showing of bad faith would make it easier to sustain a finding of breach of the more traditional contract rules, including misrepresentation, undue influence, and the like. Several of these prohibitions have counterparts for lawyers in the Code of Professional Responsibility.

"(d) the threat is a breach of the duty of good faith and fair dealing under a contract with the recipient.

"(2) A threat is improper if the resulting exchange is not on fair terms, and

"(a) the threatened act would harm the recipient and would not significantly benefit the party making the threat,

"(b) the effectiveness of the threat in inducing the manifestation of assent is significantly increased by prior unfair dealing by the party making the threat, or

"(c) what is threatened is otherwise a use of power for illegitimate ends."

The drafters of section 176 recognize that the proper limits of bargaining cannot be defined with precision. In a phrase that seems addressed specifically to lawyers, they admit that "[h]ard bargaining between experienced adversaries of relatively equal power ought not to be discouraged." On the other hand, they recognize that threats can be so improper as to amount to an abuse of the bargaining process. Threats of physical violence, wrongful seizure or detention of property, tortious interference with contractual rights, or serious economic harm may amount to this. Comment (a) prompts courts to look at the fairness of the resulting agreement as evidence of whether a particular threat was improper.

Comment (b) to Section 175 affirms that threats to commence civil litigation are not ordinarily improper because defense of a civil action is considered (as a matter of policy) a reasonable alternative to acceding to the threat. However, if a threat involves "the seizure of property, the use of oppressive tactics, or the possibility of emotional consequences," then defense in a civil action is not a reasonable alternative and the threat is improper. Illustration 2 gives an example of improper threat:

"A makes an improper threat to commence a civil action and to file a lis pendens against a tract of land owned by B, unless B agrees to discharge a claim that B has against A. Because B is about to make a contract with C for the sale of the land and C refuses to make the contract if the levy is made, B agrees to discharge the claim. B has no reasonable alternative, A's threat is duress, and the contract is voidable by B."

[*93*]

Comment (d) to Section 176 follows by acknowledging there is no impropriety in good faith threats to commence civil litigation, even if the claim should later be shown to be without foundation. However, a threat may be deemed improper and in bad faith if "the person making the threat did not believe there was a reasonable basis for the threatened process, he knew the threat would involve misuse of the process, or he realized the demand he made was exorbitant."

The reporter's notes to Comment (f) cite the case of Jamestown Farmers Elevator, Inc. v. General Mills, 552 F.2d 1285 (8th Cir. 1977), noted 54 N.D.L.Rev. 267 (1977), in which the court held that "it was an improper threat for a large corporation to threaten extensive litigation before regulatory bodies that would put a smaller company out of business." In *Farmers Elevator,* the threatening telephone conversation, as reported by an agent of a grain seller, who had previously contracted to sell grain to General Mills, went as follows:

> "We're General Mills; and if you don't deliver this grain to us, why we'll have a battery of lawyers in there tomorrow morning to visit you, and then we are going to the North Dakota Public Service [Commission]; we're going to the Minneapolis Grain Exchange and we're going to the people in Montana and there will be no more Muschler Grain Company. We're going to take your license[.]" (Jamestown Farmers Elevator, Inc. v. General Mills, 552 F.2d 1285, 1289 (8th Cir. 1977)).

The Court of Appeals held that if this threat was made, it could "make out a claim of duress against General Mills." (Id. at 1291). The court recognized that good faith insistence upon one's legal rights does not constitute duress, even if it should be found that the claim was not recognized at law. But to threaten to put a person out of business, or to deprive a person of his livelihood, or a threat of criminal or regulatory proceedings "made in order to secure another's consent to an undeserved bargain for one's own private benefit, may be sufficiently wrongful to constitute duress." (p. 1291).[31]

---

31. In support of this conclusion, the court cited Laemmar v. J. Walter Thompson Co., 435 F.2d 680 (7th Cir. 1970); Mayerson v. Washington Manufacturing Co., 58 F.R.D. 377, 383–84 (E.D.Pa.1972); Balling v. Finch, 203 Cal.App.2d 413, 21 Cal.Rptr. 490 (2d Dist. 1962); 13 Williston on Contracts, Sections 1601–07; 1612–15 (3d Ed., W. Jaeger 1970).

IV. FORMATION, INTERPRETATION AND EN-FORCEMENT OF SETTLEMENT AGREEMENTS

In general, the principles of contract law apply to settlement agreements and releases. Offer, acceptance and consideration rules apply and many of the same defenses and remedies applicable in contract law may also be applied to compromise agreements. However, because compromise agreements are contracts involving the relinquishment of a person's right to sue (a highly protected right in our society), certain problems peculiar to compromise and settlement have received special treatment by the courts.

A. OFFER AND ACCEPTANCE

Like other contracts, compromise agreements are formed by valid offer and acceptance.[32] As in general contract law acceptance must be within a reasonable time, on the terms offered. Acceptance may be implied, such as through retention of an amount tendered in full settlement of the obligation [33], or the retention of a check or draft.[34] However, forbearance from bringing suit does not in itself constitute an offer or an acceptance of compromise, unless it is communicated to the other party as such.[35]

B. CONSIDERATION

In general, the rules regarding consideration apply unchanged to settlement agreements. Consideration for the agreement is found in the compromise of amounts demanded and in the relinquishment of claims in a dispute. A subsequent finding that no legal claim was present does not invalidate a compromise if the parties believed in good faith that a valid claim existed.[36]

---

32. Wicker v. Board of Public Instruction of Dade County, 182 F.2d 764 (5th Cir. 1950).

33. Little Rock Packing Co. v. Massachusetts Bonding & Insurance Co., 262 F.2d 327 (8th Cir. 1956).

34. General Freight Transport Co. v. Riss & Co., 297 F.2d 463 (7th Cir. 1962).

35. Stoddard v. Mix, 14 Conn. 12 (1840), and Gregg v. Weathersfield, 55 Vt. 385 (1883).

36. City Street Improvement Co. v. Pearson, 181 Cal. 640, 185 P. 962 (1919), and Posey v. Lambert-Grisham Hardware Co., 197 Ky. 373, 247 S.W. 30 (1923).

C. WRITINGS AND FORMALITIES

Once the terms of the settlement are agreed upon, the lawyer's task focuses on formalizing and carrying out the agreement. As a general rule, compromise agreements are not required to be in writing to be valid. However, there are two exceptions: First, local rules and court procedures may require a writing as evidence of the agreement.[37] In these states the settlement must be signed and in writing. When writings are required, courts are likely to hold the parties strictly to the requirement, as the court in Davies v. Canco Enterprises, 350 So. 2d 23 (Fla.App.1977), which held that a settlement agreement which had been incorporated into the transcript of a deposition but which had been signed by neither party was "of no force and effect."

Second, a writing is required if the subject matter of the compromise falls within the statute of frauds. The statute, however, applies only to the subject matter of the compromise agreement and not to the antecedent claim. For example, a compromise agreement requiring one party to convey real estate to another would fall under the statute, whereas the compromise of a dispute involving ownership of land, requiring one party to pay money to the other, but involving no transfer of land, would not fall under the statute of frauds, because the subject matter of the compromise agreement is the agreement to pay money, not the conveyance of land.

It is generally good practice to make the agreement part of the record of the case. Most court requirements are satisfied by orally announcing the agreement in court as the court reporter takes it down as part of the court record.[38] However, if the agreement is in the form of a stipulation and court rules require that stipulations be written, an oral stipulation for the record will not be binding even though settlements need not otherwise be written.[39]

Some courts require attorneys to promptly notify the court when a pending action is settled. While the settlement is still

---

37. Some states require in their rules of civil procedure that "no private agreement or consent between parties or their attorneys shall be of any force unless the evidence thereof is in writing . . ." (Fla.R.Civ.P. 1.030(d)).

38. Morrow v. American Bank and Trust Co., 397 F.Supp. 803 (M.D.La. 1975).

39. Moore v. Gunning, 328 So.2d 462 (Fla.App.1976).

binding if the attorneys fail to notify the court, sanctions may be imposed against the attorneys for interfering with court proceedings (Cal. Rules for Superior Courts, Rule 226). Even when formal notice to the court is not required, documenting the agreement on the record by means of a consent judgment, a nonsuit, or a dismissal with prejudice renders the settlement more conclusive than a simple release and may therefore be desirable. Parties may usually obtain a consent judgment by appearing before the judge in chambers and having him sign a judgment order they have prepared for this purpose.[40] State statutes generally define the exact procedure to be followed.[41] Once filed, the consent judgment will appear in the same manner as a judgment rendered after a full trial. A consent judgment binds the parties both as a judgment of the court and as a contractual agreement.

A dismissal with prejudice to any further suit may be used in place of a consent judgment to also add finality to a settlement. State procedures may vary, but the procedure is illustrated in Fed.Rules Civ.Proc. Rule 41(a), requiring a stipulation signed by all the parties to be filed with the court. The stipulation must state that the action is dismissed with prejudice or it is assumed to be without prejudice.

D.   INTERPRETATION OF THE AGREEMENT

Under general rules of contract law, interpretation of settlement agreements is generally limited to the terms of the agreement itself. Extrinsic evidence is generally admissible to show that the agreement is not integrated, that the recital of facts is not accurate, that conditions precedent have not been fulfilled or that conditions subsequent have or have not occurred, that the agreement was intended to affect third parties, or that the stated consideration was never received. Extrinsic evidence may also be used to show that the agreement purports to release the claims of a minor or in some other way violates public policy.[42]

---

40. See generally Dobbs, "The Conclusiveness of Personal Injury Settlements: Basic Problems," 47 N.C.L. Rev. 665 (1963).

41. Local practice may vary. For example, N.C.G.S. § 1–209, allows the clerk of the Superior Court to enter the judgment instead of the judge.

42. See generally Havighurst, "Principles of Construction and the Parol Evidence Rule Applied to Releases", 60 N.W.U.L.Rev. 599 (1958). See also Lindsey, "Documentation of Settlements", 27 Ark.L.Rev. 27 (1973).

The intent of the parties will generally determine which claims are released when the agreement contains general language. That intent may be judged from both the language of the agreement and the circumstances surrounding its making. Usually, general language is limited by specific language; however, if the general language indicates that the dominant purpose was a general release, it may control. All claims may be released if there is no mention of specific claims because claims arising from a single cause of action cannot be made the subject of separate suits and when the suit as a unit is released all claims are usually implicitly included. Often a party will wish to release only the claim for personal injury and not property damage. If this is the intention the property damage claim should be specifically excluded from the settlement agreement. If separate consideration is stated for the release of general and specific claims, effect will be given to the general release.

Joint tortfeasor problems begin with the common law rule that the release of one joint tortfeasor releases all of the tortfeasors. This was based on the rationale that a person is entitled to only one satisfaction on a claim, and satisfaction by one tortfeasor releases all others. It was because of this problem that the covenant not to sue was developed. In a covenant not to sue, the injured party makes a contract with the tortfeasor not to bring any action against him in return for the settlement payment. Since there is no formal release, courts often hold that covenants not to sue do not operate to release the other tortfeasors.

The Uniform Contribution Among Tortfeasors Act abolished the common law rule of releases and allowed contribution among tortfeasors. In states adopting this act, a release of one tortfeasor does not release the other common tortfeasors. The amount recoverable from the remaining defendants is, however, reduced by the settling defendant's pro rata share of liability so that only one actual satisfaction is received.[43]

43. There is a voluminous literature relating to the drafting and use of releases and other settlement documents and the effect on settlements of the laws of contribution, indemnity, and comparative negligence. Helpful articles in this area include: Ann C. Livingston, "Settlements in Multiple Tortfeasor Controversies—Texas Law", 10 St. Mary's L.J. 75 (1978); Clifford Davis, "Comparative Negligence, Comparative Contribution, and Equal Portection in the Trial and Settlement of Multiple Defendant Product Cases", 10 Indiana L.Rev. 831 (1977); and James B. Sales, "Contribution and Indemnity between negligent and Strictly Liable Tortfeasors", 12 St. Mary's L.J. 323 (1980). For a more general discussion, as it relates

E. CONFLICT OF LAWS—GOVERNING LAW

Normally the conflicts of laws principles are applied to settlements as to contracts generally: the law of the state in which the compromise agreement was made will generally govern questions of validity and construction of the compromise.[44] Questions of authority may be governed by the law of the state in which a party was domiciled or the agency contract created, and matters relating to the breach of a compromise agreement are generally governed by the law of the state in which the agreement was to be performed.

However, sometimes a compromise will have a significant effect on the antecedent obligations of the parties, and certain aspects may be governed by the law of the state where those obligations were created. This is especially true in the settlement of tort claims which may be governed by the law of the place where the tort occurred.[45]

F. FEDERAL RULES OF CIVIL PROCEDURE: RULE 68 OFFERS OF COMPROMISE

FRCP 68 and similar state statutes provide procedural incentives to settle. These rules have not been used frequently in the past but there is presently a trend towards their greater use and a greater awareness of their potential impact.[46]

The essence of FRCP 68 is as follows: "At any time more than 10 days before the trial begins, a party defending against a claim may serve upon the adverse party an offer to allow judgment to be taken against him for the money or property or to the effect specified in his offer, with costs then accrued. If within 10 days after the service of the offer the adverse party serves written notice that the offer is accepted, either party may then file the offer and notice of acceptance together with proof of service thereof and thereupon the clerk shall enter judgment.

to Oregon Law, see R. Stephenson and R. Johnson, "Drafting Settlement Agreements", *Negotiation and Settlement—Oregon State Bar*, p. 121 (1980). For application to Texas law, see J.H. Edgar, "Procedural Aspects of Settlement: An Overview of Texas Law", 12 St. Mary's L.J. 279 (1980).

44. Peerless Weighing & Vending Machine Corp. v. International Ticket Scale Corp., 126 F.2d 239 (3d Cir. 1942).

45. Preine v. Freeman 112 F.Supp. 257 (D.Va.1953).

46. See Kempf, "Rule 68 Offers of Judgment: An Underused Tool", 7 Litigation 39(3) (1981) and Note, "Rule 68: A 'New' Tool for Litigation", 1978 Duke L.J. 889 (1978).

An offer not accepted shall be deemed withdrawn and evidence thereof is not admissible except in a proceeding to determine costs. If the judgment finally obtained by the offeree is not more favorable than the offer, the offeree must pay the costs incurred after the making of the offer. The fact that an offer is made but not accepted does not preclude a subsequent offer. When the liability of one party to another has been determined by verdict or order or judgment, but the amount or extent of the liability remains to be determined by further proceedings, the party adjudged liable may make an offer of judgment, which shall have the same effect as an offer made before trial if it is served within a reasonable time not less than 10 days prior to the commencement hearings to determine the amount or extent of liability." [47]

It is still unclear how substantial the offer must be in order for the rule to apply. The court of appeals for the 7th circuit has held that an offer of $450 in a case claimed to be worth $20,000 was not enough to invoke the statute. The court held the rule applies only to "good faith" offers.[48]

The most important issue surrounding Rule 68 is whether the costs to be paid by the losing party will include attorney's fees, which usually make up the greatest part of the cost of litigation. Contrary to English practice, attorney's fees in the U.S. have not generally been assessed against losing parties unless there is express statutory authorization for them.[49] Exceptions have been made to the "American rule," however, and there is a strong policy argument in favor of including the attorney's fees in the "costs incurred" provision of Rule 68. Some courts are presently awarding attorney's fees as a means of promoting the policy of the rule, though usually still in special circumstances.[50] A recent study by a judicial committee of the 7th Circuit has recommended that Rule 68 be expressly amended to include the recovery of "costs and attorney's fees incurred." (86 FRD 267, 273).

47. See generally 12 C. Wright and A. Miller, *Federal Practice and Procedure*, sec. 3001–3005, p. 56 (1973).

48. August v. Delta Air Lines, Inc., 600 F.2d 699 (7th Cir. 1979).

49. See S. Levin, "Practical, Ethical, and Legal Considerations Involved in the Settlement of Cases In Which Statutory Attorney's Fees Are Authorized", Oct. 1980 Clearinghouse Review 515.

50. Armato, Leonard, "Offers of Judgment and Compromise: Turning the Tables on Your Opponent", 55 Cal.St.B.J. 286 (July 1980). Note, "Rule 68: A 'New' Tool for Litigation", 1978 Duke L.J. 889 (1978).

G. COURT SUPERVISION AND APPROVAL OF SETTLEMENTS

The court may be involved in settlement in two ways. First through actual participation in the settlement process, and second in reviewing those settlements effected without court supervision.[51] Court participation in the mechanics of the settlement often begins in pretrial and settlement conferences. General court rules set up the framework for pretrial procedures, which may vary from a requirement of settlement discussions (Mich. Gen. Court Rules 301.1(10)), to permitting discussion of settlement by allowing consideration of any matters which may aid in the disposition of the case (FRCP 16). Some states also provide a separate procedure for settlement conferences (Cal. Rules of Court 207.5).

Local rules may further modify and clarify the place of settlement discussion in pretrial conference.

Class action settlements must be approved by the court in order to prevent legalized blackmail and protect absent class members.[52] The court must examine the terms of the agreement, not the underlying issues of the case,[53] and determine that there was no fraud or collusion in reaching the settlement and that the compromise is fair and adequate.[54] Factors which the court should consider include: (1) the relative strength of the parties,[55] (2) mutual sacrifice to avoid unprofitable litigation,[56] (3) existence of vindictive motives or pressures,[57] (4) the recommendation of counsel,[58] (5) the number of parties which object to the agreement,[59] (6) the ability of the defendant to pay a judgment greater than the settlement,[60] and (7) the business judgment of

51. For excellent treatment of the role of the judiciary in the negotiation process, see Hon. C.B. Renfrew, "Negotiations and Judicial Scrutiny in Civil and Criminal Antitrust Cases", 57 Chi.B.Rec. 130 (1975).

52. See K. Forde, "Settlement of the Class Action", 5 Litigation 23 (Fall, 1978).

53. In re Prudence Co., 98 F.2d 559 (2d Cir. 1938).

54. Percodani v. Riker-Maxson Corp., 50 F.R.D. 473 (S.D.N.Y.1970).

55. Protective Committee for Independent Stockholders v. Anderson, 390 U.S. 414, 88 S.Ct. 1157, 20 L.Ed. 2d 1 (1968).

56. Masterson v. Pergament, 203 F.2d 315 (6th Cir. 1953).

57. *Percodani,* supra,

58. Glicken v. Bradford, 35 F.R.D. 144 (S.D.N.Y.1964).

59. *Glicken,* supra.

60. Ace Heating & Plumbing Co., Inc. v. Crane Co., 453 F.2d 30 (3d Cir. 1971).

the parties, which should not be replaced by the court's unless the settlement is unfair on its face.[61]

H.   EFFECT OF NEGOTIATIONS ON STATUTES OF LIMITATIONS

One of the choices plaintiffs must make is whether to file suit before commencing settlement negotiations. Particularly in business settings, there is great reluctance to sue a fellow merchant. However, there is always a danger that negotiations may continue until the statute of limitations has run, thereby providing the other party with a defense against suit.

Absent a showing of wrongful conduct by the potential defendant, courts uniformly hold that the mere fact that settlement negotiations are underway does not of itself prevent the statute of limitations from running. This is true even where it seems clear that the defendant in fact intended to settle but did not.

Even when the defendant's actions would create justifiable reliance at one point in time, the defendant may be allowed to plead statute of limitations as a defense if his conduct was broken off leaving the plaintiff sufficient time to file his complaint.

V.   DEFECTS IN COMPROMISE AND SETTLEMENT AGREEMENTS

A.   INTRODUCTION

Despite the policy favoring settlements, a settlement agreement is considered a contract and its validity may be challenged on traditional contract defenses, including: illegality, duress, undue influence, mistake, misrepresentation, fraud, uncertainty or vagueness, lack of capacity or authority, and public policy. Again, it is important to remember that there are two actions involved, and that the defect must relate to the compromise agreement not to the antecedent claim.

B.   FRAUD, MISREPRESENTATION, AND MISTAKE

Fraud, misrepresentation, and mistake are the most common grounds for invalidating settlement agreements, especially those

---

61. *Glicken,* supra.

made by insurance carriers in settlement of tort claims. When injured parties are wrongly induced to settle for much less than the cost of the damages incurred, public policy demands that the settlement be reviewed and possibly rescinded.[62]

C. MARY CARTER AGREEMENTS

As noted above, public policy encouraging the settlement of disputes often causes the courts to interpret the law in favor of settlements. However, public policy may also dictate that certain settlement agreements must be invalidated or carefully controlled.

A particularly troublesome problem is presented in cases involving a single plaintiff and multiple defendants, where one or more of the defendants agrees to settle with the plaintiff for a guaranteed amount, which decreases in an inverse relation to the amount the plaintiff recovers from the remaining defendants. There are many variations of this standard form, but the plaintiff is always guaranteed a specific amount (often given to the plaintiff as an advance), and the defendant's liability is expressly limited. An example of such an agreement is General Motors Corporation v. Lahocki, 286 Md. 714, 410 A.2d 1039 (1980). The plaintiff broke his back when the GM van in which he was riding hit unlit wooden barricades placed in the roadway by defendant Contee Sand and Gravel, Inc. Lahocki was thrown onto the street, suffering a fractured spine. Lahocki sued Contee and GM for negligence, alleging against GM that the vehicle was "uncrashworthy". Before trial Contee and Lahocki made an agreement which provided that, "Contee would pay to the Lahockis $150,000 except in three circumstances: (1) If Contee's pro rata share of a judgment against it was in excess of $150,000 then Contee would pay this up to $250,000. (2) If final judgment was entered against GM alone, then Contee would pay nothing to the Lahockis, even if the Lahockis and GM thereafter settled the case. (3) If the Lahockis settled with GM, then the sum to be paid by Contee to the Lahockis was to be but $100,000." (id. at 1041). This agreement limited Contee's liability to a possible $250,000. If GM were found solely liable or if GM settled with Lahocki then Contee would owe nothing, mak-

---

62. See generally, Havighurst, "The Effect upon Settlements of Mutual Mistake as to Injuries", 12 Defense L.J. 1 (1963); and "Problems Concerning Settlement Agreements", 53 N.W.U.L.Rev. 283 (1958); and Dobbs, "The Conclusiveness of Personal Injury Settlements: Basic Problems", 47 N.C.L.Rev. 665 (1963).

ing it to Contee's advantage to prove GM solely liable. If GM were found not to have been liable Contee would owe $150,000. The judge was informed of the agreement but the jury was not. Because of this agreement the position of Contee in the adversarial proceeding was reversed, he was financially encouraged to assist the plaintiff, unknown to the jury. Therefore, Contee assisted Lahocki in paying the fee of an expert testifying against GM. Since Contee was still appearing as a defendant, his attorney was allowed to cross-examine Lahocki's witnesses. In doing so Contee's attorney merely had the witness repeat damaging information against GM and cure defects that Lahocki's attorney had left. Not realizing Contee's change in position, the jury found GM solely liable and awarded Lahocki $1.2 million (plus $300,000 to his wife). The court of appeals reversed, and following the trend in some states, held that these agreements are not against public policy per se, but that they must be revealed to the jury so it can evaluate the circumstances before it. These settlements, known variously as Guaranteed Verdict Agreements, Mary Carter agreements (after the case of Booth v. Mary Carter Paint Co., 202 So.2d 8 (Fla.App.1967)) or Gallagher covenants, (after City of Tucson v. Gallagher, 108 Ariz. 140, 493 P.2d 1197 (1972)), cause problems because often the defendants remain a part of the action until the case is over, while their interests have shifted from limiting the plaintiff's recovery to increasing it.[63]

Because of the potential for abuse, scholars have strongly opposed these agreements and many states have declared them void as against public policy. All courts have at least required some degree of disclosure to the jury of any such agreements. Some courts, however, have limited the usefulness of the disclosure requirement by allowing information damaging to the remaining defendants to be included in the agreement itself, therefore allowing it to come to the attention of the jury if the pact is revealed.[64]

---

63. See generally Bodine, "The Case Against Guaranteed Verdict Agreements", 29 Defense L.J. 232 (1980).

64. Contribution, where the settling defendant pays his pro rata share of the verdict, eliminates the motivation for entering into these agreements. To date, 39 states permit contribution by statute or judicial decision. See Deeley, "Denying Contribution between Tortfeasors in Arizona: A Call for Change," 1977 Arizona State L.J. 673 (1977). The 1939 version of the Uniform Contribution Among Tortfeasors Act (12 Uniform Laws Annot. 43), adopted by 10 states, compels this division. The 1955 version, adopted by nine states, permits a good faith settlement as a

VI.   SPECIAL RULES APPLICABLE
TO INSURERS

Insurers play a major role in the settlement of the majority of tort cases.   Because of the frequency with which insurers settle and the balance of power between the parties involved (by definition an insurance company and an injured plaintiff), special rules have been developed in many states and courts which apply to insurer's conduct in negotiations.   The general rule is that the insurer must weigh the insured's interest equally with its own in deciding whether to accept an offer of settlement or to commence negotiations.[65]   This has been interpreted as meaning an obligation to either bargain in good faith, or to not bargain in bad faith, or just to not act negligently.   Failure to do so may result in punitive damages.[66]

Good faith has been defined in a general contract sense to be "fair dealing [so] that neither party will do anything which will injure the right of the other to receive the benefits of the agreement."[67]   Similarly, bad faith refusal to settle has been defined as intentional disregard of the insured's financial interests, or placing its own interest above that of the insured.[68]   Negligent behavior employs the standard of a reasonable insurer in the same or similar circumstances.[69]   In California there is a statutory duty on the insurance company to negotiate in good faith in an effort to reach a settlement, (Cal.Stat., Ins. § 790.03(h)).[70]

The general conflict of interest situation occurs where a plaintiff in an insurance case (the insured) offers to take a dif-

defense to a contribution claim.   The courts of these states must find the agreement improper to allow the contribution claim.   See, Bodine, "The Case Against Guaranteed Verdict Agreements", 29 Defense L.J. 232, 249 (1980).

65.   Young v. American Casualty Co. of Reading, Pennsylvania, 416 F.2d 906 (2d Cir. 1969) certiorari denied 396 U.S. 997, 90 S.Ct. 588, 24 L.Ed.2d 490.

66.   Vernon Fire & Casualty Insurance Co. v. Sharp, 161 Ind.App. 413, 316 N.E.2d 381 (1974).

67.   Crisci v. Security Insurance Co., 66 Cal.2d 425, 429, 58 Cal.Rptr. 13, 17, 426 P.2d 173, 176 (1967).   For

further reading see Buechner, "Sliding Scale Agreements and the Good Faith Requirement of Settlement Negotiations", 12 Pacific L.J. 121 (1980).

68.   Kricar, Inc. v. General Accident Fire and Life Assurance Corp. Ltd., 542 F.2d 1135 (9th Cir. 1976) and Johnson v. Hardware Mutual Casualty Co., 109 Vt. 481, 491, 1 A.2d 817, 820 (1938).

69.   Fidelity and Casualty Co. of New York v. Robb, 267 F.2d 473 (5th Cir. 1959).

70.   For excellent treatment of the insurer's duty of care, see Waas, "Expanding The Insurer's Duty To Attempt Settlement", 49 U. of Colo. L.Rev. 251 (1978).

ferent amount than the insurance policy covers. When the plaintiff offers to settle for less than the coverage of the insurance policy in full settlement the insurer (the insurance company) may have a duty to settle within the policy limits.[71] However, the more difficult situation is where the claimant wants more than the insurance policy limits.

Factors the courts have considered as affecting the liability of a company where there is a conflict of interest are: (a) the strength of the claimant's case, (b) attempts by the insurer to induce the insured to contribute to the settlement, (c) failure by the insurer to properly investigate the case, (d) the rejection of attorney's advice by the insurer, (e) failure to inform the insured of an offer, (f) amount for which insured may be liable, and (g) the extent to which the insured induced the insurer's rejection of offers.[72]

VII.   RULES OF EVIDENCE

The rules of evidence can have a great effect on encouraging or discouraging settlement negotiations. These rules not only help determine the strength of each party's position but also govern how openly the parties may communicate during actual negotiations.

Under the common law, a general rule has been promulgated that evidence of offers to compromise disputes is not admissible to prove the offeror's liability in trial.[73] Three reasons have been given as justification for this rule. The "English" or "contract" theory is based on the view that offers are assumed to be made without prejudice and unless the offer is accepted and a contract actually formed, the offer has no evidentiary force. Another basis given is that of relevancy. The offer to compromise is viewed under this theory as demonstrating a desire for peace and not an admission of any wrong done, therefore evidence of this sort has no relevance to actual liability and is excluded. The rule has also been rationalized as a privileged exception to the evidence rules, based on the policy of the courts to encourage settlements. None of these theories generally excludes

---

71. See Cochran, "The Obligation To Settle Within Policy Limits", 41 Miss.L.J. 398 (1970).

72. Id., at 402–406.

73. See McCormick, *Handbook of the Law of Evidence*, sec. 274, p. 663 (2d ed. 1972).

from evidence admitted statements of fact or collateral statements and conduct not forming the actual compromise offer.[74]

Most of the U.S. courts follow the relevancy theory, but the effect is almost the same regardless of the theory: the courts have the difficult job of separating statements making up the actual compromise offer from those merely surrounding it. For example, at common law, if liability were conceded in the compromise and negotiations were held merely to establish the amount or worth of the damage or loss, the offer of compromise was admissible to establish liability though not as proof of the amount of the loss. The statement "O.K., I'll agree I was negligent, let's talk about damages" is admissible, while the statement, "Let's assume, just for the purposes of these negotiations, that I was negligent, what would you think the damages ought to be?" is not.

Attorneys have developed various methods for dealing with admissibility problems. One solution is to refuse to negotiate until the other side agrees in writing that anything said is without prejudice to their client's rights. Absent such agreements, attorneys can avoid admissions by phrasing all factual statements hypothetically and by including disclaimers in all writings so that the statements will be of no value as evidence. For example, "We admit, for the sake of these negotiations only, ..." An even safer method is to preface the entire statement, letter or discussion, "This is a doubtful and disputed claim, and one upon which liability, damage, and all your contentions of fact are expressly denied. Anything I say automatically includes that disclaimer."[75] This trend has resulted in less open negotiations and formed a trap for the unwary or unsophisticated lawyer who might not be careful enough in his choice of terms.

To correct this problem, Rule 408 of the Federal Rules of Evidence was enacted by congress in 1975. The rule is specifically based on the public policy favoring the compromise and settlement of disputes (see 56 F.R.D. 183, 227–228, (1972)). Using the privilege theory, rule 408 makes collateral evidence used in settlement negotations as well as the explicit offers of compromise inadmissible, thereby doing away with the common law col-

74. See Brand and Palmer, "Relevancy and Its Limits", 48 Mississippi L.J. 935, 972–973 (1977); and Waltz and Huston, "The Rules of Evidence in Settlement", 5 Litigation 11, 12 (Fall 1978).

75. Dumont v. Dinallo, 4 N.J. Super. 371, 67 A.2d 344 (1949).

lateral statement problems.[76] Notable in the rule is the use of "a valuable consideration," intended to do away with the so-called, "nuisance offers," (offers of only minimal value in relation to the size of the injury). This addition has been criticized as contributing unnecessary ambiguity to the rule; it is not yet clear how valuable the consideration must be.[77] Rule 408 also departs from the common law by including disputes as to either "validity or amount". Under rule 408, the compromise offer is inadmissible to prove either liability or the amount of liability.

The rule contains two explicit exceptions: evidence "otherwise discoverable" and a provision for "collateral use" of the evidence. The first exception was added to make sure that litigants could not avoid the admission of relevant and discoverable facts into trial by admitting them in compromise negotiations.[78] In other words, admissions in compromise negotiations are not inadmissible if they are also discovered through independent proper means.

The second exception allows evidence gained during compromise negotiations to be used, "when the evidence is offered for another purpose [other than proving liability]". The rule goes on to list examples of other proper purposes, such as the need for a jury to ascertain a witness's bias or prejudice. This exception arises most often in multiple party cases and is properly used where the statements made will be used to impeach the credibility of a person not a party to the compromise agreement. A question still exists whether courts should allow statements made during compromise negotiations to be admitted to impeach the parties to the compromise. This has not yet been clearly decided. Such use would seem to violate the policy upon which the rule is based.[79] It is important to note that neither the com-

---

76. Rule 408 reads in full: Evidence of (1) furnishing or offering or promising to furnish, or (2) accepting or offering or promising to accept, a valuable consideration in compromising or attempting to compromise a claim which was disputed as to either validity or amount, is not admissible to prove liability for or invalidity of the claim or its amount. Evidence of conduct or statements made in compromise negotiations is likewise not admissible. This rule does not require the exclusion of any evidence otherwise discoverable merely because it is presented in the course of compromise negotiations. This rule also does not require exclusion when the evidence is offered for another purpose, such as proving bias or prejudice of a witness, negativing a contention of undue delay, or proving an effort to obstruct a criminal investigation or prosecution.

77. See Waltz and Huston (1978) at 14.

78. See Report of Senate Committee on the Judiciary, Federal Rules of Evidence Service, Art. IV, p. 13.

79. See Waltz and Huston (1978) at 16.

mon law nor rule 408 applies until there is an attempt to compromise a disputed claim; both elements must be present or statements made will be held admissible.

At least 17 states have now passed rules of evidence the same as or similar to rule 408. Other states have attempted to codify the common law rules. The main difference between these rules is whether factual statements made in the compromise negotiations are admissible or not. The wise attorney will become familiar with the rules in his own jurisdiction.

Other federal rules of evidence bearing on settlement agreements are rules 409 and 410. Rule 409 states simply, "Evidence of furnishing or offering or promising to pay medical, hospital, or similar expenses occasioned by an injury is not admissible to prove liability for the injury." This rule is based not only on the policy encouraging settlement but on the policy of encouraging the prompt assistance of injured persons by the defendant or the insurance company. It should be noted, however, that the rule does not cover conduct or statements made which are not an integral part of this payment.

The Federal Rule is consistent with the common law rule in most states that evidence of medical assistance is inadmissible to establish liability of the party rendering such assistance. The states have based this on the policy encouraging such help and on the rationale that such assistance is made primarily out of humane motives and not generally as an admission of guilt.

Rule 410 deals specifically with the use of evidence gained from plea bargaining in criminal cases. This rule is much stricter than rule 408 and specifically excludes plea negotiation evidence from impeachment proceedings.

Chapter Six

THE ECONOMICS OF LITIGATION
AND SETTLEMENT

*"What needs to be done is to make an educated guess,
based largely on experience, if you have experience."* [80]

I. INTRODUCTION

Actual law practice is quite a different world than the law classroom or the appellate court. In law practice,

"[f]acts may be unavailable, obscure, disputed, or distorted. The law may be unclear, or in flux. The goals of other persons—clients, adversaries, and decision-makers, to name a few—may be cloudy or may conflict with those of the lawyer. The lawyer may be caught in a bind between two or more conflicting ethical values, or between an ethical value and a very important practical goal. Choice of the best strategy may require him to estimate and weigh probabilities. The lawyer rarely feels that he has enough time in which to do the most thorough job that he could." [81]

II. ECONOMIC ANALYSIS OF CASES:
THE MISSING LAWYER SKILL

We are conditioned by legal method to define the lawyer's functions as those of weighing facts, recognizing the issues, and applying law ("preventive law" when drafting contracts and wills or "remedial law" when suing for personal injuries or breach of contract). This conception is reflected in studies of lawyer competency. For example, an American Bar Association Task Force on Lawyer Competency defined it as the ability to:[82]

"1. analyze legal problems;

"2. perform legal research;

"3. collect and sort facts;

---

80. "Evaluation and Settlement of Personal Injury Cases" N. Shane, ed. P.L.I. (1976).

81. Meltsner and Schrag, "Report from a CLEPR Colony," 76 Colum. L.Rev. 581, 584 (1976).

82. ABA Section on Legal Education and Admission to the Bar, Report and Recommendations of the Task Force on Lawyer Competency (1979) at 9 & 10.

"4. write effectively . . .;

"5. communicate orally with effectiveness in a variety of settings;

"6. perform important lawyer tasks calling on both communication and interpersonal skills:

    "(i) interviewing,

    "(ii) counseling,

    "(iii) negotiation; and

"7. organize and manage legal work."

Curiously, the ability to determine the economic value of cases is not included in definitions of the lawyer's work. For attorneys, analyzing factual and legal aspects of a case means something less than the application of the methods of planning, research, financial analysis, and decision making routinely used in other professions.

Trial lawyers know from experience that "facts are everything". Very few cases lawyers handle turn on questions of law. This is true for civil and criminal cases, but is more apparent in the criminal setting, since there is rarely an issue whether a crime has been committed; the issue is whether the accused is the person who committed it. In this setting (as in the great majority of civil cases) facts are everything. The relative skills and diligence in fact gathering of investigators and attorneys on both sides will largely determine the outcome, both in terms of liability or guilt and in terms of remedy.[83]

Lawyers are, in a sense, trapped by the legal culture into non-quantifiable and non-objective methods of evaluating cases. The legal culture assumes that the lawyer's task is to present the facts and law in their strategically most favorable light to a judge and jury, who will determine what is truth and who will

---

83. An excellent guide to fact gathering is Robert L. Simmons, *Winning Before Trial: How to Prepare Cases for the Best Settlement or Trial Result* (Executive Reports Corp., Englewood Cliffs, New Jersey, 1974) (2 vols.). Simmons gives excellent and exhaustive treatment to interviewing witnesses (friendly, unfriendly, disinterested), investigative techniques (investigative techniques for the attorney, knowing when and how to hire an investigator), checklists of kinds of facts to search for in the most common types of cases, and use of interrogatories and other discovery techniques. For an interesting view of the fact gathering process in criminal cases, see "Special Project: A Study of the Fact Investigation Practices of Criminal Lawyers in Phoenix, Arizona", in 1981 Arizona State Law Journal 447–626.

award dollar damages commensurate with the wrong. This conception of "value" shifts the ultimate responsibility for calculating damages to judge and jury, inducing attorneys to think of case value primarily in terms of probable jury verdicts.

One example of the difficulty lawyers have in calculating case values in given in Douglas Rosenthal's study of personal injury cases in New York. Rosenthal picked 61 personal injury cases that had been settled, then selected 5 experts to independently review the actual case files and give their calculations of the settlement value of each case. The first two of the experts were experienced plaintiffs' personal injury lawyers, the third had been a plaintiff's lawyer for about 25 years but had recently begun doing insurance defense work, and the last two experts were insurance people (one an insurance defense lawyer and the other an experienced claims adjuster). This method provided 6 different settlement figures for each case, all taken from the file upon which actual settlement was based: the actual settlement amount, plus a predicted settlement value independently arrived at by each of the five experts. As illustrated by Table 6–1 the variation among these six figures is dramatic.

Table 6–1*

Activity and Recovery Scores for the Sample Clients

Client Number	Activity Score	Actual Recovery[a]	Panel Mean[b]	Panelist Evaluations[c]					Coefficient of Variability
				#1	#2	#3	#4	#5	
1	2	$ 5,800	$ 7,600	$ 6,000	$ 7,500	$ 8,500	$ 8,500	$ 7,500	0.1348
2	0	3,500	21,500	22,500	17,500	40,000	20,000	7,500	0.5490
3	8	42,500	34,000	45,000	40,000	45,000	25,000	15,000	0.3945
4	3	2,000	8,800	8,500	8,500	9,500	8,500	8,500	0.0508
5	3	4,250	3,200	1,800	4,000	4,000	3,500	2,500	0.3102
6	3	3,500	4,300	7,500	5,000	3,500	3,500	2,000	0.4836
7	4	2,000	2,200	2,300	2,000	750	4,500	1,500	0.6370
8	8	5,000	6,600	6,500	5,000	7,500	12,500	1,500	0.6070
9	1	3,000	6,900	11,000	5,800	6,000	8,500	3,000	0.4409
10	2	5,000	11,600	7,500	12,500	20,000	15,000	3,000	0.5680
11	6	3,500	2,800	1,500	4,300	2,000	4,500	1,500	0.5480
12	2	12,000	21,000	17,500	17,500	35,000	20,000	15,000	0.3820
13	3	3,500	2,600	2,000	2,750	2,500	4,500	1,000	0.5010
14	2	6,300	6,700	12,500	5,500	4,000	8,500	2,800	0.5854
15	0	3,250	4,200	2,500	3,000	7,500	4,500	3,300	0.4824
16	2	2,000	3,400	4,500	3,000	3,500	5,000	1,000	0.4580
17	1	2,900	4,800	4,700	4,500	6,000	5,500	3,000	0.2418
18	2	7,500	11,900	17,500	8,500	20,000	10,000	3,500	0.5679
19	3	2,250	10,100	15,000	13,500	8,000	10,000	4,000	0.4349
20	2	5,250	12,600	6,000	30,000	17,500	7,500	2,000	0.8950
21	4	9,000	7,400	3,500	7,500	10,000	8,500	7,500	0.3254
22	6	35,000	37,000	35,000	45,000	40,000	50,000	15,000	0.3651
23	2	14,250	15,800	17,500	11,500	25,000	10,000	15,000	0.3748
24	1	13,500	10,800	15,000	7,500	15,000	7,500	8,800	0.3630
25	4	2,250	3,400	2,100	3,250	3,000	4,500	2,500	0.2979
26	2	2,000	3,500	3,500	3,800	3,500	4,000	2,000	0.2349
27	0	2,000	3,500	3,000	3,750	3,500	3,500	3,500	0.0793
28	1	3,000	3,400	2,800	3,750	5,000	4,500	1,000	0.4639
29	5	7,000	5,000	2,500	5,500	6,000	7,500	3,500	0.4000
30	2	3,150	12,000	3,000	9,500	10,000	22,500	15,000	0.6045
31	7	8,000	9,800	12,500	10,000	12,500	10,000	4,000	0.3545
32	3	5,600	20,000	30,000	25,000	30,000	10,000	5,000	0.5863

Client Number	Activity Score	Actual Recovery[a]	Panel Mean[b]	Panelist Evaluations[c]					Coefficient of Variability
				#1	#2	#3	#4	#5	
33	6	$ 4,000	$ 7,200	$ 8,500	$ 4,800	$ 7,500	$ 7,500	$ 7,500	0.1939
34	6	2,150	2,900	2,500	3,600	2,500	4,500	1,500	0.3952
35	4	2,900	12,000	22,500	5,500	12,500	12,000	7,500	0.5480
36	0	4,500	9,300	6,500	10,000	15,000	10,000	5,000	0.4157
37	2	5,000	24,200	30,000	16,000	25,000	35,000	15,000	0.3599
38	0	8,000	4,800	6,000	6,000	7,500	3,000	1,500	0.5134
39	4	5,200	2,600	1,000	3,750	2,500	3,000	2,500	0.3946
40	0	6,500	10,900	7,000	12,500	15,000	15,000	5,000	0.4258
41	no personal injury								
42	2	3,250	4,500	3,300	4,400	7,500	5,000	2,500	0.3777
43	5	22,500	29,500	15,000	50,000	35,000	30,000	17,500	0.4809
44	2	2,300	3,000	2,000	3,500	5,000	3,000	1,500	0.4564
45	3	13,500	20,000	15,000	15,000	30,000	20,000	20,000	0.3062
46	4	23,200	21,000	20,000	27,500	17,500	20,000	20,000	0.1805
47	2	4,500	8,500	4,000	11,500	10,000	13,500	3,500	0.5310
48	3	17,000	18,000	11,000	20,000	30,000	25,000	4,000	0.5839
49	0	3,000	4,800	8,500	3,500	6,500	2,500	3,000	0.5398
50	2	4,000	3,600	6,000	3,500	6,000	3,000	2,000	0.4099
51	2	2,900	4,100	3,500	6,500	5,000	3,500	2,000	0.4171
52	1	2,200	3,200	3,300	3,500	3,500	3,500	2,000	0.2070
53	3	25,000	10,000	3,000	12,000	25,000	2,500	7,500	0.9226
54	3	2,000	4,600	6,500	3,500	7,500	4,000	1,500	0.5219
55	1	3,400	2,500	1,800	3,700	2,500	2,800	1,500	0.3527
56[d]	–	3,800	1,300	1,500	800	1,500	2,000	750	0.4042
57	7	6,950	5,800	7,500	7,500	7,500	5,000	1,500	0.4545
58	0	2,250	3,500	6,500	3,300	2,500	4,000	1,000	0.5875
59	3	3,250	4,000	4,500	3,500	5,000	4,250	2,500	0.2467
60	6	20,000	22,500	22,500	22,500	22,500	25,000	20,000	0.0785
61	3	5,500	6,000	10,000	4,750	7,500	5,000	2,500	0.4831

* *Lawyer and Client: Who's in Charge?* Douglas Rosenthal; Russell Sage Foundation: New York (1974), pp. 204–205. Reprinted by permission.

[a] Rounded to nearest 50.00
[b] Rounded to nearest 100.00
[c] The two insurance adjusters are panelist #4 and #5.
[d] Lawyer handling own claim.

[113]

For example, case number one (client number 1) is one of the few in which the panel members are comfortably close to each other in their evaluations. Compare case two, which settled for $3,500 and was evaluated at $22,500, $17,500, $40,000, $20,000, and $7,500 by the experts. Most of the cases show differences approaching this extreme.[84]

The Des Moines study described in Chapter One gives further evidence of dramatic disparities in lawyers' evaluations of cases. In the study we asked attorneys to report their opening positions. These were reported as follows:

Results of Des Moines Negotiations

Attorney's Names	Plaintiff's Opening Demand	Defendant's Opening Demand	Settlement
1. [omitted here]	$ 32,000	$10,000	$18,000
2.	$ 50,000	$25,000	no settlement
3.	$675,000	$32,150	$95,000
4.	$110,000	$ 3,000	$25,120
5.	Not reported	Not reported	$15,000
6.	$100,000	$ 5,000	$25,000
7.	$475,000	$15,000	no settlement
8.	$180,000	$40,000	$80,000
9.	$210,000	$17,000	$57,000
10.	$350,000	$48,500	$61,000
11.	$ 87,500	$15,000	$30,000
12.	$175,000	$50,000	no settlement: narrowed to $137,000—$77,000
13.	$ 97,000	$10,000	$57,500
14.	$100,000		$56,875
		Average settlement	$47,318

Notice that plaintiffs' opening demands varied from a low of $32,000 to a high of $675,000, and that the *lowest* demand by a plaintiff ($32,000) was substantially *less than* the average settlement amount ($47,318). Likewise, the range between high and low offers by defense counsel is dramatic; and the highest offer by a defendant ($50,000) is *above* the average settlement amount.

84. Douglas Rosenthal, *Lawyer and Client: Who's in Charge* (Russell Sage, 1974). A description of the method for selecting the panel and determining values is given on pages 36–37 and 202–203.

The alternative to such diverse results is for attorneys to move toward more objective methods of determining case value, adding to their legal expertise use of the financial and quantitative decision making tools currently used among business and financial experts.

III. METHODS FOR ECONOMIC EVALUATION OF CASES

In the legal profession today, lawyers use a variety of methods to formulate case values for negotiation and settlement purposes. Most are based on estimates of what a case would bring if it were decided by a jury. Despite the volumes of research on juries, however, lawyers still have no reliable method for predicting what a jury will do.[85] Thus, one of the important professional functions of lawyers is to make a best educated guess about the "value" of a case.

In evaluating routine personal injury cases, attorneys and insurance claims adjusters have developed formulas or rules of thumb that produce a value based on some multiple of "special damages" or actual medical and other costs of the injury. They decide upon an arbitrary multiplier that may be as low as two or three or as high as ten. For example, the formula of "three times special damages" has been described as allocating "one third to the lawyer, one third to the physician, and one third to the claimant." [86] In cases involving more complex damages such as continued pain and suffering, evaluators often propose an arbitrary fixed dollar amount per week for general pain and suffering; i.e., $200 per week for the period of total disability and $100 per week for the period of partial disability. These formulas provide "ballpark" figures, but they obviously ignore individual differences between cases and severely simplify issues of actual harm done.

Since predicted outcome at trial is the most common measure of case value, attorneys commonly refer to published reports of

85. Some interesting attempts have been made to quantify the standard used by a jury. See Rita James Simon and Linda Mahan, "Quantifying Burdens of Proof: A View from the Bench, the Jury, and the Classroom" 5 L. & Soc. Rev. 319–330 (1971). But see Harry Kalven, Jr., and Hans Zeisel, The American Jury (Little, Brown 1966) 182–190.

86. H. L. Ross, *Settled Out of Court*, 2nd edition, (Aldine Publishing Company, New York, 1980), p. 108.

jury verdicts for assistance in case evaluation. The most frequently used sources are verdict statistics.[87]

Rather than looking exclusively at past jury awards, an attorney may calculate case values by more direct methods. The following examples provide a format for itemizing damages for personal injury cases. These methods are improvements over "rules of thumb" and professional guesses because they are more structured and objective. However, they do not fully account for such major considerations as timing of payments and methods of evaluating subjective harm such as pain and suffering.

One widely recognized formula, developed by Robert L. Simmons, invites the attorney to subdivide the case into six categories and estimate a value for each.[88] They include:

PAV —The probable average verdict.
PPV —The probability of a plaintiff's verdict.
UV   —The uncollectible portion of the verdict.
PC   —The plaintiff's cost in obtaining verdict.
DC   —The defendant's estimated cost of defense.
I   —The value of the intangible factors.
FSV —The fair settlement value.

Expressed algebraically, the formula looks like this:

$$(PAV \times PPV) - UV - PC + DC \pm I = FSV$$

This formula uses some time value concepts and seeks to arrive at a net valuation figure for the client. This and similar methods are all useful to the extent they help the attorney ar-

---

87. Aids for predicting the *likelihood of a favorable verdict* include Jury Verdict Expectancies Service (Statewide Jury Verdicts Publishing Co.) (since 1962); J. Grossman and J. Tanenhaus, eds., Frontiers of Judicial Research 307–372 (Wiley, 1969); G. Schubert, ed., Judicial Decision-Making 111–200 (Free Press, 1963); Baade, "Jurimetrics," 28 Law & Contemp. Prob. 1 (symposium issue 1963); and S. Nagel, "The Legal Process from a Behavioral Perspective" 125–172 (Dorsey, 1969). For predicting the *amount of damages*, see Valuation Handbook Service (Statewide Jury Verdicts Publishing Co.) (since 1962); Current Money Awards (Lawyers Co-operative Publishing Co.) (since 1963); and Reeder, "Formulae for Evaluation of Damages," Law Notes (January 1967). Punitive Damages are becoming increasingly available. See, for example, Kenneth R. Redden, Punitive Damages (The Michie Co. 1980).

88. *Winning Before Trial: How to Prepare Cases for the Best Settlement or Trial Result*, Executive Reports Corporation, 1974, pp. 708–715.

rive at an objective valuation and be aware of the components of that valuation.

A more detailed listing of variables can be compiled by reading the case evaluation literature and keeping track of items thought to be important by different commentators. The following list was obtained this way:

A.   COMBINED FORMULA COMPONENTS

1. Expenses

    A. Medical

        (1) Hospital expenses

            a. surgery

            b. nurses

            c. cost of braces or other special devices

        (2) Drug expense

        (3) Doctor expense

            a. treatment at hospital or nursing home

            b. treatment as outpatient or at home

    B. Legal

        (1) Fees

            a. hours for attorneys

            b. hours for paralegals

            c. hours for non-legals

            d. or percent of award on contingent basis

        (2) Expenses

            a. discovery. This would include costs incurred in seeking factual and legal evidence and documentation, depositions, witnesses costs, etc.

            b. closing. These would include costs to collect the judgment, costs to transfer property, etc.

            c. court costs

            d. other

    C. Personal

        (1) Travel

        (2) Loss of time to parties

2. Lost Earnings
   A. Past
      (1) From total disability = wage x time not able to work at all
      (2) From partial disability = (earnings before accident − earnings after accident) x time partially disabled
   B. Future
      (1) Totally disabled = wage x future time not able to work
      (2) Partially disabled = decrease in wage (and/or earning capacity) x time partially disabled
3. Other damages
   A. Property
4. Intangibles
   A. Pain and Suffering. This is calculated by assessing the value to the plaintiff, either as a lump sum or as a multiple of damages, with regard to specific occurrences of pain and suffering as follows
      (1) Due to the injury
      (2) Due to surgery
      (3) Due to wearing braces, etc.
   B. Loss of Life's Pleasures. Calculated the same as pain and suffering
      (1) Resulting from disfigurement
      (2) Resulting from disability, loss of limb, etc.
   C. Subjective jury factors

      Add or subtract some percentage (*e.g.* 10%) from the value or add or subtract a lump sum (*e.g.* $500 each) for each factor below depending on whether it benefits or hurts plaintiff
      (1) Counsel advantage, such as skill or experience
      (2) Target defendant, such as a large corporation or one with a bad public image
      (3) Plaintiff needs the money
      (4) Defendant's financial resources

[*118*]

    (5) Plaintiff's personal profile, such as a strong sympathetic or negative image

    (6) Defendant's personal profile

5. Probabilities. Some attorneys attempt to describe estimated outcomes in terms of probabilities. These may be calculated on the basis of a systematic assessment of individual variables, or as a more intuitive, global "feeling" for what the jury is likely to do. Entering probabilities into the calculation can be done using the following three variables:

A. What is the likelihood of a favorable verdict;

B. Assuming a plaintiff's verdict, what amount of damages are likely to be awarded. Note that this may be expressed in probabilities too. For example, an attorney may estimate that if plaintiff wins, there is a 20% chance of $10,000 damages, a 60% chance of $20,000, and a 20% chance of $30,000;

C. Assuming a plaintiff's verdict, what is the likelihood of collecting the full amount of damages from the defendant.[89]

IV. AN OBJECTIVE ECONOMIC METHOD FOR CASE EVALUATION

A. INTRODUCTION

Lawyers, somewhat justifiably, resist the idea that cases can be evaluated in purely objective terms. Cases involve human beings and have unique, non-quantifiable aspects to them. Juries are also composed of human beings, and their response to the facts of individual cases cannot be understood in cold, purely objective terms. However, the presence of subjective or non-quantifiable factors (such as pain and suffering or mental anguish) should not prevent lawyers from making an accurate accounting of the objective factors. Once the objective value is established, subjective factors can be added on.

---

89. These variables are taken from 14 Am. Jur. Trials 323–326, (1966); R. L. Simmons, *Winning Before Trial: How to Prepare Cases for the Best Settlement or Trial Result*, (Executive Reports Corp., New Jersey, 1974); and the system mentioned in T. Gonzer, "Evaluating Lawsuits by Computer" in December 15, 1980 National Law Journal, pp. 17–23.

There are several items to be considered in an objective model: (1) actual costs or losses to the plaintiff; (2) future losses to the plaintiff that are certain; (3) future losses to the plaintiff that are contingent or variable; (4) relevant costs or losses to the defendant; (5) economic effects of time/money relationships; and (6) tax effects. Items 1 through 4 are detailed above, so the discussion will now turn to items 5 and 6.

B. TIME VALUE OF MONEY

A dollar now is better than a dollar a year from now; this is the basic concept behind time value calculations of money. Several factors enter into time value calculations (inflation, the risk of non-payment, and uncertain future conditions) but the basic idea is that when you consider money, the *timing* of the receipts or payments ranks second only to *amount* in importance. Suppose a beneficiary under a trust has an absolute right to receive $50,000 five years from today; a financial analyst can quickly calculate the *present value* of that right based on the value of money over time. Assuming, for illustration, an interest rate of 15% compounded annually, the value today of that sum would be $24,859.

This same principle is true when money is compounded over periods of time other than one-year intervals. It is very important to think of *periods* and not *years* when considering time value. For example, the $50,000 could have been compounded quarterly instead of annually. If this were the case, it would be necessary to consider the total number of periods (and not years), and the interest rate per period (instead of the annual interest rate). The quarterly interest rate would be 3.75% (15% divided by 4) and the money would be taken over a time frame of 20 periods (5 years times 4). The present value using this method would be $23,945—compared with $24,859 if the money were compounded on an annual basis. When using an interest rate, it is therefore very important to consider how often the interest is compounded. Using the interest rate to calculate the present value of a future sum is called *discounting* the amount; using the interest rate to determine the future value of a present sum is called *compounding* the amount.

Present and future values can be calculated by using tables or through the use of mathematical formulas. Formulas are more versatile than the tables, and attorneys must be able to use them if they are to competently represent clients in any matters involving an interplay between time and money. There are four basic variables used in time-value formulas:

PV —Used to represent the PRESENT VALUE.

FV —Used to represent the FUTURE VALUE.

i —Used to represent the rate of INTEREST per period.

n —Used to represent the number of PERIODS for which interest will be paid.

The relationship between time and money (i.e. the present value of a future sum or the future value of a present sum) is expressed in two standard formulaes:

$$FV = PV(1 + i)^n$$

$$PV = FV\left[\frac{1}{(1 + i)}\right]^n$$

If you do not have a calculator on hand, tables are used to make the time-value calculations. Table #6–2 is a listing of present values and table #6–4 is a listing of future values for $1.00 with the verticle axis representing periods and the horizontal axis representing the interest rate per period. Again, it is important to convert all calculations into periods; i.e., ten years at a quarterly rate of 8% would be converted to 40 periods (10 years times 4 periods per year) and 2% rate per period (8% divided by 4). The figures listed on the chart represent the time-value of one dollar and must be multiplied by the total dollars involved. Using tables #6–2 and #6–4 we can walk through the first example. We want to find the present value of $50,000 in five years at a 15% annual interest rate. The table to use is the one titled "Present Value of $1"; along the 5 period row, the figure for 15% is listed as .4972. This number is multiplied by $50,000 to get the present value of $24,860, which corresponds to our figure of $24,859 using the formula method. It can be easily shown that the tables allow you to calculate both from the present into the future and from the future back to the present. Using table #2 ("Future Value of $1") to find the future value of $24,860 using the same variables, the five-period figure for 15% is 2.014 which, multiplied by $24,860, is equal to $50,003— an amount corresponding to the $50,000 original figure.

Table 6-2*

Present Value of $1: $PVIF = 1/(1 + k)^t$

Period	1%	2%	3%	4%	5%	6%	7%	8%	9%	10%	12%	14%	15%	16%	18%	20%	24%	28%	32%	36%
1	.9901	.9804	.9709	.9615	.9524	.9434	.9346	.9259	.9174	.9091	.8929	.8772	.8696	.8621	.8475	.8333	.8065	.7813	.7576	.7353
2	.9803	.9612	.9426	.9246	.9070	.8900	.8734	.8573	.8417	.8264	.7972	.7695	.7561	.7432	.7182	.6944	.6504	.6104	.5739	.5407
3	.9706	.9423	.9151	.8890	.8638	.8396	.8163	.7938	.7722	.7513	.7118	.6750	.6575	.6407	.6086	.5787	.5245	.4768	.4348	.3975
4	.9610	.9238	.8885	.8548	.8227	.7921	.7629	.7350	.7084	.6830	.6355	.5921	.5718	.5523	.5158	.4823	.4230	.3725	.3294	.2923
5	.9515	.9057	.8626	.8219	.7835	.7473	.7130	.6806	.6499	.6209	.5674	.5194	.4972	.4761	.4371	.4019	.3411	.2910	.2495	.2149
6	.9420	.8880	.8375	.7903	.7462	.7050	.6663	.6302	.5963	.5645	.5066	.4556	.4323	.4104	.3704	.3349	.2751	.2274	.1890	.1580
7	.9327	.8706	.8131	.7599	.7107	.6651	.6227	.5835	.5470	.5132	.4523	.3996	.3759	.3538	.3139	.2791	.2218	.1776	.1432	.1162
8	.9235	.8535	.7894	.7307	.6768	.6274	.5820	.5403	.5019	.4665	.4039	.3506	.3269	.3050	.2660	.2326	.1789	.1388	.1085	.0854
9	.9143	.8368	.7664	.7026	.6446	.5919	.5439	.5002	.4604	.4241	.3606	.3075	.2843	.2630	.2255	.1938	.1443	.1084	.0822	.0628
10	.9053	.8203	.7441	.6756	.6139	.5584	.5083	.4632	.4224	.3855	.3220	.2697	.2472	.2267	.1911	.1615	.1164	.0847	.0623	.0462
11	.8963	.8043	.7224	.6496	.5847	.5268	.4751	.4289	.3875	.3505	.2875	.2366	.2149	.1954	.1619	.1346	.0938	.0662	.0472	.0340
12	.8874	.7885	.7014	.6246	.5568	.4970	.4440	.3971	.3555	.3186	.2567	.2076	.1869	.1685	.1372	.1122	.0757	.0517	.0357	.0250
13	.8787	.7730	.6810	.6006	.5303	.4688	.4150	.3677	.3262	.2897	.2292	.1821	.1625	.1452	.1163	.0935	.0610	.0404	.0271	.0184
14	.8700	.7579	.6611	.5775	.5051	.4423	.3878	.3405	.2992	.2633	.2046	.1597	.1413	.1252	.0985	.0779	.0492	.0316	.0205	.0135
15	.8613	.7430	.6419	.5553	.4810	.4173	.3624	.3152	.2745	.2394	.1827	.1401	.1229	.1079	.0835	.0649	.0397	.0247	.0155	.0099
16	.8528	.7284	.6232	.5339	.4581	.3936	.3387	.2919	.2519	.2176	.1631	.1229	.1069	.0930	.0708	.0541	.0320	.0193	.0118	.0073
17	.8444	.7142	.6050	.5134	.4363	.3714	.3166	.2703	.2311	.1978	.1456	.1078	.0929	.0802	.0600	.0451	.0258	.0150	.0089	.0054
18	.8360	.7002	.5874	.4936	.4155	.3503	.2959	.2502	.2120	.1799	.1300	.0946	.0808	.0691	.0508	.0376	.0208	.0118	.0068	.0039
19	.8277	.6864	.5703	.4746	.3957	.3305	.2765	.2317	.1945	.1635	.1161	.0829	.0703	.0596	.0431	.0313	.0168	.0092	.0051	.0029
20	.8195	.6730	.5537	.4564	.3769	.3118	.2584	.2145	.1784	.1486	.1037	.0728	.0611	.0514	.0365	.0261	.0135	.0072	.0039	.0021
25	.7798	.6095	.4776	.3751	.2953	.2330	.1842	.1460	.1160	.0923	.0588	.0378	.0304	.0245	.0160	.0105	.0046	.0021	.0010	.0005
30	.7419	.5521	.4120	.3083	.2314	.1741	.1314	.0994	.0754	.0573	.0334	.0196	.0151	.0116	.0070	.0042	.0016	.0006	.0002	.0001
40	.6717	.4529	.3066	.2083	.1420	.0972	.0668	.0460	.0318	.0221	.0107	.0053	.0037	.0026	.0013	.0007	.0002	.0001	*	*
50	.6080	.3715	.2281	.1407	.0872	.0543	.0339	.0213	.0134	.0085	.0035	.0014	.0009	.0006	.0003	.0001	*	*	*	*
60	.5504	.3048	.1697	.0951	.0535	.0303	.0173	.0099	.0057	.0033	.0011	.0004	.0002	.0001	*	*	*	*	*	*

*The factor is zero to four decimal places.

Table 6-3 *

Present Value of an Annuity of $1 Per Period for n Period: $PVIFA = \sum_{t=1}^{n} \frac{1}{(1+k)^t} = \frac{1 - \frac{1}{(1+k)^n}}{k}$

Number of payments	1%	2%	3%	4%	5%	6%	7%	8%	9%	10%	12%	14%	15%	16%	18%	20%	24%	28%	32%
1	0.9901	0.9804	0.9709	0.9615	0.9524	0.9434	0.9346	0.9259	0.9174	0.9091	0.8929	0.8772	0.8696	0.8621	0.8475	0.8333	0.8065	0.7813	0.7576
2	1.9704	1.9416	1.9135	1.8861	1.8594	1.8334	1.8080	1.7833	1.7591	1.7355	1.6901	1.6467	1.6257	1.6052	1.5656	1.5278	1.4568	1.3916	1.3315
3	2.9410	2.8839	2.8286	2.7751	2.7232	2.6730	2.6243	2.5771	2.5313	2.4869	2.4018	2.3216	2.2832	2.2459	2.1743	2.1065	1.9813	1.8684	1.7663
4	3.9020	3.8077	3.7171	3.6299	3.5460	3.4651	3.3872	3.3121	3.2397	3.1699	3.0373	2.9137	2.8550	2.7982	2.6901	2.5887	2.4043	2.2410	2.0957
5	4.8534	4.7135	4.5797	4.4518	4.3295	4.2124	4.1002	3.9927	3.8897	3.7908	3.6048	3.4331	3.3522	3.2743	3.1272	2.9906	2.7454	2.5320	2.3452
6	5.7955	5.6014	5.4172	5.2421	5.0757	4.9173	4.7665	4.6229	4.4859	4.3553	4.1114	3.8887	3.7845	3.6847	3.4976	3.3255	3.0205	2.7594	2.5342
7	6.7282	6.4720	6.2303	6.0021	5.7864	5.5824	5.3893	5.2064	5.0330	4.8684	4.5638	4.2883	4.1604	4.0386	3.8115	3.6046	3.2423	2.9370	2.6775
8	7.6517	7.3255	7.0197	6.7327	6.4632	6.2098	5.9713	5.7466	5.5348	5.3349	4.9676	4.6389	4.4873	4.3436	4.0776	3.8372	3.4212	3.0758	2.7860
9	8.5660	8.1622	7.7861	7.4353	7.1078	6.8017	6.5152	6.2469	5.9952	5.7590	5.3282	4.9464	4.7716	4.6065	4.3030	4.0310	3.5655	3.1842	2.8681
10	9.4713	8.9826	8.5302	8.1109	7.7217	7.3601	7.0236	6.7101	6.4177	6.1446	5.6502	5.2161	5.0188	4.8332	4.4941	4.1925	3.6819	3.2689	2.9304
11	10.3676	9.7868	9.2526	8.7605	8.3064	7.8869	7.4987	7.1390	6.8052	6.4951	5.9377	5.4527	5.2337	5.0286	4.6560	4.3271	3.7757	3.3351	2.9776
12	11.2551	10.5753	9.9540	9.3851	8.8633	8.3838	7.9427	7.5361	7.1607	6.8137	6.1944	5.6603	5.4206	5.1971	4.7932	4.4392	3.8514	3.3868	3.0133
13	12.1337	11.3484	10.6350	9.9856	9.3936	8.8527	8.3577	7.9038	7.4869	7.1034	6.4235	5.8424	5.5831	5.3423	4.9095	4.5327	3.9124	3.4272	3.0404
14	13.0037	12.1062	11.2961	10.5631	9.8986	9.2950	8.7455	8.2442	7.7862	7.3667	6.6282	6.0021	5.7245	5.4675	5.0081	4.6106	3.9616	3.4587	3.0609
15	13.8651	12.8493	11.9379	11.1184	10.3797	9.7122	9.1079	8.5595	8.0607	7.6061	6.8109	6.1422	5.8474	5.5755	5.0916	4.6755	4.0013	3.4834	3.0764
16	14.7179	13.5777	12.5611	11.6523	10.8378	10.1059	9.4466	8.8514	8.3126	7.8237	6.9740	6.2651	5.9542	5.6685	5.1624	4.7296	4.0333	3.5026	3.0882
17	15.5623	14.2919	13.1661	12.1657	11.2741	10.4773	9.7632	9.1216	8.5436	8.0216	7.1196	6.3729	6.0472	5.7487	5.2223	4.7746	4.0591	3.5177	3.0971
18	16.3983	14.9920	13.7535	12.6593	11.6896	10.8276	10.0591	9.3719	8.7556	8.2014	7.2497	6.4674	6.1280	5.8178	5.2732	4.8122	4.0799	3.5294	3.1039
19	17.2260	15.6785	14.3238	13.1339	12.0853	11.1581	10.3356	9.6036	8.9501	8.3649	7.3658	6.5504	6.1982	5.8775	5.3162	4.8435	4.0967	3.5386	3.1090
20	18.0456	16.3514	14.8775	13.5903	12.4622	11.4699	10.5940	9.8181	9.1285	8.5136	7.4694	6.6231	6.2593	5.9288	5.3527	4.8696	4.1103	3.5458	3.1129
25	22.0232	19.5235	17.4131	15.6221	14.0939	12.7834	11.6536	10.6748	9.8226	9.0770	7.8431	6.8729	6.4641	6.0971	5.4669	4.9476	4.1474	3.5640	3.1220
30	25.8077	22.3965	19.6004	17.2920	15.3725	13.7648	12.4090	11.2578	10.2737	9.4269	8.0552	7.0027	6.5660	6.1772	5.5168	4.9789	4.1601	3.5693	3.1242
40	32.8347	27.3555	23.1148	19.7928	17.1591	15.0463	13.3317	11.9246	10.7574	9.7791	8.2438	7.1050	6.6418	6.2335	5.5482	4.9966	4.1659	3.5712	3.1250
50	39.1961	31.4236	25.7298	21.4822	18.2559	15.7619	13.8007	12.2335	10.9617	9.9148	8.3045	7.1327	6.6605	6.2463	5.5541	4.9995	4.1666	3.5714	3.1250
60	44.9550	34.7609	27.6756	22.6235	18.9293	16.1614	14.0392	12.3766	11.0480	9.9672	8.3240	7.1401	6.6651	6.2402	5.5553	4.9999	4.1667	3.5714	3.1250

Table 6-4 *

Future Value of $1 at the End of n Periods $FVIF_{k,n} = (1 + k)^n$

Period	1%	2%	3%	4%	5%	6%	7%	8%	9%	10%	12%	14%	15%	16%	18%	20%	24%	28%	32%	36%
1	1.0100	1.0200	1.0300	1.0400	1.0500	1.0600	1.0700	1.0800	1.0900	1.1000	1.1200	1.1400	1.1500	1.1600	1.1800	1.2000	1.2400	1.2800	1.3200	1.3600
2	1.0201	1.0404	1.0609	1.0816	1.1025	1.1236	1.1449	1.1664	1.1881	1.2100	1.2544	1.2996	1.3225	1.3456	1.3924	1.4400	1.5376	1.6384	1.7424	1.8496
3	1.0303	1.0612	1.0927	1.1249	1.1576	1.1910	1.2250	1.2597	1.2950	1.3310	1.4049	1.4815	1.5209	1.5609	1.6430	1.7280	1.9066	2.0972	2.3000	2.5155
4	1.0406	1.0824	1.1255	1.1699	1.2155	1.2625	1.3108	1.3605	1.4116	1.4641	1.5735	1.6890	1.7490	1.8106	1.9388	2.0736	2.3642	2.6844	3.0360	3.4210
5	1.0510	1.1041	1.1593	1.2167	1.2763	1.3382	1.4026	1.4693	1.5386	1.6105	1.7623	1.9254	2.0114	2.1003	2.2878	2.4883	2.9316	3.4360	4.0075	4.6526
6	1.0615	1.1262	1.1941	1.2653	1.3401	1.4185	1.5007	1.5869	1.6771	1.7716	1.9738	2.1950	2.3131	2.4364	2.6996	2.9860	3.6352	4.3980	5.2899	6.3275
7	1.0721	1.1487	1.2299	1.3159	1.4071	1.5036	1.6058	1.7138	1.8280	1.9487	2.2107	2.5023	2.6600	2.8262	3.1855	3.5832	4.5077	5.6295	6.9826	8.6054
8	1.0829	1.1717	1.2668	1.3686	1.4775	1.5938	1.7182	1.8509	1.9926	2.1436	2.4760	2.8526	3.0590	3.2784	3.7589	4.2998	5.5895	7.2058	9.2170	11.703
9	1.0937	1.1951	1.3048	1.4233	1.5513	1.6895	1.8385	1.9990	2.1719	2.3579	2.7731	3.2519	3.5179	3.8030	4.4355	5.1598	6.9310	9.2234	12.166	15.916
10	1.1046	1.2190	1.3439	1.4802	1.6289	1.7908	1.9672	2.1589	2.3674	2.5937	3.1058	3.7072	4.0456	4.4114	5.2338	6.1917	8.5944	11.805	16.059	21.646
11	1.1157	1.2434	1.3842	1.5395	1.7103	1.8983	2.1049	2.3316	2.5804	2.8531	3.4785	4.2262	4.6524	5.1173	6.1759	7.4301	10.657	15.111	21.198	29.439
12	1.1268	1.2682	1.4258	1.6010	1.7959	2.0122	2.2522	2.5182	2.8127	3.1384	3.8960	4.8179	5.3502	5.9360	7.2876	8.9161	13.214	19.342	27.982	40.037
13	1.1381	1.2936	1.4685	1.6651	1.8856	2.1329	2.4098	2.7196	3.0658	3.4523	4.3635	5.4924	6.1528	6.8858	8.5994	10.699	16.386	24.758	36.937	54.451
14	1.1495	1.3195	1.5126	1.7317	1.9799	2.2609	2.5785	2.9372	3.3417	3.7975	4.8871	6.2613	7.0757	7.9875	10.147	12.839	20.319	31.691	48.756	74.053
15	1.1610	1.3459	1.5580	1.8009	2.0789	2.3966	2.7590	3.1722	3.6425	4.1772	5.4736	7.1379	8.1371	9.2655	11.973	15.407	25.195	40.564	64.358	100.71
16	1.1726	1.3728	1.6047	1.8730	2.1829	2.5404	2.9522	3.4259	3.9703	4.5950	6.1304	8.1372	9.3576	10.748	14.129	18.488	31.242	51.923	84.953	136.96
17	1.1843	1.4002	1.6528	1.9479	2.2920	2.6928	3.1588	3.7000	4.3276	5.0545	6.8660	9.2765	10.761	12.467	16.672	22.186	38.740	66.461	112.13	186.27
18	1.1961	1.4282	1.7024	2.0258	2.4066	2.8543	3.3799	3.9960	4.7171	5.5599	7.6900	10.575	12.375	14.462	19.673	26.623	48.038	85.070	148.02	253.33
19	1.2081	1.4568	1.7535	2.1068	2.5270	3.0256	3.6165	4.3157	5.1417	6.1159	8.6128	12.055	14.231	16.776	23.214	31.948	59.567	108.89	195.39	344.53
20	1.2202	1.4859	1.8061	2.1911	2.6533	3.2071	3.8697	4.6610	5.6044	6.7275	9.6463	13.743	16.366	19.460	27.393	38.337	73.864	139.37	257.91	468.57
21	1.2324	1.5157	1.8603	2.2788	2.7860	3.3996	4.1406	5.0338	6.1088	7.4002	10.803	15.667	18.821	22.574	32.323	46.005	91.591	178.40	340.44	637.26
22	1.2447	1.5460	1.9161	2.3699	2.9253	3.6035	4.4304	5.4365	6.6586	8.1403	12.100	17.861	21.644	26.186	38.142	55.206	113.57	228.35	449.39	866.67
23	1.2572	1.5769	1.9736	2.4647	3.0715	3.8197	4.7405	5.8715	7.2579	8.9543	13.552	20.361	24.891	30.376	45.007	66.247	140.83	292.30	593.19	1178.6
24	1.2697	1.6084	2.0328	2.5633	3.2251	4.0489	5.0724	6.3412	7.9111	9.8497	15.178	23.212	28.625	35.236	53.108	79.496	174.63	374.14	783.02	1602.9
25	1.2824	1.6406	2.0938	2.6658	3.3864	4.2919	5.4274	6.8485	8.6231	10.834	17.000	26.461	32.918	40.874	62.668	95.396	216.54	478.90	1033.5	2180.0
26	1.2953	1.6734	2.1566	2.7725	3.5557	4.5494	5.8074	7.3964	9.3992	11.918	19.040	30.166	37.856	47.414	73.948	114.47	268.51	612.99	1364.3	2964.9
27	1.3082	1.7069	2.2213	2.8834	3.7335	4.8223	6.2139	7.9881	10.245	13.110	21.324	34.389	43.535	55.000	87.259	137.37	332.95	784.63	1800.9	4032.2
28	1.3213	1.7410	2.2879	2.9987	3.9201	5.1117	6.6488	8.6271	11.167	14.421	23.883	39.204	50.065	63.800	102.96	164.84	412.86	1004.3	2377.2	5483.8
29	1.3345	1.7758	2.3566	3.1187	4.1161	5.4184	7.1143	9.3173	12.172	15.863	26.749	44.693	57.575	74.008	121.50	197.81	511.95	1285.5	3137.9	7458.0
30	1.3478	1.8114	2.4273	3.2434	4.3219	5.7435	7.6123	10.062	13.267	17.449	29.959	50.950	66.211	85.849	143.37	237.37	634.81	1645.5	4142.0	10143.
40	1.4889	2.2080	3.2620	4.8010	7.0400	10.285	14.974	21.724	31.409	45.259	93.050	188.88	267.86	378.72	750.37	1469.7	5455.9	19426	66520	*
50	1.6446	2.6916	4.3839	7.1067	11.467	18.420	29.457	46.901	74.357	117.39	289.00	700.23	1083.6	1670.7	3927.3	9100.4	46890.	*	*	*
60	1.8167	3.2810	5.8916	10.519	18.679	32.987	57.946	101.25	176.03	304.48	897.59	2595.9	4383.9	7370.1	20555.	56347.	*	*	*	*

*FVIF > 99,999

Table 6-5 *

Sum of an Annuity of $1 Per Period for n Periods $\quad FVIFA_{kn} = \sum (1+k)^{n-1} = \dfrac{(1+k)^n - 1}{k}$

Number of Periods	1%	2%	3%	4%	5%	6%	7%	8%	9%	10%	12%	14%	15%	16%	18%	20%	24%	28%	32%	36%
1	1.0000	1.0000	1.0000	1.0000	1.0000	1.0000	1.0000	1.0000	1.0000	1.0000	1.0000	1.0000	1.0000	1.0000	1.0000	1.0000	1.0000	1.0000	1.0000	1.0000
2	2.0100	2.0200	2.0300	2.0400	2.0500	2.0600	2.0700	2.0800	2.0900	2.1000	2.1200	2.1400	2.1500	2.1600	2.1800	2.2000	2.2400	2.2800	2.3200	2.3600
3	3.0301	3.0604	3.0909	3.1216	3.1525	3.1836	3.2149	3.2464	3.2781	3.3100	3.3744	3.4396	3.4725	3.5056	3.5724	3.6400	3.7776	3.9184	4.0624	4.2096
4	4.0604	4.1216	4.1836	4.2465	4.3101	4.3746	4.4399	4.5061	4.5731	4.6410	4.7793	4.9211	4.9934	5.0665	5.2154	5.3680	5.6842	6.0156	6.3624	6.7251
5	5.1010	5.2040	5.3091	5.4163	5.5256	5.6371	5.7507	5.8666	5.9847	6.1051	6.3528	6.6101	6.7424	6.8771	7.1542	7.4416	8.0484	8.6999	9.3983	10.146
6	6.1520	6.3081	6.4684	6.6330	6.8019	6.9753	7.1533	7.3359	7.5233	7.7156	8.1152	8.5355	8.7537	8.9775	9.4420	9.9299	10.980	12.135	13.405	14.798
7	7.2135	7.4343	7.6625	7.8983	8.1420	8.3938	8.6540	8.9228	9.2004	9.4872	10.089	10.730	11.066	11.413	12.141	12.915	14.615	16.533	18.695	21.126
8	8.2857	8.5830	8.8923	9.2142	9.5491	9.8975	10.259	10.636	11.028	11.435	12.299	13.232	13.726	14.240	15.327	16.499	19.122	22.163	25.678	29.731
9	9.3685	9.7546	10.159	10.582	11.026	11.491	11.978	12.487	13.021	13.579	14.775	16.085	16.785	17.518	19.085	20.798	24.712	29.369	34.895	41.435
10	10.462	10.949	11.463	12.006	12.577	13.180	13.816	14.486	15.192	15.937	17.548	19.337	20.303	21.321	23.521	25.958	31.643	38.592	47.061	57.351
11	11.566	12.168	12.807	13.486	14.206	14.971	15.783	16.645	17.560	18.531	20.654	23.044	24.349	25.732	28.755	32.150	40.237	50.398	63.121	78.998
12	12.682	13.412	14.192	15.025	15.917	16.869	17.888	18.977	20.140	21.384	24.133	27.270	29.001	30.850	34.931	39.580	50.894	65.510	84.320	108.43
13	13.809	14.680	15.617	16.626	17.713	18.882	20.140	21.495	22.953	24.522	28.029	32.088	34.351	36.786	42.218	48.496	64.109	84.852	112.30	148.47
14	14.947	15.973	17.086	18.291	19.598	21.015	22.550	24.214	26.019	27.975	32.392	37.581	40.504	43.672	50.818	59.195	80.496	109.61	149.23	202.92
15	16.096	17.293	18.598	20.023	21.578	23.276	25.129	27.152	29.360	31.772	37.279	43.842	47.580	51.659	60.965	72.035	100.81	141.30	197.99	276.97
16	17.257	18.639	20.156	21.824	23.657	25.672	27.888	30.324	33.003	35.949	42.753	50.980	55.717	60.925	72.939	87.442	126.01	181.86	262.35	377.69
17	18.430	20.012	21.761	23.697	25.840	28.212	30.840	33.750	36.973	40.544	48.883	59.117	65.075	71.673	87.068	105.93	157.25	233.79	347.30	514.66
18	19.614	21.412	23.414	25.645	28.132	30.905	33.999	37.450	41.301	45.599	55.749	68.394	75.836	84.140	103.74	128.11	195.99	300.25	459.44	700.93
19	20.810	22.840	25.116	27.671	30.539	33.760	37.379	41.446	46.018	51.159	63.439	78.969	88.211	98.603	123.41	154.74	244.03	385.32	607.47	954.27
20	22.019	24.297	26.870	29.778	33.066	36.785	40.995	45.762	51.160	57.275	72.052	91.024	102.44	115.37	146.62	186.68	303.60	494.21	802.86	1298.8
21	23.239	25.783	28.676	31.969	35.719	39.992	44.865	50.422	56.764	64.002	81.698	104.76	118.81	134.84	174.02	225.02	377.46	633.59	1060.7	1767.3
22	24.471	27.299	30.536	34.248	38.505	43.392	49.005	55.456	62.873	71.402	92.502	120.43	137.63	157.41	206.34	271.03	469.05	811.99	1401.2	2404.6
23	25.716	28.845	32.452	36.617	41.430	46.995	53.436	60.893	69.531	79.543	104.60	138.29	159.27	183.60	244.48	326.23	582.62	1040.3	1850.6	3271.3
24	26.973	30.421	34.426	39.082	44.502	50.815	58.176	66.764	76.789	88.497	118.15	158.65	184.16	213.97	289.49	392.48	723.46	1332.6	2443.8	4449.9
25	28.243	32.030	36.459	41.645	47.727	54.864	63.249	73.105	84.700	98.347	133.33	181.87	212.79	249.21	342.60	471.98	898.09	1706.8	3226.8	6052.9
26	29.525	33.670	38.553	44.311	51.113	59.156	68.676	79.954	93.323	109.18	150.33	208.33	245.71	290.08	405.27	567.37	1114.6	2185.7	4260.4	8233.0
27	30.820	35.344	40.709	47.084	54.669	63.705	74.483	87.350	102.72	121.09	169.37	238.49	283.56	337.50	479.22	681.85	1383.1	2798.7	5624.7	11199.9
28	32.129	37.051	42.930	49.967	58.402	68.528	80.697	95.338	112.96	134.20	190.69	272.88	327.10	392.50	566.48	819.22	1716.0	3583.3	7425.6	15230.2
29	33.450	38.792	45.218	52.966	62.322	73.639	87.346	103.96	124.13	148.63	214.58	312.09	377.16	456.30	669.44	984.06	2128.9	4587.6	9802.9	20714.1
30	34.784	40.568	47.575	56.084	66.438	79.058	94.460	113.28	136.30	164.49	241.33	356.78	434.74	530.31	790.94	1181.8	2640.9	5873.2	12940.	28172.2
40	48.886	60.402	75.401	95.025	120.79	154.76	199.63	259.05	337.88	442.59	767.09	1342.0	1779.0	2360.7	4163.2	7343.8	22728	69377	*	*
50	64.463	84.579	112.79	152.66	209.34	290.33	406.52	573.76	815.08	1163.9	2400.0	4994.5	7217.7	10435	21813	45497	*	*	*	*
60	81.669	114.05	163.05	237.99	353.58	533.12	813.52	1253.2	1944.7	3034.8	7471.6	18535	29219	46057	*	*	*	*	*	*

*FVIFA > 99,999

[C5348]

A third method of calculating the time value of money is with
the aid of a small electronic calculator. A calculator equipped
with basic financial functions has keys to enter any three of the
four basic variables, and the calculator will calculate the value
of the fourth variable. These calculators are inexpensive and
provide by far the easiest method of computing the time value of
money.[90]

Using the methods just described, an attorney is able to figure the present value or the future value of any one payment or
receipt, or of a schedule of many payments and receipts by figuring each amount separately. There are cases, however, where
even these relatively easy methods would prove to be tedious.
For example, using a 12% annual interest rate, what is the present value of the stream of lost wages of a worker who has been
injured and will not be able to work for 5 years if his monthly
wage was $1,348.00? This problem would require multiple indi-
vidual calculations if done by the single payment method. This
kind of a problem, however, is a special case—where the stream
of payments is called an *annuity*. An annuity is a series of payments of a fixed amount for a specified number of periods.[91]
The following variables are used in annuity calculations:

> PVA —The present value of an annuity.
> FVA —The future value of an annuity.
> i   —The interest rate per period.
> n   —The total number of periods.
> p   —The fixed payment per period.

The following formulas govern the relationship of the time value
of annuities:

$$FVA = p \left[\frac{(1 + i)^n - 1}{i} \right]$$

$$PVA = p \left[\frac{1 - \frac{1}{(1 + i)^n}}{i} \right]$$

90. Stuart M. Speiser has written
an article entitled "Computing Future
Earnings on Hand-held Calculators"
relating to this application which can
be found in 84 *Case and Comment* p.
3 (1979).

91. *For the purposes of this discussion we will deal with an annuity*

*where the payment is made at the
end of each period, called a regular
or a deferred annuity. For cases
where the payments are made at the
beginning of the period—an annuity
due—some slight modifications
must be made. See your calculator
handbook for instructions.*

Tables can also be used to ease the calculation of annuities. Table #6–5 lists future values of annuities with a $1.00 payment per period, and table #6–3 lists the same information for the present values of annuities. These tables are organized in the same manner that tables #6–2 and #6–4 were organized. Working with the example of the lost wages, we would first convert the 5 year time span into the number of periods—60 one-month periods. The interest rate per period would be 1% (12% / 12), and the figure from the table would be 44.950. Multiplying this figure by the $1,348.00 fixed payment, the present value of this stream of payments, or annuity, is $60,599.34. Notice the difference in this and in the absolute sum of the 60 payments of $1,348—$80,880. This $20,000 difference is due entirely to the effects of the time value of money.

Here again, the easiest way to calculate annuities is to use a financial calculator. Most such calculators provide keys for entering values of the known variables, and the calculator gives you the value of the unknown variable. Calculators are especially useful with weekly payments because the number of periods considered will often be very high, and the interest per period will often be only a small fraction not found on the tables.

C. THE APPROPRIATE RATE OF INTEREST FOR TIME-VALUE CALCULATION USE

The interest rate used in the time value calculations greatly affects the ultimate outcomes, and thus a key factor in the reliability of the calculations is the appropriateness of the interest rate variable. The rate used should usually be the value of money to your client. The rate may be based on saving or borrowing rates of the individuals involved, or an established rate may be used, such as a fixed amount above or below the current prime rate. The key "ingredients" in an interest rate figure are the inflation factor and the risk factor. For example, in a scenario with no risk of non-payment and with no inflation, an individual might be willing to lend money at a rate of 3%. This would be a base amount to which would be added an amount representing expected inflation—say 12%, and an amount for risk coverage, which for this example might be 2%. Under these circumstances, a rate of 17% would be a good rate of interest to use.[92]

---

92. *See* Bingham, *Financial Management Theory and Practice*, p. 118 (Dryden, 1979). The plaintiff and defendant will not necessarily have the same discount rate because they may be receiving different returns on their investments, and they may have different estimates of inflation rates.

D.   THE TAX ASPECTS OF SETTLEMENT

The day is past when lawyers could ignore the tax implications of settlements. At present levels of taxation, the economic value of a settlement for the plaintiff or the defendant can routinely vary by as much as 50%, depending upon the tax treatment of the money or property involved.

The tax effects in a settlement agreement depend upon two primary factors: (1) the characterization of the values exchanged for tax purposes, and (2) the timing of payments.

To the defendant, there is a large saving if the payment is deductible from gross income (i.e. if the payment qualifies as an income tax deduction) rather than being payable with after-tax dollars.

The cost of a payment by the defendant is also conditioned by the timing of taxation. If the payment is deductible, can it be deducted all in this tax year, or must it be amortized or depreciated over a number of years?

For the plaintiff, the question is whether money received will be taxed, and if so at what rate. If it is tax exempt, there is, of course, no tax to be paid. If it is characterized as ordinary income, it will be subject to the plaintiff's regular tax rate. If it is characterized as capital gain, it will be subject to tax, but at a more favorable rate than ordinary income.

The interests of the parties are often at odds on tax issues, because most of the tax rules are structured to give favorable treatment at one end of the transaction or the other, but not at both. A paying party may wish to deduct a payment in the current tax year, while the receiving party may wish to receive the income in a future year, or to spread it over a number of years when he will either have less earnings than at present (as might be the case in a personal injury case where the payments are compensation for injuries causing a loss of a job) or when the effects of a high inflation rate will make the payments less painful. Thus, tax aspects of the transaction should be explicitly studied and consciously structured.

See E. Mishan, *Economics for Social Decisions*, p. 112–140 (Praeger, 1972); and Dinwiddy, *Elementary Mathematics for Economists*, pp. 199–216 (Oxford, 1967).

The best available reference work for settlement purposes is Gersham Goldstein, *Index to Federal Tax Articles* (Boston: Warren, Gorham and Lamont, 1980). This Index is an excellent and exhaustive report of the literature on taxation, listed according to type of transaction.

CHAPTER NOTES

1. *When to Use Facts: Fact Development and Argumentation*

Many attorneys are conditioned in their use of facts by the dictum of trial lawyers that the element of surprise is still a major source of strength at trial; attorneys deduce from this that the cautious strategist will withhold his best facts in anticipation of trial, saving them for the coup de grace which, at some exquisite moment in trial, will dramatically win the case for them. The more helpful response to this mentality is to observe that for any group of 10 cases, 9 are likely to be settled without trial. If attorneys in those cases have reserved their best facts for trial, then they are guilty of settling those cases without the benefit of their most powerful facts. The withholding attorneys have put themselves in the awkward position of arguing for a value on the case which is not fully supported, because they are holding back the most persuasive factual evidence. They are twice harmed: first in their failure to put forth their best cases, and second in their attempt to sell a value for the case which cannot be supported by the facts they do present.

2. *Inflation and Productivity as Factors in Damage Awards*

Damage awards in some states may now reflect inflation and anticipated productivity increases. The issue in these states is how to calculate these factors. For inflation, the Alaska Supreme Court has adopted a "total offset" method which assumes that the inflation rate and discount rate cancel each other out, so there is no reduction for discount rate and no increase for inflation. For a Pennsylvania case allowing both types to be awarded, see Kaczkowski v. Bolubasz, 491 Pa. 561, 421 A.2d 1027 (1980).

3. *Zero-Sum Games*

A civil dispute presents the best opportunity for a negotiated settlement when the parties recognize that they depend upon each other to avoid a mutually destructive outcome. This kind of relationship is known among bargaining theorists as a non-zero-sum game. It appears that the possibilities of a reciprocal relationship between parties in conflict is obvious to some people and obscure to others. See T.C. Schelling, *The Strategy of Conflict* vi–vii (Cambridge: Harvard Univ. Press, 1980 ed.) Recognition of this relationship by the parties does not necessarily diminish the prospects for trial; in fact, one of the issues to be bargained is whether this case should be brought to trial.

A zero-sum game is any game where the losses equal the winnings. Examples are hiring quotas (where each job given to a person in a preferred category means one less job for non-preferred persons); athletic contests (in which one team or person wins and the other loses); trial verdicts (except that there is imbalance in the costs of prosecuting the case, which means that one party may have payed grossly more than the other regardless of which side won or lost). Lester Thurow points out that "distributional issues are highly contentious" (Thurow, *The Zero-Sum Society* (Penguin Books: New York, 1980), p. 18). He implies that distributional methods are not very efficient because they are not good at loss allocation: they give an all or nothing solution, which means both sides are in an all or nothing contest. He says "the essence of problem solving is loss allocation."

4. Preparation: How Much Preparation Must Be Completed Before Opening (or Closing) Settlement Negotiations?

Most trial attorneys reason that until you have prepared a case for trial you should not settle, since you cannot know what it is worth in settlement. This premise is troublesome, because if you cannot settle a case until it is ready for trial, then you have already incurred the major expenses of litigation, and there is proportionately less benefit to both to settle.

5. Risk-Averison and Risk-Seeking Behavior as an Explanation of Why Institutional Defendants Sometimes Prefer Trial.

Economists have suggested that the economic choices we make are influenced by our attitudes toward risk. Individuals who prefer certainty to chance are labeled risk-averse, while individuals who prefer to gamble on certain outcomes are labeled risk-preferring. While the studies of the psychology of preferences have been largely experimental, they suggest that when people are forced to make risky choices, they lose their objectivity and end up making irrational selections.

One of the most intriguing findings is that our attitude toward risk is significantly influenced by the nature of problem: if we stand to gain some benefit (for example, we are given a choice of receiving $80 outright or an 85% chance of receiving $100 and a 15% chance of receiving nothing), we tend to be risk-averse and to choose certainty ($80 in our pocket) over chance (an 85% chance of receiving $100). But if we face a loss, we tend to select the risk of loss (an 85% chance of losing $100) over a certain loss ($80).

The implications of this simple model for settlement negotiations are intriguing. The model suggests that plaintiffs, who are generally seeking to gain some benefit (compensation for a past loss), are more likely to be risk-averse and to prefer a lesser outcome that is certain to the possibility of a higher outcome that carries some risk of failure. By contrast, the model suggests that defendants, who are generally seeking to avoid a loss, would prefer the risk of a higher loss at trial than the certainty of a lesser present loss. The psychology of preferences offers a powerful hypothesis that plaintiffs are psychologically predisposed to seek settlement and defendants are psychologically predisposed to resist settlement in favor of trial.

An excellent recent treatment of this perspective is given in Daniel Kahneman and Amos Tversky, "The Psychology of Preferences", Scientific American (January 1982 at 160).

6. *Structured Settlements*

In a serious injury case in which a claim for substantial future damages is being made, a single lump-sum payment is the normal method of settlement. An alternate method, however, is the use of a structured settlement which focuses on the timing and the amount of a series of payments rather than the amount of a single payment. Such settlements offer advantages to both parties. See C.F. Krause, "Structured Settlements For Tort Victims", 66 A.B.A.J. (1980) at 1527–1529; and J.S. Granelli, "Structuring the Settlement" National Law Journal (February 16, 1981), for a discussion of the benefits of structured settlements as well as an example of a structured settlement in a $45 million liability suit. A California company is seeking to register the phrase "structured settlement" as a trademark. This application has been challenged and is pending before the U.S. Trademark Trial and Appeal Board (N.L.J. March 30, 1981, page 3).

In 1977, the National Conference of Commissioners on Uniform State Laws produced a Uniform Periodic Payments Act which deals with structured judgments of cases involving large amounts of damages tried under the act, by which the courts fashion a periodic installment judgment. See "Structured Settlements and the Uniform Periodic Payments Act" by Marvin E. Verbeck and Stanley J. Michaels in the Fall 1978 F.I.C. Quarterly (pp. 17–28) and "Periodic Payments of Bodily Injury Awards" by Roger C. Henderson in the June 1980 issue of the A.B.A. Journal (vol. 66, pp. 734–737). Both examine structured settlements as they would be organized under this act.

7. Taxation of Settlements: An Outline

The treatment of plaintiffs in personal injury cases is governed by the Internal Revenue Code, Section 104(a)(2), which excludes from income the amount of any damages received by suit or settlement agreement on account of personal injuries or sickness.

The general rule on taxation of payments by defendants is they may deduct amounts only if the amounts represent ordinary and necessary expenses for the carrying on of a trade or business, or if they are ordinary and necessary expenses for a person in his or her production and collection of income or the management, conservation, or maintenance of property held for production and collection of income. Businesses may not deduct amounts relating to capital expenditures, acquisition of property, disposition of a capital asset, defenses of title, or recovery of property. Depreciation or amortization of such expenditures, however, may be deducted.

Tax treatment of selected actions are outlined in the following table:

Table 6–6 Taxation of Settlement Agreements

Action	Plaintiff	Defendant
1. Assault	Excludes compensatory and punitive	Apply general test
2. Battery	Excludes compensatory and punitive	Apply general test
3. Negligently caused injuries	Excludes compensatory and punitive	Apply general test

[132]

Action	Plaintiff	Defendant
4. Strict Liability injuries	Excludes compensatory and punitive	Apply general test
5. Workmen's Compensation	Excludes compensatory and punitive but not "wage differential payments" unless Title VII and no personal damage	Apply general test
6. Recompense for past/future *individual* earnings	Excludes compensatory and punitive, even if annuity	Apply general test
7. Recompense for injuries to wife	Excludes compensatory and punitive	Apply general test
8. Reimbursement for medical expenses	Excludes compensatory and punitive, unless Plaintiff has deducted already	Apply general test
9. No fault insurance benefits	Excludes compensatory and punitive	Apply general test
10. Alienation of affections	Excludes compensatory and punitive	Apply general test
11. Surrender of custody of minor	Excludes compensatory and punitive	Apply general test
12. False imprisonment	Excludes compensatory and punitive	Apply general test
13. Infliction of mental stress	Excludes compensatory and punitive	Apply general test
14. Libel	Excludes compensatory only	Deduct
15. Slander	Excludes compensatory only	Deduct
16. Defamation	Excludes compensatory only	Deduct
17. Fraud	Excludes compensatory only	Apply general test
18. Deceit	Excludes compensatory only	Apply general test
19. Invasion of privacy	Excludes it *after* it occurs; cannot exclude if paid in advance	Apply general test
20. Loss of profits treated as returned capital	Excludes	Deduct lost profits separately

Action	Plaintiff	Defendant
21. Loss of profits as lost goodwill	Excludes	Deduct lost profits separately
22. Wrongful death	Excludes	Apply general test
23. Embarrassment, etc. from improper termination of employment	Excludes, but maybe not embarrassment alone	Deduct
24. Infringement of a U.S. patent	Excludes	Apply general test
25. Recoveries for antitrust violations	Excludes compensatory only	Apply general test
26. Breach of contract or fiduciary duties	Excludes	Deduct if no money or property received
27. Unrecovered losses	Excludes	Apply general test
28. Person, legal expenses for production or collection of income, property	Excludes	Deduct
29. Injury to person's *business* reputation or judgment	Taxable income	Deduct
30. Lost *business* profits, earnings	Taxable income	Deduct
31. Breech of employment contract	Taxable income but plaintiff can deduct legal fees	Deduct
32. Claims for unpaid rent	Taxable income	Apply general test
33. Claims for unpaid salaries	Taxable income	Apply general test
34. Claims for unpaid dividends	Taxable income	Apply general test
35. Interest earned on *any* damages	Taxable income except annuities where plaintiff has no right to the P.V.	Apply general test
36. Title VII damages for back pay	Taxable only if no personal damage is involved	Apply general test
37. Damage to income	Taxable income	Apply general test

[*134*]

Action	Plaintiff	Defendant
38. Payments in excess of basis	Taxable income	Apply general test
39. Fine, penalty for violation of the law	Taxable income	Apply general test
40. Legal expenses in re violation of the law		Deduct
41. Business torts		Deduct
42. Business or income producing activities		Deduct Deduct

*

Appendix I

RESEARCH METHODOLOGY: THE BYU LEGAL NEGOTIATION PROJECT

The objective of this study was to obtain descriptions of attorneys engaged in negotiation within the context of the legal system. Prior to developing the research instruments, a survey of relevant literature in the social sciences and legal domains was conducted. We then selected metropolitan areas as test sites, and proceeded to make contact with leaders of the Bar in each area to obtain their permission and cooperation in the research. For our first test area, we also solicited from Bar leaders names of respected, experienced attorneys to serve as advisors to the project.

We then conducted a total of 47 structured, one-hour, tape recorded interviews with members of the Bar in our test area. In the course of these interviews, attorneys were asked to name traits of effective and ineffective attorney/negotiators. These interviews were subsequently transcribed as an aid to analysis. These interviews were used, along with the literature previously mentioned, to develop a set of hypotheses about negotiator effectiveness and to derive three sets of descriptive scales for use in mailed questionnaires. Our work during this time was reviewed and made more relevant to the legal context by the advisory committee.

The mailed questionnaire was designed not only to test hypotheses available from the literature and from attorney interviews, but also to provide raw material from which a valid empirical description of negotiators behavior could be drawn whether or not anticipated by our hypotheses. Section I of the questionnaire asked for basic demographic data about the respondent. It then directed the respondent to think of the last attorney with whom they had negotiated, and, without naming the attorney, to provide basic demographic information about the attorney and about the subject-matter involved in the negotiation. The respondent was then asked, in Section II of the questionnaire, to rate the behavior of that attorney according to three sets of scales. The first set was an adjective checklist of 77 items, including many of the items commonly used in the adjective checklist (Gough and Heilbrun, 1965), supplemented by items derived from the attorney interviews. They were rated on scales of zero (not characteristic) to five (highly characteristic).

The second set of scales consisted of 43 bipolar adjective pairs selected in part from such scales as Sherwood's Self Concept Inventory (Sherwood, 1962) and in part from concepts obtained in the attorney interviews. These scales were rated from 1 (extremely characteristic on one pole of the scale) to 7 (extremely characteristic at other pole). The last set of scales in the questionnaire had twelve items concerning the apparent goals or objectives of the rated attorney.

Section III of the questionnaire asked for a fuller description of the subject-matter of the negotiation. Questions included whether the matter was a transaction (such as negotiation of a contract or business agreement) or a legal dispute (defined as a case which could be pursued through litigation); whether the case went to trial; how it was resolved if it did not go to trial; if it was settled by negotiated agreement, how many days before trial was it settled; if it went to trial, what were the primary reasons; and whether opposing counsel could have done more to promote a negotiated settlement.

Section IV asked the respondent to rate the reputation and performance of the rated attorney as a negotiator and, if the case went to trial, his or her effectiveness as a litigator.

The questionnaire was mailed to a random sample of one thousand licensed attorneys in the Phoenix, Arizona metropolitan area. Each attorney was mailed a copy of the questionnaire accompanied by a cover letter signed by the President of the County Bar Association. Follow-up letters were sent and telephone calls made to members of the sample who had not responded within two weeks. A total of 351 usable questionnaires were returned for a response rate of 35%.

Results were coded and analyzed according to standard statistical routines, including factor analysis, multiple regression analysis, and discriminant analysis. In addition, the data were analyzed according to Q methodology as conceived by Stephenson (1935) and Thomson (1935) and articulated by Brown (1980). Q Methodology is a technique of factor analysis involving the transpose of the R matrix (where a single matrix of data are factored by columns and then again by rows) under the special condition that the measuring unit is the same both for rows and columns (Brown 1980, p. 13).

Q methodology was applied in response to our discontent with some of the limitations of R technique. We found that the standard factor analyses defined negotiator behavior in terms of its constituent parts, but it provided no information about the relative significance of the parts to negotiator effectiveness nor about the functional relationship of the parts to each other.

In our first application of Q methodology, we limited the analysis to an inverted factor analysis (SPSS, Nie et al., 1975:470n) of three groups of data: descriptions of negotiators rated as effective, average, or ineffective. The inverted analysis produced two principle factors for each group, with each factor representing negotiating characteristics operantly defined in terms of the behavior of the subjects as determined by the rankings of actual negotiator characteristics as reported by rating attorneys (See Brown 1980 pp. 22–23). Thus, the factors represent actual patterns of reported negotiating behavior as contrasted to pre-determined categories developed by the researchers for testing or evaluation. (See also Brown 1980 p. 28 for further justification and interpretation of the kind of data obtained by Q methodology).

*

Appendix II

TABLES

The tables present, in rank order, the mean rating for effective, average, and ineffective attorneys according to their classification as cooperative or competitive negotiators. Since all attorneys were described by identical questionnaire items, the interpretation of each negotiator type depends upon comparison of the *rank order* of the higher scoring items for each type. The rank order was determined by computing a mean (average) score for each group on each item, then ranking items for each group in order of the mean score.

THE ADJECTIVE CHECKLIST

The adjective checklist presented 75 adjectives and asked the responding attorney to rate the extent to which the adjective described the negotiator being rated regardless of whether it added or detracted from his effectiveness as a negotiator. Six ratings were possible: zero, 1, 2, 3, 4, and 5. Thus for each adjective such as bluffer, rude, tough, etc. the responding attorney would indicate with a zero, 1, 2, 3, 4, or 5 the extent to which each adjective is characteristic of the attorney being rated. In analyzing the data, the scores of all attorneys in each type and level of effectiveness were averaged, giving a composite score on that item. With a zero to five range, the highest rating possible is 5.00. The items are presented in rank order on pages 142 and 143.

THE BIPOLAR ADJECTIVE SCALES

The bipolar adjective scales there were 43 items rated on a scale of 1 to 7. The 26 highest rated items were selected for analysis. These ratings are given on pages 144 and 145.

APPENDIX 2

Effective Cooperative Adjective Checklist (Phoenix Q–Analysis)	Effective Aggressive Adjective Checklist (Phoenix Q–Analysis)	Average Cooperatives Adjective Checklist (Phoenix Q–Analysis)
1. Experienced	1. Convincing	1. Ethical
2. Realistic	2. Experienced	2. Trustworthy
3. Ethical	3. Perceptive	3. Rational
4. Rational	4. Rational	4. Personable
5. Perceptive	5. Analytical	5. Cautious
6. Trustworthy	6. Creative	6. Realistic
7. Convincing	7. Ambitious	7. Self-controlled
8. Analytical	8. Dominant	8. Careful
9. Fair	9. Forceful	9. Discreet
10. Creative	10. Realistic	10. Sociable
11. Self-controlled	11. Tough	11. Objective
12. Versatile	12. Self-controlled	12. Legally astute
13. Personable	13. Clever	13. Analytical
14. Adaptable	14. Poised	14. Fair
15. Wise	15. Ethical	15. Loyal
16. Objective	16. Legally astute	16. Perceptive
17. Poised	17. Adaptable	17. Helpful
18. Careful	18. Versatile	18. Deliberate
19. Organizing	19. Egotistical	19. Experienced
20. Legally astute	20. Trustworthy	20. Organizing
21. Helpful	21. Personable	21. Dignified
22. Discreet	22. Smooth	22. Warm
23. Loyal	23. Organizing	23. Conservative
24. Sociable	24. Sociable	24. Adaptable
25. Warm	25. Demanding	25. Wise
26. Deliberate	26. Wise	26. Moderate
27. Dignified	27. Masculine	27. Poised
28. Patient	28. Manipulative	28. Ambitious
29. Smooth	29. Careful	29. Forceful
30. Forceful	30. Fair	30. Patient
31. Clever	31. Argumentative	31. Smooth
32. Masculine	32. Deliberate	32. Clever
33. Ambitious	33. Cautious	33. Convincing
34. Moderate	34. Stern	34. Creative
35. Cautious	35. Bluffer	35. Demanding
36. Obliging	36. Helpful	36. Versatile
37. Sympathetic	37. Objective	37. Gentle
38. Tough	38. Dignified	38. Masculine
39. Forgiving	39. Suspicious	39. Forgiving
40. Dominant	40. Discreet	40. Obliging
41. Praising	41. Patient	41. Argumentative
42. Gentle	42. Warm	42. Dominant
43. Conservative	43. Headstrong	43. **Bluffer**
44. Stern	44. Loyal	44. Sympathetic
45. Demanding	45. Picky	45. Praising
46. Manipulative	46. Impatient	46. Suspicious
47. Suspicious	47. Selfish	47. Picky
48. Idealistic	48. Obliging	48. Tough
49. Bluffer	49. Moderate	49. Evasive
50. Picky	50. Evasive	50. Egotistical
51. Argumentative	51. Praising	51. Idealistic
52. Egotistical	52. Greedy	52. Stern
53. Sentimental	53. Conniving	53. Headstrong
54. Impatient	54. Unpredictable	54. Impatient
55. Unpredictable	55. Quarrelsome	55. Complaining
56. Headstrong	56. Loud	56. Impulsive
57. Rude	57. Sympathetic	57. Manipulative
58. Selfish	58. Irritating	58. Greedy
59. Impulsive	59. Intolerant	59. Staller
60. Evasive	60. Sarcastic	60. Quarrelsome
61. Hostile	61. Conservative	61. Unpredictable
62. Greedy	62. Hostile	62. Timid
63. Staller	63. Forgiving	63. Selfish
64. Sarcastic	64. Impulsive	64. Sentimental
65. Rebellious	65. Staller	65. Intolerant
66. Intolerant	66. Gentle	66. Irritating
67. Quarrelsome	67. Rebellious	67. Hostile
68. Loud	68. Complaining	68. Conniving
69. Irritating	69. Idealistic	69. Loud
70. Conniving	70. Sentimental	70. Sarcastic
71. Timid	71. Rude	71. Reckless
72. Reckless	72. Reckless	72. Rebellious
73. Complaining	73. Spineless	73. Feminine
74. Feminine	74. Feminine	74. Rude
75. Spineless	75. Timid	75. Spineless

TABLES

Average Aggressive Adjective Checklist (Phoenix Q-Analysis)	Ineffective Cooperative Adjective Checklist (Phoenix Q-Analysis)	Ineffective Aggressive Adjective Checklist (Phoenix Q-Analysis)
1. Argumentative	1. Ethical	1. Irritating
2. Ambitious	2. Complaining	2. Egotistical
3. Demanding	3. Personable	3. Argumentative
4. Bluffer	4. Fair	4. Quarrelsome
5. Egotistical	5. Gentle	5. Headstrong
6. Sociable	6. Conservative	6. Impatient
7. Ethical	7. Trustworthy	7. Greedy
8. Evasive	8. Masculine	8. Demanding
9. Legally astute	9. Staller	9. Loud
10. Suspicious	10. Obliging	10. Intolerant
11. Greedy	11. Demanding	11. Complaining
12. Cautious	12. Cautious	12. Rude
13. Headstrong	13. Deliberate	13. Conniving
14. Impatient	14. Experienced	14. Sarcastic
15. Personable	15. Patient	15. Impulsive
16. Complaining	16. Moderate	16. Suspicious
17. Quarrelsome	17. Forgiving	17. Unpredictable
18. Unpredictable	18. Argumentative	18. Evasive
19. Trustworthy	19. Idealistic	19. Hostile
20. Rational	20. Sociable	20. Bluffer
21. Loyal	21. Suspicious	21. Manipulative
22. Masculine	22. Irritating	22. Ambitious
23. Forceful	23. Rational	23. Picky
24. Discreet	24. Bluffer	24. Selfish
25. Obliging	25. Timid	25. Rebellious
26. Impulsive	26. Discreet	26. Reckless
27. Intolerant	27. Warm	27. Tough
28. Irritating	28. Sympathetic	28. Dominant
29. Picky	29. Dignified	29. Stern
30. Staller	30. Poised	30. Staller
31. Analytical	31. Helpful	31. Forceful
32. Smooth	32. Self-controlled	32. Masculine
33. Moderate	33. Legally astute	33. Clever
34. Realistic	34. Unpredictable	34. Experienced
35. Manipulative	35. Egotistical	35. Loyal
36. Dominant	36. Headstrong	36. Spineless
37. Careful	37. Careful	37. Cautious
38. Fair	38. Impatient	38. Sociable
39. Adaptable	39. Impulsive	39. Careful
40. Self-controlled	40. Analytical	40. Legally astute
41. Conservative	41. Realistic	41. Self-controlled
42. Deliberate	42. Objective	42. Smooth
43. Clever	43. Picky	43. Deliberate
44. Dignified	44. Praising	44. Organizing
45. Experienced	45. Sentimental	45. Ethical
46. Tough	46. Evasive	46. Idealistic
47. Perceptive	47. Perceptive	47. Personable
48. Praising	48. Adaptable	48. Conservative
49. Patient	49. Ambitious	49. Versatile
50. Hostile	50. Quarrelsome	50. Dignified
51. Forgiving	51. Wise	51. Poised
52. Sarcastic	52. Organizing	52. Timid
53. Organizing	53. Convincing	53. Rational
54. Objective	54. Creative	54. Discreet
55. Creative	55. Intolerant	55. Moderate
56. Warm	56. Stern	56. Trustworthy
57. Selfish	57. Spineless	57. Analytical
58. Idealistic	58. Selfish	58. Perceptive
59. Poised	59. Greedy	59. Sentimental
60. Versatile	60. Sarcastic	60. Gentle
61. Conniving	61. Hostile	61. Fair
62. Sympathetic	62. Smooth	62. Creative
63. Helpful	63. Forceful	63. Sympathetic
64. Stern	64. Clever	64. Praising
65. Wise	65. Tough	65. Adaptable
66. Gentle	66. Conniving	66. Realistic
67. Loud	67. Reckless	67. Obliging
68. Convincing	68. Versatile	68. Wise
69. Rebellious	69. Manipulative	69. Forgiving
70. Rude	70. Loyal	70. Patient
71. Timid	71. Rebellious	71. Objective
72. Sentimental	72. Dominant	72. Helpful
73. Spineless	73. Rude	73. Convincing
74. Reckless	74. Loud	74. Warm
75. Feminine	75. Feminine	75. Feminine

APPENDIX 2

Effective/Cooperatives
Bipolar Adjective Scales
(Phoenix Q–Analysis)

1. Dishonest / Honest — 6.69
2. Discourteous / Courteous — 6.56
3. Disregarded customs and courtesies of the bar / Adhered to customs and courtesies of the bar — 6.46
4. Unintelligent / Intelligent — 6.34
5. Disinterested in the needs of his clients / Knew the needs of his clients — 6.22
6. Unfriendly / Friendly — 6.18
7. Distrustful / Trustful — 6.04
8. Unreasonable / Reasonable — 6.02
9. Insincere / Sincere — 6.00
10. Devious / Tactful — 5.96
11. Devious / Forthright — 5.92
12. Min. prepared on factual elements of the case / Thoroughly prepared on the factual elements — 5.89
13. Unwilling to share information / Willing to share information — 5.79
14. Obstructed / Facilitated — 5.71
15. Used threats / Did not use threats — 5.64
16. Emotional / Logical — 5.62
17. Unsure of the value of the case / Accurately estimated the value of the case — 5.61
18. Min. prepared on legal elements of the case / Thoroughly prepared on the legal elements of the case — 5.47
19. Disinterested in my position / Probed my position — 5.45
20. Disinterested in the needs of my client / Knew the needs of my client — 5.39
21. Took one position and refused to move from it / Was willing to move from original position — 5.35
22. Ineffective trial attorney / Effective trial attorney — 5.34
23. Unskillful in reading my cues / Skillful in reading my cues — 5.33
24. Passive / Active — 5.23
25. Uncooperative / Cooperative — 5.23
26. Took an unrealistic initial position / Took a realistic initial position — 5.14
27. Revealed information gradually / Revealed information early — 5.12
28. Not careful about timing & sequence of actions / Careful about timing & sequence of actions — 5.09
29. Emotionally involved / Emotionally detached — 5.05
30. Disinterested in my personality / Got to know my personality — 5.03
31. Formal / Informal — 4.98
32. Used take it or leave it / Did not use take it or leave it — 4.97
33. Rigid / Flexible — 4.94
34. Did not consider my needs / Considered my needs — 4.92
35. Passive / Aggressive — 4.78
36. Arrogant / Modest — 4.59
37. Willing to stretch the facts / Unwilling to stretch the facts — 4.41
38. Unconcerned about how I would look in the eyes of my client / Concerned about how I would look — 4.29
39. Unwilling to stretch the rules / Willing to stretch the rules — 4.09
40. Narrow range of bargaining strategies / Wide range of bargaining strategies — 3.76
41. Made a high opening demand / Made a low opening demand — 3.72
42. Defended / Attacked — 3.63
43. Did own factual investigation and preparation / Hired an investigator for investigation — 3.27

Effective/Aggressives
Bipolar Adjective Scales
(Phoenix Q–Analysis)

1. Passive / Aggressive — 6.05
2. Defended / Attacked — 6.04
3. Ineffective trial attorney / Effective trial attorney — 6.00
4. Unintelligent / Intelligent — 6.00
5. Min. prepared on factual elements of the case / Thoroughly prepared on the factual elements — 5.82
6. Passive / Active — 5.73
7. Disinterested in the needs of his client / Knew the needs of his client — 5.38
8. Dishonest / Honest — 5.09
9. Disregarded customs & courtesies of the bar / Adhered to the customs & courtesies of the bar — 5.05
10. Min. prepared on legal elements of the case / Thoroughly prepared on the legal elements — 4.77
11. Not careful about timing & sequence of actions / Careful about timing & sequence of actions — 4.78
12. Unskillful in reading my cues / Skillful in reading my cues — 4.59
13. Tactless / Tactful — 4.41
14. Disinterested in my position / Probed my position — 4.41
15. Emotional / Logical — 4.36
16. Narrow range of bargaining strategies / Wide range of bargaining strategies — 4.36
17. Disinterested in my personality / Got to know my personality — 4.32
18. Took one position and refused to move from it / Was willing to move from original position — 4.32
19. Unsure of the value of the case / Accurately estimated the value of the case — 4.29
20. Emotionally involved / Emotionally detached — 4.23
21. Unfriendly / Friendly — 4.14
22. Did own factual investigation & preparation / Hired an investigator for investigation — 4.05
23. Unwilling to stretch the rules / Willing to stretch the rules — 4.05
24. Discourteous / Courteous — 4.00
25. Unreasonable / Reasonable — 3.95
26. Formal / Informal — 3.95
27. Distrustful / Trustful — 3.91
28. Insincere / Sincere — 3.86
29. Unwilling to share information / Willing to share information — 3.61
30. Obstructed / Facilitated — 3.55
31. Used take it or leave it / Did not use take it or leave it — 3.55
32. Revealed information gradually / Revealed information early — 3.55
33. Uncooperative / Cooperative — 3.50
34. Willing to stretch the facts / Unwilling to stretch the facts — 3.45
35. Unconcerned about how I would look in the eyes of my client / Concerned about how I would look — 3.43
36. Did not consider my needs / Considered my needs — 3.41
37. Disinterested in the needs of my client / Knew the needs of my client — 3.23
38. Rigid / Flexible — 2.91
39. Used threats / Did not use threats — 2.91
40. Arrogant / Modest — 2.27
41. Took an unrealistic initial position / Took a realistic initial position — 2.18
42. Made a high opening demand / Made a low opening demand — 2.14
43. Devious / Forthright — 3.73

Average/Cooperatives
Bipolar Adjective Scales
(Phoenix Q–Analysis)

1. Dishonest / Honest — 6.23
2. Unfriendly / Friendly — 5.93
3. Disregarded customs and courtesies of the bar / Adhered to customs and courtesies of the bar — 5.87
4. Disinterested in the needs of his client / Knew the needs of his client — 5.85
5. Discourteous / Courteous — 5.82
6. Devious / Forthright — 5.57
7. Insincere / Sincere — 5.55
8. Uncooperative / Cooperative — 5.51
9. Distrustful / Trustful — 5.39
10. Unintelligent / Intelligent — 5.37
11. Min. prepared on factual elements of the case / Thoroughly prepared on the factual elements — 5.37
12. Unreasonable / Reasonable — 5.30
13. Used threats / Did not use threats — 5.19
14. Tactless / Tactful — 5.17
15. Formal / Informal — 5.12
16. Took one position and refused to move from it / Was willing to move from original position — 4.94
17. Unwilling to share information / Willing to share information — 4.94
18. Obstructed / Facilitated — 4.93
19. Emotional / Logical — 4.70
20. Arrogant / Modest — 4.67
21. Disinterested in my personality / Got to know my personality — 4.66
22. Passive / Active — 4.65
23. Ineffective trial attorney / Effective trial attorney — 4.60
24. Disinterested in my position / Probed my position — 4.60
25. Rigid / Flexible — 4.55
26. Emotionally involved / Emotionally detached — 4.55
27. Used take it or leave it / Did not use take it or leave it — 4.49
28. Did not consider my needs / Considered my needs — 4.48
29. Unwilling to stretch the rules / Willing to stretch the rules — 4.46
30. Min. prepared on legal elements of the case / Thoroughly prepared on the legal elements — 4.29
31. Passive / Aggressive — 4.22
32. Not careful about timing & sequence of actions / Careful about timing & sequence of actions — 4.23
33. Revealed information gradually / Revealed information early — 4.20
34. Unskillful in reading my cues / Skillful in reading my cues — 4.20
35. Disinterested in the needs of my client / Knew the needs of my client — 4.20
36. Unconcerned about how I would look in the eyes of my client / Concerned about how I would look — 3.87
37. Took an unrealistic initial position / Took a realistic initial position — 3.80
38. Unsure of the value of the case / Accurately estimated the value of the case — 3.78
39. Willing to stretch the facts / Unwilling to stretch the facts — 3.68
40. Defended / Attacked — 3.63
41. Did own factual investigation & preparation / Hired an investigator for investigation — 3.35
42. Narrow range of bargaining strategies / Wide range of bargaining strategies — 3.33
43. Made a high opening demand / Made a low opening demand — 2.98

TABLES

Average Aggressives Bipolar Adjective Scales (Phoenix Q–Analysis)	
1. Disinterested in the needs of his clients	
Knew the needs of his clients	5.08
2. Passive	
Aggressive	5.34
3. Min. prepared on factual elements of the case	
Thoroughly prepared on the factual elements	5.03
4. Unintelligent	
Intelligent	4.97
5. Passive	
Active	4.91
6. Defended	
Attacked	4.83
7. Disregarded customs & courtesies of the bar	
Adhered to customs & courtesies of the bar	4.40
8. Ineffective trial attorney	
Effective trial attorney	4.35
9. Dishonest	
Honest	4.26
10. Unfriendly	
Friendly	4.23
11. Not careful about timing & sequence of actions	
Careful about timing & sequence of actions	4.00
12. Formal	
Informal	3.97
13. Min. prepared on legal elements of the case	
Thoroughly prepared on the legal elements	3.95
14. Unwilling to stretch the rules	
Willing to stretch the rules	3.94
15. Disinterested in my personality	
Got to know my personality	3.91
16. Disinterested in my position	
Probed my position	3.86
17. Insincere	
Sincere	3.71
18. distrustful	
Trustful	3.66
19. Discourteous	
Courteous	3.63
20. Emotional	
Logical	3.62
21. Emotionally involved	
Emotionally detached	3.60
22. Willing to stretch the facts	
Unwilling to stretch the facts	3.60
23. Tactless	
Tactful	3.57
24. Used threats	
Did not use threats	3.54
25. Unwilling to share information	
Willing to share information	3.54
26. Took one position and refused to move from it	
Was willing to move from original position	3.51
27. Unskillful in reading my cues	
Skillful in reading my cues	3.50
28. Used take it or leave it	
Did not use take it or leave it	3.34
29. Uncooperative	
Cooperative	3.26
30. Unsure of the value of the case	
Accurately estimated the value of the case	3.24
31. Obstructed	
Facilitated	3.23
32. Devious	
Forthright	3.20
33. Revealed information gradually	
Revealed information early	3.14
34. Unconcerned about how I would look in the eyes of my client	
Concerned about how I would look	3.14
35. Unreasonable	
Reasonable	3.11
36. Did own factual investigation & preparation	
Hired an investigator for investigation	3.03
37. Made a high opening demand	
Made a low opening demand	2.94
38. Disinterested in the needs of my client	
Knew the needs of my client	2.83
39. Narrow range of bargaining strategies	
Wide range of bargaining strategies	2.69
40. Rigid	
Flexible	2.66
41. Did not consider my needs	
Considered my needs	2.60
42. Took an unrealistic initial position	
Took a realistic initial position	2.57
43. Arrogant	
Modest	2.40

Ineffective Cooperatives Bipolar Adjective Scales (Phoenix Q–Analysis)	
1. Passive	
Aggressive	4.93
2. Defended	
Attacked	4.63
3. Passive	
Active	4.51
4. Disinterested in the needs of his client	
Knew the needs of his client	3.96
5. Dishonest	
Honest	3.89
6. Willing to stretch the facts	
Unwilling to stretch the facts	3.85
7. Min. prepared on factual elements of the case	
Thoroughly prepared on the factual elements	3.74
8. Formal	
Informal	3.63
9. Min. prepared on the legal elements of the case	
Thoroughly prepared on the legal elements	3.59
10. Unwilling to stretch the rules	
Willing to stretch the rules	3.56
11. Emotionally involved	
Emotionally detached	3.52
12. Disregarded customs & courtesies of the bar	
Adhered to customs & courtesies of the bar	3.42
13. Did own factual investigation & preparation	
Hired an investigator for investigation	3.41
14. Revealed information gradually	
Revealed information early	3.33
15. Discourteous	
Courteous	3.26
16. Not careful about timing & sequence of actions	
Careful about timing & sequence of actions	3.11
17. Unintelligent	
Intelligent	3.04
18. Used take it or leave it	
Did not use take it or leave it	2.96
19. Unconcerned about how I would look in the eyes of my client	
Concerned about how I would look	2.96
20. Used threats	
Did not use threats	2.96
21. Emotional	
Logical	2.93
22. Ineffective trial attorney	
Effective trial attorney	2.89
23. Took one position and refused to move from it	
Was willing to move from original position	2.89
24. Distrustful	
Trustful	2.85
25. Unfriendly	
Friendly	2.85
26. Disinterested in my position	
Probed my position	2.81
27. Obstructed	
Facilitated	2.74
28. Unsure of the value of the case	
Accurately estimated the value of the case	2.74
29. Devious	
Forthright	2.70
30. Disinterested in my personality	
Got to know my personality	2.70
31. Unwilling to share information	
Willing to share information	2.67
32. Insincere	
Sincere	2.52
33. Tactless	
Tactful	2.41
34. Made a high opening demand	
Made a low opening demand	2.37
35. Unskillful in reading my cues	
Skillful in reading my cues	2.19
36. Rigid	
Flexible	2.19
37. Arrogant	
Modest	2.19
38. Did not consider my needs	
Considered my needs	1.96
39. Uncooperative	
Cooperative	1.93
40. Narrow range of bargaining strategies	
Wide range of bargaining strategies	1.85
41. Disinterested in the needs of my client	
Knew the needs of my client	1.81
42. Unreasonable	
Reasonable	1.74
43. Took an unrealistic initial position	
Took a realistic initial position	1.74

Ineffective Aggressives Bipolar Adjective Scales (Phoenix Q–Analysis)	
1. Dishonest	
Honest	6.89
2. Devious	
Forthright	6.44
3. Distrustful	
Trustful	6.33
4. Unwilling to share information	
Willing to share information	6.33
5. Discourteous	
Courteous	6.11
6. Disregarded customs & courtesies of the bar	
Adhered to customs & courtesies of the bar	6.11
7. Insincere	
Sincere	6.00
8. Unfriendly	
Friendly	6.00
9. Uncooperative	
Cooperative	5.89
10. Disinterested in the needs of his client	
Knew the needs of his client	5.89
11. Emotional	
Logical	5.67
12. Used threats	
Did not use threats	5.56
13. Obstructed	
Facilitated	5.44
14. Tactless	
Tactful	5.44
15. Took one position and refused to move from it	
Was willing to move from original position	5.33
16. Unintelligent	
Intelligent	5.22
17. Unreasonable	
Reasonable	5.22
18. Disinterested in my personality	
Got to know my personality	5.11
19. Min. prepared on factual elements of the case	
Thoroughly prepared on the factual elements	5.11
20. Rigid	
Flexible	5.11
21. Formal	
Informal	5.11
22. Emotionally involved	
Emotionally detached	5.00
23. Disinterested in my position	
Probed my position	5.00
24. Revealed information gradually	
Revealed information early	4.78
25. Arrogant	
Modest	4.67
26. Unsure of the value of the case	
Accurately estimated the value of the case	4.67
27. Took an unrealistic initial position	
Took a realistic initial position	4.56
28. Willing to stretch the facts	
Unwilling to stretch the facts	4.56
29. Min. prepared on legal elements of the case	
Thoroughly prepared on the legal elements	4.56
30. Used take it or leave it	
Did not use take it or leave it	4.22
31. Not careful about timing & sequence of actions	
Careful about timing & sequence of actions	4.22
32. Disinterested in the needs of my client	
Knew the needs of my client	4.11
33. Unskillful in reading my cues	
Skillful in reading my cues	4.11
34. Did not consider my needs	
Considered my needs	4.11
35. Ineffective trial attorney	
Effective trial attorney	3.78
36. Made a high opening demand	
Made a low opening demand	3.56
37. Unwilling to stretch the rules	
Willing to stretch the rules	3.56
38. Defended	
Attacked	3.44
39. Passive	
Active	2.89
40. Narrow range of bargaining strategies	
Wide range of bargaining strategies	2.78
41. Unconcerned about how I would look in the eyes of my client	
Concerned about how I would look	2.78
42. Passive	
Aggressive	2.56
43. Did own factual investigation & preparation	
Hired an investigator for investigation	2.11

THE MOTIVATIONAL OBJECTIVES

There were 12 items in the motivational objectives list, which also asked for ratings on a scale of 1 to 7. All ratings above 4.0 (i.e. all positive characteristics) were used in this analysis. The highest rated attributes from each list are given in tables accompanying the discussion of each level of negotiator effectiveness.

Effective Cooperatives
Objectives
(Phoenix Q–Analysis)

1. Conducting himself ethically — 6.09
2. Maximizing settlement for his client — 5.58
3. Getting a fair settlement — 5.24
4. Meeting his client's needs — 4.97
5. Satisfaction in exercise of legal skills — 4.84
6. Avoiding litigation — 4.54
7. Maintaining or establishing good personal relations with you — 4.50
8. Improving reputation with you — 3.25
9. Obtaining profitable fee for himself — 3.05
10. Improving reputation in his Firm — 3.04
11. Improving reputation among bar members — 2.83
12. Outdoing or outmaneuvering you — 2.77

Effective Aggressives
Objectives
(Phoenix Q–Analysis)

1. Maximizing settlement for his client — 5.86
2. Obtaining profitable fee for himself — 4.67
3. Outdoing or outmaneuvering you — 4.59
4. Conducting himself ethically — 4.32
5. Satisfaction in exercise of legal skills — 4.01
6. Meeting his client's needs — 3.68
7. Getting a fair settlement — 3.68
8. Improving reputation with his Firm — 3.31
9. Improving reputation among bar members — 3.05
10. maintaining or establishing good personal relations with you — 2.69
11. Avoiding litigation — 2.59
12. Improving reputation with you — 2.55

TABLES

Average Cooperatives
Objectives
(Phoenix Q–Analysis)

1. Maximizing settlement for his client — 5.35
2. Conducting himself ethically — 5.09
3. Getting a fair settlement — 4.65
4. Meeting his client's needs — 4.27
5. Maintaining or establishing good personal relations with you — 4.02
6. Avoiding litigation — 4.00
7. Satisfaction in exercise of legal skills — 3.63
8. Obtaining profitable fee for himself — 3.20
9. Improving reputation in his Firm — 3.15
10. Outdoing or outmaneuvering you — 3.11
11. Improving reputation with you — 3.07
12. Improving reputation among bar members — 2.61

Average Aggressives
Objectives
(Phoenix Q–Analysis)

1. Maximizing settlement for his client — 5.83
2. Outdoing or outmaneuvering you — 4.97
3. Meeting his client's needs — 4.23
4. Obtaining profitable fee for himself — 4.17
5. Improving reputation in his Firm — 3.97
6. Satisfaction in exercise of legal skills — 3.84
7. Conducting himself ethically — 3.49
8. Getting a fair settlement — 3.34
9. Avoiding litigation — 3.14
10. Improving reputation among bar members — 2.80
11. maintaining or establishing good personal relations with you — 2.54
12. Improving reputation with you — 2.38

Ineffective Cooperatives
Objectives
(Phoenix Q–Analysis)

1. Conducting himself ethically — 5.56
2. Maximizing settlement for his client — 5.33
3. Meeting his client's needs — 4.44
4. Getting a fair settlement — 4.33
5. Maintaining or establishing good personal relations with you — 4.33
6. Satisfaction in exercise of legal skills — 4.22
7. Obtaining profitable fee for himself — 3.56
8. Avoiding litigation — 3.44
9. Outdoing or outmaneuvering you — 2.78
10. Improving reputation with you — 2.67
11. Improving reputation among bar members — 2.67
12. Improving reputation in his Firm — 1.86

Ineffective Aggressives
Objectives
(Phoenix Q–Analysis)

1. Maximizing settlement for his client — 4.96
2. Outdoing or outmaneuvering you — 4.81
3. Obtaining profitable fee for himself — 4.50
4. Improving reputation in his Firm — 3.42
5. Conducting himself ethically — 3.26
6. Meeting his client's needs — 3.23
7. Satisfaction in exercise of legal skills — 2.63
8. Improving reputation among bar members — 2.48
9. Getting a fair settlement — 2.37
10. Avoiding litigation — 2.19
11. Maintaining or establishing good personal relations with you — 2.19
12. Improving reputation with you — 1.96

[C5423]

*

[*147*]

Appendix III

TRANSCRIPT OF THE PERSONAL INJURY NEGOTIATION [93]

TRANSCRIPT A PERSONAL INJURY NEGOTIATION

DEFENDANT: I appreciate your coming over. It's very gracious of you to come to my office. I wish you'd sit down here and we'll see if we can get rid of this case.

PLAINTIFF: Thank you Sam. I don't know, we'll see. I think it's worth a try.

DEFENDANT: Well we've both been around a long time. We've handled a lot of these so I think we can cut through a lot of the preliminaries, can't we?

PLAINTIFF: I think so.

DEFENDANT: All right. If you don't mind then, would you tell me what your special damages are?

PLAINTIFF: Sure. We have medical damages which are listed in the letter I sent to you.

DEFENDANT: Have they changed since that time?

PLAINTIFF: Not really, and they total $11,035. We have the emergency room at $188, x-rays of $320, therapy at $571, anesthesia $173, operating room costs $974, doctors and specialists $2,045, and there's his private room from June 1, '75 to August 28, '75, $6,281.

DEFENDANT: I would expect this boy to have a private room even if he had his toenails clipped.

PLAINTIFF: Well, I think it was justified in this case. He had a very, very serious injury. He comes from a family where that would be consistent. I see no particular problem with that. Then of course there's the back brace and the crutches and the prescriptions—all of that adds up to $11,035.

DEFENDANT: Well hasn't most of that been covered by his own insurance?

93. Copyright © 1977 Brigham Young University and Gerald R. Williams. All rights reserved. This is a negotiation between two experienced attorneys. Videotapes of this negotiation and the divorce negotiation that follows it are available at cost from the author.

PLAINTIFF: Well, so what?

DEFENDANT: Well is he really out of pocket?

PLAINTIFF: Well, I don't really know the full extent to which he's out of pocket, but I'm going to assume he's out of pocket the whole amount—$11,035. Now I think before we even get to the question of damages we ought to try to talk about liability. That might be a good starting point.

DEFENDANT: Well let me get a little more on damages if you don't mind—just on these specials. Is he going to have any more medical bills that you know of?

PLAINTIFF: I think it's very, very likely.

DEFENDANT: Is he under treatment now?

PLAINTIFF: He's been released by his doctor, but the doctor has said this in the last paragraph and I think you have a letter from Dr. Clark, it said "December 18, 1976, the patient came in for his last checkup today."

DEFENDANT: What was that date again?

PLAINTIFF: December 18, 1976. "Several plastic surgery operations continuing from October to November of this year have been successful and the scar is not present." I think what he meant there was the scar on his face. He has the other scars. I would say maybe that is an overstatement on the part of the doctor because the scar to a certain extent is there.

DEFENDANT: Well Dr. Clark is a well-known plastic surgeon and I think he's pretty reliable.

PLAINTIFF: He's done a good job.

DEFENDANT: Yes, and I don't think that he would be conservative. I think he's trying to call it the way he sees it.

PLAINTIFF: I think so, but I still think it's an overstatement. It says, "the patient walked on his own but will not be able to engage in active sports with strenuous activities. His back bothers him every so often and he has occasional relapses, but his recovery at this time has probably progressed as far as it can." I think it's quite likely that he's going to have back trouble the rest of his life and I really think that arthritis is a good possibility, particularly with the broken bones. There's no way we can say that he won't have any more medical expenses but at least we've reached a point at which I think we can negotiate. We don't have every fact and we never will.

DEFENDANT: Well, there is nothing planned by way of medical treatment at this time, is there?

PLAINTIFF: Not that we know of. No I think he's really very lucky to be here and he's in fairly good shape.

DEFENDANT: I understand that he's out dating the girls again.

PLAINTIFF: Well, I'm not acquainted with that. What have you been doing, watching his love life?

DEFENDANT: We have to take a look at what people are doing, you know that.

PLAINTIFF: Well, as you know he was at the time this occurred, he was engaged to be married and he lost that girl, basically because of the scar on his face.

DEFENDANT: She wasn't worth keeping then.

PLAINTIFF: That may be so. I don't see any dollar damages from that, other than the general damages that he should get for suffering and pain.

DEFENDANT: He isn't claiming any loss of income.

PLAINTIFF: Oh yes. He is claiming loss of income. He was gainfully employed and he was earning I think it was $160 every two weeks in his job and he was no longer able to keep that job and so yes there are a loss of earnings here. I haven't really sat down and computed those completely.

DEFENDANT: But John do you take that very seriously? Joe Curtis, Jr. the son of a governor and the grandson of a senator isn't going to spend his career working as a gym attendant.

PLAINTIFF: No, but that is a loss. That is an income source which triggers another potential loss in this case.

DEFENDANT: How long had he had the job?

PLAINTIFF: Well let me explain that potential loss and that is that his dad told him that if he could graduate with a masters degree with no help from him, he'd give him $50,000 to start off with for his own business until he could go into politics and it looks like this accident has probably lost that for him because he had to borrow the money for this year's tuition and unless something occurs that enables him to pay that back, he's going to be $50,000 out. So I think that's a matter that we've got to come to grips with in this negotiation.

[*151*]

DEFENDANT: Frankly, I can't give him much credit for that because I can't believe his father when knowing that the boy's education has been interrupted by an accident is going to hold him to that bargain. I'm sure that his father's going to bend the rules. He's got the money. His family is well-known. They're exceedingly wealthy and I think that this loss of the $50,000 upon getting his degree is consequential damage at most and I can't see his father failing to do that if the boy wants to buckle down and go back to school.

PLAINTIFF: I think that this is a point that you might raise with his father but as far as I know he is in jeopardy of losing that $50,000 and that has to be brought into our discussion.

DEFENDANT: Do you think the jury would be entitled to take that into consideration?

PLAINTIFF: Why not?

DEFENDANT: Don't you think that it's just a consequential damage and not an actual damage?

PLAINTIFF: I think there's a good chance that the jury might be very interested in that fact. They may not award him that $50,000 but I think it would greatly increase the amount of general damages that he would receive.

DEFENDANT: What do you think the case is worth?

PLAINTIFF: Well I don't really know yet. I'd like to first talk about some liability and see if we can arrive at some understanding as to the percentages. Have you given this some thought?

DEFENDANT: Well, with this darn new comparative negligence doctrine we both have to consider liability and comparative negligence in the sense that some damages are going to be awarded here and it's a matter of where the jury's going to draw the line. So I would say yes you're going to get something in this case but I don't think that that concedes liability in the old sense where we used to worry about contributory negligence being a bar.

PLAINTIFF: Yes. I think we're trying to come to grips with this case before the statute—I might be in some trouble because there was a peg to hang the contributory negligence hat on but I think that the clear responsible party in this case is your client. Let me explain why.

DEFENDANT: All right.

PLAINTIFF: Then maybe you can tell me why I'm wrong. I think if we can come to grips with that first we might be able to tackle the problem of how much. In the first place your man was a part-time ambulance driver. Okay, there's nothing wrong with having a part-time ambulance driver but on the other hand I'm not so sure he was as well qualified to be doing this very serious work as he might be, particularly when I see what happened. He had no particular background for this. He didn't seem to be psychologically right for the situation, and I'll explain why in just a moment. There's no reason why he can't be driving at dawn because he has to go when the problem occurs and in this case it was a food poisoning problem. But still, being a part-time man I'm not sure he understood the full responsibility he had—no use of red lights, no sirens, moving along and then he was in an area that was kind of unfamiliar to him. He kept getting his map out. He really should have sat down ahead of time and mapped out where he was going.

DEFENDANT: Now how did that contribute to the accident? He had to look at a map—he wasn't looking at the map at the time of the accident—what difference could that make?

PLAINTIFF: Well what he says, if you'll look at his statement carefully, is that he was quite surprised when he saw the, as he says the dad-gummed sheep wandering around. He was very surprised by what he saw. He shouldn't have been surprised because if he'd been paying attention to the road, and if he hadn't been looking at his maps as he was driving along he probably would have seen the sheep. I think that that is when he really started to get into trouble and I think that's the first act of some negligence. Now he showed his immaturity and his inattention to what he should have been doing and his inexperience by being more concerned about the lambs on the road than he was observing the rules of safety. Instead of stopping or instead of slowing down, he decided the thing to do was to move onto the left-hand side of the road so that he wouldn't hit those sheep.

DEFENDANT: Now what's so unreasonable about that? Incidentally, I'm going to tell old Harvey that you consider him immature at age 63, but here's a man who lives in the country, he's accustomed to livestock, he knows the sheep are going up in the mountains at this season of the year and he sees a herd and he slows down. He was driving carefully enough to see those sheep. Now this indicated some care on his part, at least up to that time.

PLAINTIFF: But he says he was surprised when he saw the sheep because he was looking at his map. I think he had a duty not to be looking at a map while he was driving an ambulance going to help somebody who's in trouble.

DEFENDANT: But John you're not suing him for hitting a sheep. He was careful then; he missed the sheep.

PLAINTIFF: We're suing him because he was negligent; because he didn't observe the proper safety rules, because he got over on the left-hand side of the road. He found sheep more important than people. He found—I think you'll admit that that's a problem.

DEFENDANT: Well, let's look at it at the moment that he moved over there to avoid those sheep. There were no people around at that time. His only duty at that time was to avoid those sheep, and he certainly had that duty didn't he. And he moved over to the left-hand side of the road because the sheep were bunched on the right-hand side. At that time there was no duty to people because there were no people there and then your boy came racing around that corner in that little red Triumph, probably around 70 miles an hour. Now really, could Harvey have expected that sort of thing? Why wasn't your boy watching out for sheep or anything else that might be on the road?

PLAINTIFF: Where did you get this idea that our boy was traveling 70 miles an hour?

DEFENDANT: Well I think that we've got a statement here from that cyclist, the guy that was camping out with his girlfriend.

PLAINTIFF: I think that man—

DEFENDANT: Didn't he estimate the speed at 70 miles an hour?

PLAINTIFF: Let's take a look at our statements on that. Let's see what he really did say. You're talking about Harley Davidson?

DEFENDANT: Yeah, what a name. I wonder what his real name is. You're not going to rely on him are you? I doubt if you'll even find him.

PLAINTIFF: We have to rely on who we have—we don't make our witnesses—

DEFENDANT: Any cyclist that goes under the name of Harley Davidson is probably off in New Mexico by now. Are you going to bring him at the trial?

PLAINTIFF: Okay, here's what the statement says. He saw the entire accident and testified that the ambulance was not only being driven recklessly prior to the collision but had been so driven for a mile or so before the accident. He also claims the ambulance was weaving and that a front wheel looked like it was loose and wobbling. If he's the one you're relying on, I'm very happy. You're the one that brought him up and I think that he has stated—

DEFENDANT: John, I'm pulling your leg. It wasn't Harley Davidson, it was the sheep herder.

PLAINTIFF: Okay and the sheep herder is the one that they can't find. In fact they looked up his address and we can't even locate him.

DEFENDANT: John would it change your position at all if I tell you I found the sheep herder? The sheep herder will testify that he was going 70 miles an hour.

PLAINTIFF: Okay I don't consider that to be crucial. I consider it to be a factor that we should take into consideration. I would give you something on that point.

DEFENDANT: All right, here's you boy, been out partying all night, going home at dawn. . . . How about the blood test? How much had he been drinking?

PLAINTIFF: .08—which is not legally drunk.

DEFENDANT: Not legally drunk—not under the influence?

PLAINTIFF: No he would not be considered legally under the influence at .08.

DEFENDANT: Well I think I can bring in medical witnesses that will testify that this boy's reflexes were slowed down, his perception was affected, that he was not able to drive normally under .08 influence of alcohol.

PLAINTIFF: Let's talk about how this happened. My man was in the lane which was assigned to him, he was driving along. All of a sudden he sees an ambulance coming at him in his lane. Now really who's to blame for that situation—I mean in large part?

DEFENDANT: Who had the last clear chance?

PLAINTIFF: Well I think that's one of the issues in the case. I'm not sure what this particular statute has done to last clear chance in the state of California but I suspect that it has seriously damaged its use as a defense in a case like this. I think what we get down to . . ..

DEFENDANT: Not yet John. The last clear chance doctrine has not been eliminated yet.

PLAINTIFF: No, I don't think it's been eliminated.

DEFENDANT: My next point is do you want the Supreme Court to decide in this case?

PLAINTIFF: Well, the Supreme Court might have to if we can't settle it. I think you and I can probably eventually arrive at some settlement in this case but before we can even talk reason about settlement, we've got to figure out who has liability and in what percentage. Now I don't expect that we will agree completely but we might be able to come to some close understanding and let's see what it means in dollars and cents.

DEFENDANT: All right. Let me, just to help us move this thing along, ask you this. Assume that there was 100 percent liability—no reduction for comparative negligence what would you evaluate this case at?

PLAINTIFF: Let me stop and do a little figuring.

DEFENDANT: All right.

PLAINTIFF: I would call this case about $180,000.

DEFENDANT: How do you figure that?

PLAINTIFF: Well you've got to take into consideration a lot of subjective factors here. We have a man whose health and vitality, whose ability to work in athletics to present a very strong and positive image, whose confidence is vastly more important than the ordinary plaintiff that you might have. His future was all tied up in politics. It's very unusual to find a man who looked to this kind of a life as his life.

DEFENDANT: Who does he think he is, a Kennedy?

PLAINTIFF: Well I'm not going to make any comparisons. I'm just taking his case exactly as it is. Now I think he's put in jeopardy the money that his father otherwise would have put into his political career. I think his father probably wouldn't be heartless about the situation, but I don't think his father would feel nearly as strongly that he has a political career because of this accident. So I think we've got a $50,000 factor there. Now we've got $11,035 in this case. I would think with those special damages and with general damages we're probably talking $75–80,000 for that in addition to the other things that I mentioned. I think we've got loss of earnings which we really can't decide fully. I think that's a big unknown in the case and one reason why I'm very hesitant to put a dollar figure on it. It depends on whether he regains his memory and his faculties. Because if he doesn't, then I think we're talking about a case of perhaps in the three quarter million category, and I think at this point I'd be very reluctant to give this case away at even $175–180,000. I think I would have to know a lot more about the impairment of his faculties, because if he really can't learn, if he can't retain, if he can't have a memory, I believe that there's a good chance that he's not going to have the kind of career that he's looking forward to. Perhaps practicing law or whatever and if that's the case he's probably left with a very low income his entire life. We've got to find out what that is and then compute it to its present dollar value, and that's why I think that's something I've probably got to examine a little more. If you're willing to negotiate on the basis that he has had a permanent injury to his mental faculties I think we can perhaps get someplace.

DEFENDANT: John I'm not willing to negotiate on that assumption and I think you don't believe he has a permanent damage to his mental faculties or you wouldn't be talking to me today.

PLAINTIFF: Why?

DEFENDANT: You wouldn't want to settle this case this soon if you thought he had permanent damage to his brain.

PLAINTIFF: Well you're the one that invited me to your office and I accepted to come.

DEFENDANT: I know, but I didn't force you over and the fact that you're here to talk about settlement, I think, is pretty strong evidence that you're not very confident about any permanent loss of memory. Sure the boy was shaken up, but he's back in school, isn't he?

[*157*]

PLAINTIFF: Yes, he's back in school.

DEFENDANT: And he's getting along all right in school, my investigators tell me and I think that it's only a gift of nature that some of these accidents and other occurrences in our lives can be blotted out and if he doesn't remember all the details of the accident, I think he's just fortunate, but he seems to be getting along all right in school so I cannot give him any credit for a permanent loss of memory.

PLAINTIFF: Well you have a lot of confidence I'm sure in Dr. Clark and Dr. Clark says that the patient seems confused and is obviously suffering from short mental blackouts, including occasional lapses of memory and noticeable amnesia. Those are very, very serious things.

DEFENDANT: May I see that letter?

PLAINTIFF: Yes.

DEFENDANT: Thank you. But he also says this: "It is possible that consistent use of alcohol has somewhat been responsible for this condition and appears to be similar to a loss of mental abilities caused by amphetamine abuse. While the patient admits he's a social drinker, he denies taking drugs other than aspirin for headache." Now this is a rich young playboy. Let's not kid ourselves. You're representing a rich young playboy. He'd done plenty of drinking. We don't know what drugs he's played around with, but the doctor here gives us the key that this lapse of memory that he's complaining about is the kind of thing normally caused by amphetamine abuse and . . . .

PLAINTIFF: Caused . . . therein lies something I think we probably can't agree to but I would grant this to you that his own activities have been a partial cause of his problem.

DEFENDANT: You know it would have been useful if I had had that medical report before we met today. I just suspected the alcohol. I guessed at it. I didn't have that report.

PLAINTIFF: That's good. I want you to have all the facts and . . . .

DEFENDANT: Well I'm not surprised at it and I appreciate your showing it to me today.

PLAINTIFF: But as far as I can tell, the doctor does say that part of the cause of his problem, that part of it is the accident. After all, the injury was to the head as well as to the body and even putting aside that problem you've got a man who is probably destined to go through life with a bad back and that's a very serious problem. It probably has taken away anything as streuous as golf and tennis and contact sports for the rest of his life.

DEFENDANT: Well he's had his time on the football field and very few of us that have played football have come out without some bumps or bruises to our backs which show up in later life and I don't think you can blame all of his back troubles on this particular incident. Yes it probably did exacerbate some earlier problem but I think the indications are that he'd had a football injury and sure it reinjured it but I don't think you can blame all of his back troubles on poor old Harvey.

PLAINTIFF: Getting back to the original question that I've been trying to address, and that is the extent of liability in spite of the things you've brought out and I think those things would result in a finding by a jury, if a jury were given the facts, of some contribution to liability on the part of my client. I think, nevertheless that the great bulk of the liability would be the part of your client. After all, just consider a jury there and we've got diagrams and an ambulance coming on the wrong side of the road and smashing head-on into an automobile which is traveling with the right-of-way and causing very, very serious injury. It seems to me that we probably have about a 90/10 situation.

DEFENDANT: But John, who smashed into whom? Harvey's ambulance was barely moving. Your guy came along at 70 miles an hour and smashed into an ambulance.

PLAINTIFF: Well I think that's a very unique theory Sam. Your man is driving on the wrong side of the road.

DEFENDANT: Sure enough but he was barely crawling along because he was in a herd of sheep. Your guy came barreling down the road, around the curve at 70 miles an hour. Now my man,

PLAINTIFF: What's the speed limit there, 55?

DEFENDANT: 55 everywhere now.

PLAINTIFF: The 75 miles an hour had no relationship to any issue of approximate cause in this at all.

[*159*]

DEFENDANT: He didn't even slow down. He was so far out of it that he didn't even see that ambulance until he was on top of it.

PLAINTIFF: What he saw, he saw, but he saw it too late to do anything about it. He didn't even have time to swerve he said.

DEFENDANT: Sure because he was so tired and sleepy and so hungover that he couldn't have reacted, and don't you think the jury's going to, we're going to have a bunch of housewives on there. You know how people feel about drugs and liquor now. Don't you think those housewives on that jury, these mothers of little kids are going to be affected by that? The rich young playboy been out for a night of carousing, sure he was hurt but don't you think those things are going to cut it down?

PLAINTIFF: Sam, let me just ask you one question. How do you assess the responsibility here?

DEFENDANT: Oh probably about 75% your boy's fault.

PLAINTIFF: I don't think there's much use in our talking. If that is your position then my feeling is that I want a judge involved.

DEFENDANT: I want a jury.

PLAINTIFF: I want a judge and a mandatory settlement conference that might make some sense. I don't think there's any judge in this that will lend any credence to that assessment of 75 percent responsibility on the part of my client, no way. And if you really are hung up with the figure then I say there's no use talking.

DEFENDANT: All right. We can call it off if you want to.

PLAINTIFF: I think it's probably wise.

[End of Negotiation]

QUESTIONS TO THE TWO ATTORNEYS
ABOUT THE NEGOTIATION

MODERATOR: Gentlemen, that was a very interesting negotiation to watch and I think that we're as emotionally involved as maybe you are by this point. I think the first thing we'd like to know is how each of you think the case would have come out. Would it have gone to trial, if so with what result, if not with what result? And could I ask for a prediction from both of you maybe beginning with the plaintiff's lawyer and moving to the defendant's.

PLAINTIFF: Yes, I'd be glad to predict. Based on my experience I think a trier of fact would have found the defendant, Harvey Walker, at least 80–90 percent responsible for this accident. I think that the reason there would be 10–20 percent on the part of my client is that he was not totally free from fault and he certainly had been drinking too much. There were a number of problems. Nevertheless, I don't think those were the basic cause of the accident and I really think that we would have prevailed at a fairly significant level in this case. The amount— I haven't really studied these facts enough to know, it's a very complex thing and you've got to be prepared in a negotiation like this before you can make a prediction, but I think it would have been a significant verdict in my judgment well over $100,000 and depending on how this memory thing went and whether the man's life was completely ruined, it could have been a very big case.

DEFENDANT: I think the outcome would have depended primarily upon the loss of memory. I think that's the most important element in the case. With the facts that we had I don't think that there was a strong case for that. I don't think that it could have been supported on the medical data which we have received and if the case had gone that way, if the medical evidence had been against the loss of memory, then I don't think the verdict would go over $100,000. I think the jury would probably come in at around 60 or 65 percent liability and I think that my man would have had to pay something more than his insurance coverage but not very much more. He had $50,000 coverage plus $2,000 medical and a little property damage.

PLAINTIFF: There's a very good chance, incidentally, that at some point along the line we would have settled for the coverage. That would be fairly common.

MODERATOR: It's interesting that negotiations broke down for example to hear from you Mr. [DEFENDANT] that you think the jury would have come out around 65 percent liability by your client or by the defendant and yet you took a position that was at the other end of the scale in terms of liability and let negotiations break down on it. Why did you do that?

[*161*]

DEFENDANT: He gave up too soon. I would have kept the negotiations going in real life. I'd have cajoled or bullied or begged or something and I'd have kept him talking. It's normal to take a position such as I did. You've got to have room for bargaining. There's a lot of poker playing in this game. I think that I also would have used the family position particularly here for bargaining. The boy comes from a very responsible and well-known family but his father's made a lot of political enemies. He's been elected to office so he has a lot of people who are strongly for him but a lot of people who are strongly against him and I think that I'd have used the fact that perhaps his father wouldn't want this case to go to trial. Now this has nothing to do with the merits of the law suit but it has a lot to do with the merits of negotiating a settlement. And I think I'd have held out for a low figure, up to the day before the trial. And at that point I think that the boy's father and grandfather because of their political connections and their positions in the community would have compelled the boy to settle. They wouldn't want this boy to go into trial and have it spread all over the newspapers about drugs and alcohol and all that sort of thing. Now this is perhaps unfair, but it's the way settlements are sometimes made and I'd have played that to the hilt.

PLAINTIFF: I might say that if I had known the limits of coverage it may have made a difference in the way the negotiation would have proceeded but I don't find negotiations to be too fruitful when one side takes a position that really is clearly opposite the way the facts point and I think that's what happened in this case. I think the assessment of 75/25 made it pretty difficult to achieve a meaningful discussion of what the damages might be, but by breaking off negotiations you don't foreclose settling cases. Usually you don't settle a case in the first negotiation anyway.

DEFENDANT: Well, I think that John would have assumed that if I suggested 25/75 he would expect me to go 50/50 just in bargaining. And in getting me above 50/50 would depend upon his skill and the pressures that he could put on me by showing the weaknesses of my case, but these numbers of 50/50 or 80/20 don't mean very much unless you know what amounts you're speaking of. You've got to apply those ratios to a particular figure. I think his figure of $183,000 would have been cheap if this had been another kind of a boy, somebody who didn't have a wealthy family and a reputation to protect, and a boy who was working at his life's career instead of just earning a little money to stay in college. It would have made a lot of difference. Then he'd have been talking about half a million dollars and I'd have been talking about a great deal more also. But I think the case ultimately would have gone for . . .. I don't think he would have taken the policy limits frankly, but I think the case might have settled for around $75,000.

MODERATOR: Referring again to the evaluation of the case, both of you had information which was detrimental to your clients, and while this didn't come out as it shouldn't, I was wondering if you regard this in your evaluation of the case or do you disregard it and seek the best possible result for your client, or do you look for what would be a just settlement considering those facts?

DEFENDANT: In settling a case, the first obligation of a lawyer is to know everything he can possibly know about his own case and about the other lawyer's case as well. You don't try to settle a case unless you have had your investigators out and obtained the medical reports, you've had in a case like this, you've even had an investigator follow this young man, take movies of him if necessary, and you don't go into a settlement conference unless you are completely aware of the strengths and weaknesses of each side. You sometimes try to minimize them and you try to bully and cajole and intimidate and you try to make things appear a little better than they are. This is a poker game and you do your best to put the best front on your case and you try to make the other fellow think that his weaknesses are bigger than he really ought to consider them.

PLAINTIFF: But you don't, I don't think, ever ever mislead when you ask a question and it's a fact that is not privileged and if asked properly that question has to be answered truthfully and honestly. On the other hand, it's not necessary to reveal all of the weaknesses of your case in a negotiation and I think you have a duty to your client that's stronger than that but certainly I don't think one should ever even with the implication mislead someone on the facts.

DEFENDANT: No, I didn't mean that.

PLAINTIFF: I know you didn't and I wasn't suggesting that but I think that's part of the rest of your question and that certainly was one of the troublesome aspects of this case because there were hidden facts that were very, very difficult.

[*163*]

MODERATOR: Do you take those facts into account as you evaluate the case and ask for a result on the basis of those facts or do you disregard them?

PLAINTIFF: I would, particularly if they're discoverable facts. I would not assume that Sam would not learn everything that was unprivileged, and I didn't see anything really privileged in this case. So I think before it was over he would know the case, and if I know that the man is thorough and he's going to do that I'm happy to save time by opening my files and thoroughly acquainting him, provided he's willing to give me the same privilege which he usually is.

DEFENDANT: You have to rely on your instincts and intuition as well. I didn't know this guy had been drinking. My file did not include the medical report. I just suspected it and so I played my hand that way and sure enough he turned over to me a medical report that indicated what I suspected and you often have to do this. You just use your intuition in some cases in this situation.

PLAINTIFF: Usually before a negotiation takes place, all of the special damages and all the medical reports have been not only provided the other side but have been thoroughly discussed, gone over so that they have these facts before you sit down and negotiate.

DEFENDANT: In addition, I would have had some medical reports from doctors who examine on my behalf and would've furnished copies of those reports to him.

MODERATOR: Mr. [DEFENDANT] you indicated when you got the medical report that you wished you would have had it before and things would have been different. Now I don't know if you were aware that Mr. [PLAINTIFF] did not have the traffic report. Would you feel an obligation to share not specifically that item but in a negotiation some other item you have that he does not have access to?

DEFENDANT: You notice that I had to ask for the medical report. He'd have gotten the accident report if he'd have asked for it. But the accident report would have been available to him simply on application, so he could have subpoenaed it.

MODERATOR: Sure, this was just for purposes of this problem. We gave one student one item and another student another item. In evaluating the case, Mr. [PLAINTIFF] I'm sure you listed the specials and you briefly went through things as to how

[*164*]

you arrived at your final figure. What fascinates me and what I'd like you to comment on and then Mr. [DEFENDANT] is how do you value the intangibles in the case, such as a broken engagement, such as the loss of $50,000 or pain and suffering, how do you put a price tag on that?

PLAINTIFF: Well, it's very, very difficult to do that but you start with your medical damages and that provides you with a basic tangible fact and then you evaluate the nature of the injuries. Was there scarring, where was the scarring, what were the problems that were caused by this accident, what's the likelihood of problems in the future, in what way has it impaired the person's ability to enjoy life and to function in a fine way in the future and out of all of that you sort of make a guess and you might even do it through a multiple of the medical bill although that is overvalued I think in the whole profession. I've had cases where I've received an amount for general damages that was twenty times medical. I've had cases where I couldn't get two times medical, so you can't really use that to any great extent, but in this case I think we had a very, very serious type of injuries and I think that it's quite likely that we would have been at a fairly high multiple for general damages as compared with medical damages.

DEFENDANT: The insurance companies frequently use a multiple rule of thumb—three or four times the specials when they try to settle cases and this is a very, very rough figure because there may be a serious injury where the medical expenses are quite low. The loss of earnings is a very important factor. It wasn't important in this case. The loss of the engagement I think is minimal. That isn't worth anything.

PLAINTIFF: I agree.

DEFENDANT: The additional surgery to get rid of the scar on the face would be significant, and if I were the plaintiff's lawyer I would make something of that, the additional time, the pain, the expense, all this sort of thing.

PLAINTIFF: And a facial injury is a more important injury for purposes of getting general damages than say a body scar.

DEFENDANT: It's dramatic, but he'd gotten a good result from the plastic surgery so that helps minimize it quite a bit. And I would argue if I were trying this before a jury that yes the boy's got a scar on his face and what's he doing about it. He's now campaigning against liquor and drugs and he can say

[*165*]

see what it did to me and I mean you try to turn it the other way and I would point out that this chap intends to be a politician and you tend to try to make positive results from negative problems and this is what I think he would do as a politician. I think he'd seize on this opportunity, get on the bandwagon, compaign against drugs and liquor, see what it did to me! You know it isn't going to be the kind of thing that's going to make a jury give him a lot of money, so a scar on the face can work either way.

PLAINTIFF: I think one of the real strong elements of damage for this plaintiff was this back injury. Back injuries are really tough and they impair your whole style and entire balance of life. I think there's a good chance of weaving an argument not only to the attorney in negotiations but to a jury that for every year of his life he's entitled to something because of that back injury.

MODERATOR: When you were discussing the back injury, Mr. [DEFENDANT] brought up the possibility that this might be a prior football injury. You kind of tended not to say anything about that. Just briefly would you have revealed to him any information that you had that may or may not have caused this accident by a prior football injury?

PLAINTIFF: Yes, because he would have discovered that. He would've gotten all the medical records and he would've discovered that it was merely a back strain, there were no bones involved, no problem of that kind. I don't think it would have assisted him very much at all.

MODERATOR: At the outset you both seemed interested in guiding the discussion in a particular direction. Was your interest in getting information in those areas or scoring these areas or do you ever think about momentum in a negotiation, in an interaction?

PLAINTIFF: I think you do think about momentum. We all come into things with our own preconceived notions as to what is effective and what is logical and you don't always agree. For my own part I like to figure out what the liability situation is and then I like to get into the damage question and then I like to put the two together. It just makes more logical sense to me and I'm more comfortable practicing law that way and perhaps that's why I tried to guide it in that direction, not because of a desire for a momentum.

DEFENDANT: From my standpoint, I didn't want to be tied down to a set agreement on the liability at the beginning. I wanted to test out certain areas, to try to point out, not point out—he was already aware of them, but to at least emphasize weaknesses in his case. I know I'm going to have to pay some money in this case so I want to try to throw him off balance in his approach. I want to intimidate him if I can. I want to bring in ideas about the results which he may not have anticipated such as my argument about the political effects here and the family desire not to have a trial and this sort of thing. I would use those arguments to try to make him worry a little bit about what a jury's going to do instead of starting out here on a mathematical basis—well we've got 80 percent liability and the damages are $180,000, therefore you pay me $150–160,000—whatever they be. His is a more limited approach than mine because he's interested in getting the money and I can swing wildly here trying to find weaknesses and to throw him off balance so that he will lose a little confidence in his case.

MODERATOR: Gentlemen, thank you very much. That's a very nice end for a very interesting negotiation.

DEFENDANT: You're tough John!

*

Appendix IV

TRANSCRIPT OF THE DIVORCE NEGOTIATION *

Attorney for Mrs. Barbara Smith . . . David Findley**

Attorney for Mr. Tom Smith . . . Christine Tanner**

Chris—David I really appreciate your call and coming over. I think it's very useful to get together now before you prepare an answer to our complaint. I'm really concerned for both of the Smiths. I think this is a case with a lot of young children and two young people who have a lot of needs. I think if we can work something out at this juncture without getting ourselves into a litigation stance we can do a favor for both of our clients.

Dave—Well I think it's a good idea, Mrs. Tanner. May I call you Chris, is that your first name?

Chris—That will be fine.

Dave—I think we had a case together a few years ago. Do you recall?

Chris—Yes, I remember.

Dave—I appreciate your offer to sit down and visit about this matter. We had a fun time before but I didn't get to know you that well. How long have you been practicing?

Chris—About five years.

Dave—I see. Do you do a lot of domestic relations work?

Chris—Enough. It keeps me busy.

Dave—How long have you known Tom? Has he been an old client?

Chris—No, Tom was referred to me by another divorce client.

Dave—I see. Have you done any work for the Smiths prior to this time?

** Noms de negociation

[*169*]

Chris—Not in this area. I had some few contacts with Tom in connection with an investment he was considering a few years back, but it never came to fruition.

Dave—Did you meet Barbara at the time?

Chris—No, I have not met Barbara yet. I assume she's been into your office to see you.

Dave—Yes she came in to see me. She was referred to me by a brother of hers who's been a good client of mine for years. He's a politician, but Barbara is a lot different personality than he is.

Chris—Well yes, she had received the complaint I assume by the time that she saw you.

Dave—Yes and she was rather distraught and depressed when she came in but I managed to get some salient facts from her and I think probably that we're at a point where we can begin to talk some matters and see if there is any solution to any of the problems. Do you think there is any chance for these parties to reconcile?

Chris—Well I've discussed that with my client. Of course, it's one of the first things that I always try to talk about and my impressions from him are that he would be willing to discuss it. He still has a lot of feelings for his wife, and he has been, of course he's in a position now of being extremely hurt by the way things have gone and that puts him in probably a less favorable position for talking in terms of divorce than it would for talking in terms of reconciliation. I would like very much to see them attempt something. From what he tells me, however, Barbara may not have a good deal of interest in that area. What are your feelings from talking with her?

Dave—I don't know. She seems to feel that there is no chance to reconcile at least at this point.

Chris—That's the impression I get from Tom from her side of things. He says that he would be willing to do anything that might help. He has asked me to refer to him some names of some psychologists and marriage counselors and I have some people that I work with in my practice that I would be glad to refer them to, but he was very uncertain as to whether Barbara would cooperate or have any interest.

Dave—The marriage you know is of substantial duration— fifteen years, and I think she told me they have four children.

Chris—Five.

Dave—Five children, and all of them are fairly young and I don't think—at least I didn't recall—that they've ever had any counseling.

Chris—No they haven't and on the one hand the ages of the children makes me very interested in encouraging them to do that. But on the other hand as you say the duration of the marriage and the length of time the breakdown has apparently been occurring makes me a little bit pessimistic also about the possibilities there.

Dave—When you met with Tom initially, did he give you any idea of what he wanted. Does he want the children, the house, the furniture?

Chris—Well I think Tom's major concern is for the children. He's a very dedicated father and like a lot of young fathers these days, he has a very deep commitment to raising them. He's spent a great deal of time with them, worked very hard at building relationships with all of them and especially with the younger ones. He's, from what I can see of him, a very nurturing person and I think he has real concerns about some of the things that have been occurring in Barbara's life.

Dave—I would be the first to agree that the last at least short period of time has not been too stable in her life. I guess you know his background in terms of employment and his working hours.

Chris—Yes.

Dave—It doesn't seem to be too compatible.

Chris—Well actually he's in a rather favorable situation. First of all he tells me that he now has some seniority on service and may be able to have some say in taking his shifts. He anticipates the possibility of obtaining some part-time household help so that he can accomplish his employment. Right now, as you know, he's working during the night hours while the children are asleep and he presently as I understand it has made arrangements while Barbara is gone with a neighbor to come and sleep at night. He indicated that he was exploring possibilities of making that permanent or of obtaining some kind of a visiting nurse situation so that someone could sleep with the children regularly.

Dave—Now when you served, or at least prepared the papers for service upon Barbara I noticed that you did file a summons and complaint but you didn't serve her with a restraining order. She would like to come back and be with the children. Would you have any objection—her coming back and living with the children and Tom finding another place?

Chris—Actually moving into the home? I suppose at this point that's something we need to think about very carefully because Tom does have real reservations about the influence that Barbara is on the children, particularly the older girls at this point in their lives. Of course the younger children have a strong relationship with their mother but at the same time they've been let down by her and—

Dave—Well I appreciate his concern but you know Barbara has been having a lot of children in her home. Apparently she's qualified and capable.

Chris—Well and that's been one of the bones of contention unfortunately because Tom has felt particularly since she has taken up some of her outside activities and some of her new social relations that she's neglected the responsibilities she's committed herself to and really you know we didn't serve her with a restraining order partly because we thought there was very little necessity. She has not shown any strong interest in or commitment to visiting the children and continuing that relationship and Tom realizes that she's in a state of upheaval and he also realizes that she's spending a lot of time probably finding herself.

. . .

Dave—Had he ever discussed with her prior to the time of filing the papers any difficulties or problems? It looked like he jumped to a lot of conclusions.

Chris—Well there is a possibility that he jumped to conclusions. Unfortunately the type of conclusions he jumped to are based on some facts which were very highly charged. I suppose Barbara has related to you the incidents.

Dave—Does he have any evidence of her unfaithfulness?

Chris—No, not hard evidence.

Dave—Has he ever found or caught her with anyone else?

Chris—Well there was an incident—did Barbara tell you about the incident in the park?

Dave—Well just briefly. She was so upset and nervous. You know she didn't feel like talking much about anything. She was very concerned and upset that she wasn't back in the house with the children and that's really what she'd like to do.

Chris—Apparently one evening while Tom was at work he was called by a fellow dispatcher who had located Barbara with her tennis player friend in his car in the middle of the night, and I think that that incident—again, Tom was extremely hurt, and—

Dave—Did Tom ever see her with this young tennis player?

Chris—He arrived on the scene of that incident and saw them together. As far as I know he's not convinced of any infidelity and he—although he indicates that he would be willing to pursue that line if he felt it was necessary in this litigation. I don't think that he would be inclined to do that for any reason other than real necessity. I hope we won't come to that. I think that would be very unfortunate for Barbara and especially for the children.

Dave—Now what about Tom and his problems. Does he have a drinking problem? She complains that all he wants to do is come home and drink beer and watch television.

Chris—No, I don't think that's a drinking problem. I expect he has a fatigue problem. I'm sure that with the shift he works that—and the long hours he works—five children is a lot of children to support on a policeman's salary and Tom works very hard and I suspect that this may have been one of the areas that caused their marriage to get into trouble. They're both very young and vital and yet Barbara is someone who has in a lot of respects some time on her hands. It might have been very useful a few years back if she'd had more—or taken more advantage of maybe an opportunity to go back to school and so forth. Has she expressed any interest to you in getting some college classes or vocational training or . . ..

Dave—You know she's totally untrained to do anything. Based on the income of the two parties, it would appear to me that if they did go ahead and complete the divorce by a decree being entered, both of them would have to work to support themselves and the children and I think she has the desire— she's expecting some inheritance, but she doesn't know when that's going to come.

Chris—Yes Tom indicated that was very substantial. To what extent can Barbara look forward to relying on that for income or support?

Dave—Well, I really don't know. There might be some contingencies upon that inheritance. She hasn't got any of it yet.

Chris—That's a testamentary bequest from a relative I understand?

Dave—Yes, that's her father. He had an art collection and how sellable it is, I don't know. It might not have any value—it might be a valuable piece of property.

Chris—Has it been appraised?

Dave—They don't have any appraisal yet. He just passed away and they haven't even completed the inventory to file with the probate court. Which brings up a big issue and that is that Barbara doesn't have any money to pay a retainer fee. Can Tom take care of some attorney fees?

Chris—Number one I don't think Tom is able. In fact we had to spend a little time working out a plan for him that was compatible with his limited income and his extensive commitments with the house and the expenses of the children. In addition, Tom is under the gun to some extent through somewhat rash expenditures that Barbara made. I think it is part of her general state of unrest in the last few months. Tom tells me she's run up in excess of a thousand dollars on their local charge accounts and of course the accounts are in Tom's name at the present time and .   . ..

Dave—She didn't tell me anything about this. She says that Tom takes the money and controls it and she has little or nothing to do with it.

Chris—Well, and perhaps this is another area where some counseling might be in effect because I do get the impression from Tom that he is perhaps overly rigid in his control of the finances. Partly it's necessary because of the limited income, but perhaps if Barbara had taken and had more responsibility for the funds, she might be a little more responsive to their needs. What happened was that Tom has a Mastercharge account that they use for family emergencies and he frankly doesn't even know how she got the card. It's his impression that she took the card out of his wallet.

TRANSCRIPT OF DIVORCE NEGOTIATION

Dave—I see. She didn't tell me anything about this. She did say that he took the car and she needs some transportation.

Chris—There are two vehicles. There's the '74 Pontiac and a Datsun which is a pick-up truck which Tom uses most of the time for his transportation. I do understand that she needs transportation and I'll talk to Tom about that and he indicates that . . ..

Dave—Tom has both cars now. Which one does he prefer to keep? Which one does he use?

. . . Tom asked her to move out after the incident in the park.

Dave—Well she's with her mother. Her mother lives here. Her mother had to come and pick her up the other night. It was kind of embarrassing to her and she's having difficulty explaining all the circumstances.

I'm sure she is, and I've got to keep her mother out of the program if we can, because the less she knows about it all I think the better we're going to have it for all parties concerned. But we sure need to get this car. Which car do you think she could get and when do you think we could make arrangements for her to get it?

Chris—Well why don't I give Tom a call and get a final decision from him as to whether he thinks he can manage with that pickup and if he thinks he can handle, of course he is transporting the older girls to their music lessons and . . ..

Dave—Well she could take care of all this and that would be no problem. She's done that all the time while Tom's been working or sleeping. I mean she's had to do everything with the children. That's how . . . I really can't understand now why Tom thinks that she can't take care of the kids. For fifteen years he's never been concerned about it.

Chris—Well he has been concerned . . ..

Dave—All he thinks about is his job and TV and beer.

Chris—No, for about the last six months to a year, Tom has been very concerned and Tom has had to get more involved and that's one of the reasons he's very concerned about the children . . ..

Dave—Yes but she tells me, Chris, that he has never taken time to discuss any of these problems with her. She tells me the first impression she gets that something is wrong is when he comes and takes the car away from her.

Chris—Yes but David you've got to realize . . ..

Dave—And she denies anything happening in that park.

Chris—Yes but you must admit I think that the situation . . ..

Dave—You don't think that she would go chase around with an eighteen year old boy do you?

Chris—She has been David. She's been doing it for over six months and that's why Tom has had to get involved . . ..

Dave—What proof does Tom have of it?

Chris—3:00 a.m. in the morning in a dugout in a deserted park, a 30 year old woman . . .

Dave—Yeah, that's hearsay. Tom wasn't there, he didn't see it, he doesn't know what's going on.

Chris—Tom did.

Dave—Tom was working.

Chris—Tom was called by his fellow dispatcher and came to the park. He saw the couple leave the dugout together.

Dave—Well I'd like to solve this thing amicably but I don't know. I'm not going to sit here you know, let my client go without a car, live with her mother and him just take everything.

Chris—He doesn't want to take everything. He's willing to let her have a car, he's willing to help her get on her feet. His major concern is that she is not fit at this point in her life because of her own needs and he acknowledges that they are real but he feels that they interfere with her ability to perform as a mother.

Dave—What proof does he have that the children have been neglected?

Chris—All right, first of all the older girls as you know have apparently been taken by their mother during the morning hours, leaving the nursery school children in the care of her assistants at nursery school—young children themselves—alone for hours at a time.

Dave—Who's telling you this Chris, because when I talk to Barbara she denies this.

Chris—OK well some of this information comes from the children, David. As I said before I think that the children's needs and so forth, especially the older children . . ..

Dave—Have you visited with the children?

Chris—I have talked with the two older girls and have some real concerns about their attitude towards their mother right now. Their mother has been attempting to perform or to behave really more as a peer. I don't know whether she's going through a second adolescence or she's seeing these girls grow up and she resents their youth and beauty but she's out with them and their friends at times of the day when those young children are home alone. She has actually left those nursery school children; that's why I asked you if she'd contacted the parents because I think some of the parents have been very distressed by the reports of the nursery school children about being left alone.

Dave—Well in order that I can substantiate some of these facts or at least determine that there's any substance to the allegations, do you have any objection if I visit with these five children in my office?

Chris—I would certainly have objection if the children don't have independent representation. I think at this point I have not attempted to examine them. I've talked to them in their father's presence, very preliminarily when Tom first contacted me. And I don't think it would be either in their best interest or their parents' best interest for them to be examined privately by either one of us. I think that we ought to contact the court for an evaluation with a view to independent counsel. Now are we still talking post-reconciliation efforts here? Are you suggesting that we need to resolve some of these possible factual discrepancies before we proceed on that or . . ..

Dave—Well my concern is I've got to get my client out of her mother's house and I need to get her back in her own. She doesn't even have any clothes to wear.

Chris—She's got over $500 worth of brand new ones sitting in the closet which Tom is making the payments on.

Dave—If she could make arrangements to get them, that would be fine. But I've got a client who is sitting home with her mother, nothing to do. She can't run her little nursery business at home. She's got five children all of whom need their mother. And what about Tom, is he working now?

[*177*]

Chris—I'm sympathetic to the situation you describe except to the extent that Barbara's brought it on herself.

Dave—Well I don't think she has.

Chris—Well I think she has. I think she's been working up to it . . ..

Dave—I don't think you can blame her for everything that's happened. She's obviously been neglected at home, you know.

Chris—I agree that you can't blame Barbara for the problems in the home but I think that the way Barbara has handled the problems in the home indicate a pretty basic lack of readiness to accept responsibility of parenthood. And this is a woman with five children who is running around with an eighteen year old tennis player.

Dave—Well now that's your statement and I don't think we have any proof of that and when you say running around with an eighteen year old tennis player—what are they doing, where are they going? You know I'm having a hard time convincing her of that.

Chris—I'm sure she perceives it very differently, but the perception of her children and of her husband and of the neighbors would indicate that appearances are such that she's engaged in activities that are very inappropriate for a woman in her situation.

Dave—Well let's do this Chris. I have a court appearance downtown in ten minutes and I've got to go. Can we just kind of at least see if there is any way to decide on some immediate solutions?

Chris—All right first of all, we have no objections to Barbara picking up her personal things. I'm quite sure from what Tom has told me . . ..

Dave—I'd rather first determine whether she can get back in the house.

Chris—From what Tom has told me I am quite sure that he would not be willing at this point in time . . . now let me finish . . . to consider her moving back in, partly because he and Barbara were under such tension between them that they couldn't stay there together.

Dave—Well they couldn't live together, but isn't Tom in a much better position to find another place to live? His working hours are such that he'd be a lot better downtown in some motel where he can sleep during the day.

Chris—David it would be impossible for me right now to convince Tom that anybody can give his children what they need besides him. Those kids have been let down and left alone so much that he has been spending every spare minute trying to build them back up—put that family back together. And he has been working hard at it; he's been doing without some of his sleep in order to manage it; he's been financially keeping himself on a very austere schedule so he can make all the payments. But what I'm suggesting is that we ought to proceed with some of the counseling efforts in an attempt to get first of all to get not only the facts and what may be in dispute there but also to get at what the party's real emotional status is. Now from what Tom has told me, Barbara's attitude toward the marriage is that it's dead and gone and finished. Now from what you're telling me here today that may not be the case.

Dave—I'm not so sure that's the case. Maybe she told Tom that, and I know her conversations with him in the last few days has led her to believe that maybe there is no hope because he's making accusations against her that just absolutely cannot be proven. I think that what we've got to do is get these parties back together if we can so that she can get with the children. Would you have any objection to having a conference with Tom and Barbara and the children?

Chris—No, I think that would be a very good idea.

Dave—Could we set that up in my office in the morning at 9:00?

Chris—All right.

Dave—And can I call Dr. Cole and see what his schedule looks like to examine .   .   ..

Chris—Let me give Tom a call right now—I can probably get him off of his shift at noon and call you back and find out if that's satisfactory.

Dave—Okay now Barbara doesn't have any transportation. Do you think you could check with Tom and I could call you back later in the day and see if she could get one of these cars?

Chris—I will check on the cars.

Dave—She doesn't even have any money for gasoline. Do you think we could get some money from him?

[*179*]

Chris—Well what kind of work is she doing. You mentioned she was working part time.

Dave—Well you know she's trying to get back in the house to get her nursery going.

Chris—Frankly David I just don't know, I understand gas is a very real need but Tom is put to it. He does not make enough money and you've acknowledged he doesn't make enough money to support two separate households.

Dave—Well they've got a lot of equity in the house, they've got cars free and clear and they've got snowmobiles.

Chris—And I think we can look to, should we be talking about an ultimate breakdown, we can look to a situation where Tom is going to be willing to make the kind of concessions that are going to let Barbara get herself back together and get herself in a position to be economically independent.

Dave—Have you discussed any ultimate division of property with Tom?

Chris—We have discussed preliminarily. I don't have the monthly expense figures yet and I need those before we can be talking about that.

Dave—Is Tom in good health?

Chris—Tom is in good health and I understand Barbara is as well.

Dave—Well Barbara is in excellent health unless he is alleging that she's got psychological or psychiatric problems. And if that be the case, we might need some substantial maintenance or alimony from him.

Chris—Those are in relationship to her activities as a mother and wife largely and rather than having . . ..

Dave—Well does Tom feel she is a fit and proper person to have the children?

Chris—Not at this point in time.

Dave—But he has over the last fourteen and a half years?

Chris—No, he has not over the last six months to eighteen months. He has been seeing a deterioration in her treatment of the children that has disturbed him greatly. That's been a major source of conflict and it has been getting worse. I think this blow up with the tennis player is the culmination of a long series of events that have had him very disturbed.

Dave—Well, has he told you of any of the complaints that Barbara has been vociferously mentioning against him?

Chris—Yes, in fact he feels it to have been, well obviously he feels she has been a little unreasonable in that she expects him to work a ten hour shift at work, come home and spend time with the children, be a good father to them, and on top of that to have the energy and time to go out and play with her and he's very frequently tired. . . .

Dave—Do you know how long it's been since he's taken her out to dinner?

Chris—Well they haven't been getting along for quite a while.

Dave—Well sure. He's obviously has been ignoring her and the children totally. She says that he doesn't care about the kids. The only thing he cares about is his work, beer and football.

Chris—No that's not true. Tom cares. . . .

Dave—He comes home and he sits on the couch and watches football games and drinks beer until he goes to sleep and that's it. She says he hasn't even kissed her goodnight or good morning in the last six years.

Chris—Well you know that's a pretty . . ..

Dave—You know just for him to run up and kick her out of the house. You know, take the car, take the children. . . . You know I think we need some immediate solutions to these problems and I'm going to have to go to the court for relief if we can't get something done.

Chris—We don't have any immediate solutions. David you know that. We're talking about a long-standing . . ..

Dave—It looks like to me that we're just wasting our time talking about this.

Chris—Well I think we've made some progress. We've talked about—at least what I heard you say earlier was that we had some area to work in and that . . ..

Dave—Well if we get some immediate relief for her I think we can but I think that the immediate relief ought to be visitation with the children. We've got a conference set up in my office in the morning at 9:00 if your client will agree. I'll talk with Dr. Cole. If we can get a car to Barbara at least we're making some progress.

Chris—Okay and we are amenable to visitation. We were talking before about a returning of Barbara to the home in custody which Tom isn't willing to consider now but I think visitation is a good place to start.

Dave—Now when you talk to him can you ask him what resources he has for some attorney fees?

Chris—I'd be happy to talk to him about it although David I'll be very candid with you right now. Tom feels like the injured party and under the law in this jurisdiction I think Tom can establish that he's the injured party and I should alert you to the fact . . ..

Dave—She's entitled to representation and she has no funds. Her mother has offered to pay me an attorney's fee and I won't take money from her.

Chris—David she's an able-bodied woman and employment is available. I acknowledge the disability she's under with no training and Tom acknowledges that and we need to talk about the possibilities of training for her, but she can make sufficient to support her needs so long as he is maintaining the home and children. That's temporary, but I think that's as much as he can do at this point in time.

Dave—Well you see at the present time, he has control of all the assets. He has the house, the furniture, fixtures, appliances; he has both cars and he has the children.

Chris—Yes and he's also bearing the burden of some debts which Barbara has incurred and . . ..

Dave—She's been working too and he hasn't spent any money on her. She tells me he hasn't given her a gift in five years.

Chris—He hasn't spent any money on himself either David. $11,000 a year and five children . . ..

Dave—I appreciate that—with five children it doesn't go very far.

Chris—Tom has not asked any more of Barbara than he's been willing to perform on his own and perhaps that's wrong. They're different people. . . .

Dave—Chris I'm going to have to run in just a minute.

TRANSCRIPT OF DIVORCE NEGOTIATION

Chris—I understand you have an appointment.

Dave—I think the marriage has deteriorated. I don't think it's beyond repair and I think you and I have a duty to help them reconcile if we can. And I think in the attempt to reconcile these people we need to get these people together at least in my office in the morning and I'd like to get her back in the house with the children. . . .

Chris—Well we're agreeable to visitation and I think you can inform her of that before the conference that maybe we can work something out.

Dave—Well can I give her any hope that maybe she can move back in the house with the children?

Chris—I would be very reluctant David. That frankly—quite candidly that's the area in which my client is the least flexible at this point.

Dave—Well don't you think, we've got three children three, six, and ten, don't you think those smaller children would be better with their mother—he's working at night and sleeping the days.

Chris—David do you know what would impress my client a great deal would be, I think, would be some interest and some real effort on the part of your client to rebuild those relationships with the children and I think visitation is the place to start there.

Dave—I appreciate what you're saying Chris. Barbara tells me that he never pays any attention to how good of a mother she is. She's a good cook. She prepares meals, she takes care of the children, and he doesn't pay any attention to that and never compliments her.

Chris—But David at the same time she's been emotionally erratic; she's been extremely disassociated from the family. She's been gone a long time.

Dave—But I think it's been brought on and increased by his total neglect. I mean she feels unloved, unneeded, and . . . . .

Chris—That may be but some of the preliminary information that I have from that examination that Barbara underwent indicates that there may be good grounds to believe that at this point in her life motherhood is not the thing that Barbara can do very well. She's got too many other needs.

[183]

Dave—She tells me she loves the children and at all costs, above anything else which she desires in life, she wants the children to be with her and she seems sincere.

Chris—Well we've got problems in that area David and I think we have made some good progress. We've got a face-to-face conference which we can monitor. We're willing to turn over a car. We can discuss which one tomorrow. We're willing to arrange some regular visitation and we're willing to enter into some counseling on both sides. Is that what you perceive?

Dave—Well I think we got a lot done in that area. I think probably what each of our clients needs to understand is that if we get fighting for custody of the children it's going to be expensive. The minimum bar fee at least in our office for contested custody cases is $2,000. Barbara doesn't have any money so it looks like to me that we could use all the assets of the parties fighting for the children.

Chris—At this point, very much so.

Dave—You see, she tells me he has never taken any interest in the children and now he wants custody of them and he works all night and sleeps all day.

Chris—He's always taken an interest. When the marriage was working, he could depend on Barbara to perform the home-making tasks. For the last year, Barbara has become less and less dependable in that area and he has started to take over.

. . .

Dave—Okay, listen Chris, I've got to leave for court. I appreciate the hospitality of your office. You look great. Hope things go well for you.

Chris—Well thanks. It's nice to see you and I'll look forward to tomorrow morning.

Dave—Okay, now, do you want me to call this afternoon to check on the Dr. Cole appointment?

Chris—Yes I will do that this afternoon as well.

Dave—What time do you think you can reach him?

Chris—I can get him at noon so by the time you get back and

. . .

Dave—Hey that would be super. So if you'll call him and give me a jingle I'll appreciate it okay?

Chris—Right, goodbye.

Dave—Bye-bye.

Chris—Nice to see you.

Question and Answer Session held immediately following the Negotiating Session

Q—Ms. Tanner and Mr. Findley, we've enjoyed watching your demonstration of the negotiation. There are four of us who have been scribbling questions all the way through and I'm sure we won't have a chance to ask all we'd like to. I think maybe the most interesting place to begin would be to ask both of you to read the future and answer two questions if you would. One is how do you think the conference tomorrow morning at 9:00 will go, or would go if it were held; and then assuming that reconciliation were out of the question, how do you think the case would be ultimately resolved? I wonder if you would begin Ms. Tanner and then Mr. Findley following her response.

Chris—We may not have sufficient facts to be certain about the answer to that first question, and the reason I say that is that I do not recall in examining the fact situation how much we know about the position of the children. My expectation is that at least the older children would probably have an impact on the resolution of this case and particularly on that conference. The reason I agreed to the conference with the children there was my recollection and I may be mistaken but that the children had some pretty realistic and mature evaluations of their mother's behavior and of the reasons for the breakdown of the marriage. It would be my expectation that those could be brought out in that conference which might make Barbara a little more realistic in assessing her functions as a mother and her real desire and ability to continue with the children at least at this point in time. Should reconciliation efforts break down at the end of this particular conference, I wouldn't be at all surprised to see this case in a pretty bitter custody dispute. Partly because some of the information that didn't come out entirely in conference but which I have in the fact situation indicates that Tom at least is willing to go the full route on that at this point. He might soften up but he's mad enough and hurt enough about I suppose in some respects the sexual insult implied by Barbara's activity that he feels very strongly about keeping those children and I have to acknowledge this on a realistic basis in a fault jurisdiction that kind of behavior is going to give him a much stronger

[185]

case when you're talking about a custody dispute. Now the economics are another thing, however. We do have limited economics and frankly that will influence custody litigation a great deal but at this point in the negotiations if reconciliation is a failure, I wouldn't be surprised to see us litigate it.

Dave—Thank you. When I suggested the conference, the thing I wanted to pursue totally throughout the negotiation was what I consider to be the urgency and the expense and I really felt that I needed to push constantly to get my client back in the house with the children, get her stabilized as much as she could immediately. I have this exact fact situation in Colorado except I represented Tom, and the wife and mother ultimately changed her name and left town; never have seen or heard from her since. I always said at that time I'd like to have been her lawyer because I could do her a better job than that which she got done for her. I really would conjecture that Tom nor the children probably wouldn't show up for the conference but I wanted to push for that conference and I think it would be good if they would come. I think it would help inform my client particularly of the facts and circumstances and help her to understand maybe what the children feel. The children will always tell each parent that they want to live with them but when they get behind the closed doors in the judges chambers then they'll tell the truth and they'll tell really with whom they want to live. And in our jurisdiction if the child is eleven or twelve or older the judge will pretty much take their desires and give it priority consideration. So I would like to avoid that if that's what the children are going to say and it gives me a preview of what they would say to a judge if they're going to tell me in my office with their father and mother present that they'd rather live with one or the other that helps me to understand what they'd do if they get to a judge. So that was kind of the idea of the conference and with this type of a situation I think you need to make some decisions early and get the solutions implemented immediately because this type of a situation would deteriorate. If we got the mother of Barbara involved in the case then it really gets disastrous. I love mothers in law and I think they're fine but they can really be tough to deal with in domestic relations matters. Now in reference to the proposed reconciliation I really doubt under the circumstances that they could put this thing back together. There are too many problems both with Tom and with Barbara. And statistically you know about one out of ten marriages where people are married during high school or right after end up in divorce today. So statistically they're fighting an uphill battle to reconcile their problems. What would happen if they didn't reconcile, I think really would be dependent upon recommendation of professionals. That's either social service agency or the welfare department. In Colorado we have the Diagnostic Center at the University of Colorado and they do extensive investigations into the children and to the parents and they make recommendations—seldom ever split custody and I wouldn't recommend a split custody in this case. I think the children all should be with one or the other parent. But I think that ultimately with the children would go the house, furniture, fixtures, appliances. I think obviously each of them would be able to keep that equity or that money which they had prior to the marriage. He would I think be entitled to first an offset on the house equity for the money he had at the time of the marriage and I think secondly, she'd be entitled to whatever inheritance she's getting from her father.

Q—Do you agree that it would have ended up in a bitter custody fight or could you assess the probability or possibility of it?

Dave—I think really it would depend on how much she was infatuated with this young tennis player. In my case it was a young seminary student and they ultimately got married and you never know what's going to happen with these people. They were both married right out of high school and neither one of them had a chance to associate with other people, to date, to mature in romance and love and it would just really I think depend on how much and how sincere she was in having the custody of the children. If she sincerely wanted those children above everything else, then I think it would be a real custody battle.

Q—Mr. Findley, I'd like to direct a question to you. Of course, in watching the negotiations I tend to identify with Ms. Tanner and I want to know when you first came in you sat down and made some pleasantries and remarks, commented on how attractive she was looking and then throughout the negotiation you seemed to be a real gentleman in not interrupting even when you might appear frustrated with trying to get a word in edgewise. Now would this be something that would be typical of your negotiating style or would it be unique to your negotiating with women attorneys?

Dave—Well there are more and more women attorneys and I have no problem negotiating with them. I'd have to say that in my fifteen years of practicing law I have never gone to a law-

[*187*]

yer's office to negotiate face-to-face on a domestic relations matter. Most negotiations are done by telephone. I really prefer to negotiate by telephone. Two reasons, the first is that it's a great time saver, and if you have a good active practice you just can't run to other lawyers' offices to sit down and spend an hour talking about a domestic relations case. Chris and I both know and understand these facts and we know essentially probably what the outcome would be and I'm not so sure we'd spend this much time in a personal conference in her office or my office. And one of my frustrations would be one of time and maybe spending this much time on this particular case under these circumstances. I was frustrated. I'd like to have interrupted her many times and I think maybe if she had been a fellow man lawyer I might have interrupted more. I might have been a little more forceful or persuasive. She's so sweet and kind and she'd just go right on and I didn't feel good maybe in interrupting as much as I would have liked to have done.

Q—Chris when you have negotiated have you had an opportunity to negotiate with another woman attorney and if so what were the differences in negotiating with another woman as compared to another man attorney?

Chris—I'm sorry to say, and perhaps it's a function of practicing in a town of moderate size that I have not had occasion to negotiate with another woman attorney. My expectation is that there would be few differences other than perhaps—I have had the experience of negotiating with male attorneys and this is particularly true in a commercial negotiation situation—I have found some male attorneys to be somewhat nonplussed by a woman on the other side of the table. And I think there is a slight tendency and it varies from lawyer to lawyer to be somewhat more courteous and somewhat more tolerant in what they'll take from a woman from what they'll take from a man and quite frankly I'll use that if I am aware that an attorney is reluctant to interrupt me or is reluctant to press home a point when I won't discuss it, I'm perfectly willing to take advantage of that situation if I feel that I can. Perhaps that edge would be gone if the opponent were a woman who you know had no reservations about pulling out all the stops. And to some extent in litigation I have found this an advantage from time to time—it's less and less true as a new breed of lawyers is being trained who have trained with women and feel no compunctions or reservations about doing all of the usual things.

Dave—I think a lot of that, just back to that question, I'm not so sure that the female-male negotiation is important. A big factor in negotiating is the relative experience of each of the attorneys in the area, and you find lawyers that have been practicing law for many many years and are concentrating in this area. It's frustrating to get with a lawyer who hasn't done much in this practice. Secondly, if you have a real busy practice and you get a domestic relations case that's referred in by a good client, sometimes you're not as inclined as you should be to give that case the amount of time that's necessary. Where on the other side, maybe Tom's lawyer has only been practicing law two or three years, might not have much of a practice, might have a lot of time, they might want to make a federal case out of this set of facts and that's a real important element in negotiation.

Q—Mr. Findley, as the negotiation progressed you began to emphasize, well all through the negotiations you emphasized the immediate solutions to problems now such as the need for money, the need for present transportation, visitation or getting Barbara back into the house. Why did you emphasize those immediate needs and Ms. Tanner what was your reaction to that and why did you emphasize the long-term needs?

Dave—First I think when an attorney represents a client he must be able to produce for her results immediately and if I were able to have gotten for her that day a car or some visitation rights, in other words I've got to hold my client together. I've got to have her have confidence in me. I've got to have her see some actual results of what I'm doing. And when she's with her mother with no car and no kids, no house, nothing, I've got to begin to put these things back together for her. So my negotiations were always stressing urgency for her and I felt that if I could get her the car today the conference with the children tomorrow and some hope of getting back in the house then I could have a good rapport with my client and she'd feel like I was doing a good job for her. I think that is very important in client-attorney relationships and I think that was why I was pushing hard to get these things done. Secondly, these domestic relations matters—the most critical time is when they begin. When they made a decision to file an action for divorce, they made a big decision. Then you need to "hold them together" while these matters are being pursued and you're getting through the temporary orders, the permanent orders and getting the matter concluded. So I stressed the urgency all the

[*189*]

way through the negotiations to begin to get her some of these things which would stabilize her and give her some confidence.

Chris—And on the other hand, I was in the position of representing a client who had at the moment the things which he was most ultimately concerned, namely the children and the home and an ability to care for the children and the home. Whereas I would have been extremely uncomfortable both as a person and if I had to justify my position before a court in denying a mother the opportunity to visit with her small children. My client was totally unwilling and I could not on his behalf permit that woman back in the home at this particular time, and it is to his advantage and looking towards the long range adjudication of interests to maintain the status quo with him caring for the children. Particularly since I felt that on the facts of the situation there was a strong possibility the wife might lose interest and might change her name and leave town and the longer she remained outside the home the stronger that possibility became. So I was willing to make concessions on the visitation and on the car, partly because if you can acquiesce on things which aren't going to hurt you will frequently improve your image so to speak and your client's image should you ultimately have to enter into judicially supervised negotiations.

Dave—Just as an addendum to that, I think that both lawyers felt the urgency and the need to keep the children together and they both understood that they needed a father and needed a mother, and it certainly was uppermost in my mind to keep her available and keep her in town so she could see the children and could continue that rapport.

Q—Just real briefly to both of you I know that this is a problem negotiated by students in class and many of the students ended up splitting custody of the children. Would this have been acceptable to either of your clients, or would you have done that in this divorce case?

Chris—I'm always very reluctant to consider a split custody situation. I think it has real potential pitfalls for the children involved and frankly I would at this point on this fact situation have recommended it in this situation. I agree with what you said about all of the children belonging with one parent or another.

Dave—The most difficult part of domestic relations is custody problems, absolutely. Money is replaceable, the car can be replaced, the house can be rebuilt, but when it comes to the children, that's where the most emotions come into play in domestic relations matters and I have never been one to recommend split custody. I have found few judges that will, save and except it's from a recommendation through a Social services department, a welfare department, or the child diagnostic center. If they recommend it then the judge feels that he can do it, but I have found few judges who would do that on their own.

Q—Let me ask about the relationship with respect to believing each other's version of the facts. In a couple of the negotiations that we have watched, there was always a presumption that whatever the other attorney represented was his good faith statement of the facts and I noticed in this case Mr. Findley that you would attack the version of the facts that Ms. Tanner would give to you. Is that a usual tactic and then may I ask you Ms. Tanner how you responded to that and how you felt inside?

Dave—Well in negotiations and especially in domestic relations matters I don't take anything at face value. I don't just believe something because someone says it happened and particularly in trying these kinds of cases, they'll let more hearsay evidence in than in any other type of litigation. They want to know everything, the judges do, and they never sustain an objection as to hearsay and I think this is a time when it begins early to put them on notice that you're not going to just let them put anything in that someone said or told them. And I wanted to put her on a strict burden of proof right then that I wanted to see some actual evidence that she had done these things.

Chris—And that was my reaction. That was what I saw immediately was that he was going to be very hard nosed about proof of facts which made me uncomfortable in this situation because I foresaw the probable necessity of doing some very unpleasant things in the way of detective work and the kind of evidence which personally I don't enjoy having to amass and present before a fact-finding body, but he put me on notice—that was accomplished.

Q—I think that is as many questions as we have time for. Thank you both very much.

Dave—Thank you.

Chris—Thank you.

*

BIBLIOGRAPHY

AMERICAN BAR ASSOCIATION, *Model Code of Professional Responsibility* (1969, 1980).

ABA *Opinions of the Committee on Professional Ethics.*

ARMATO, Leonard, "Offers of Judgment and Compromise: Turning the Tables on Your Opponent" (55 Cal.St.B.J. 286, July 1980).

AUBERT, Vilhelm, "Competition and Dissensus: Two Types of Conflict and Conflict Resolution" (7 J. of Conflict Resolution 26–42, 1963).

BACHARACH, Samuel B. and Edward J. Lawler, *Bargaining: Power, Tactics, and Outcomes* (San Francisco: Jossey-Bass Inc., 1981).

BAER, Harold & Broder, Aaron J., *How to Prepare and Negotiate Cases for Settlement* (Prentice-Hall, Inc., 1967).

BARNETT, Leslie J., "Deductibility of Attorneys' Fees: New Developments" (59 ABA Jour. 661, 1973).

BARTOS, O., "How Predictable are Negotiations?" (2 Journal of Conflict Resolution 481–496, 1967).

BARTOS, Otomar J., *Process and Outcome of Negotiations* (New York: Columbia University Press, 1974).

BARTOS, Otomar, "Simple Model of Negotiation" (In Zartman, *The Negotiation Process* 13–27, 1978).

BELLOW, Gary, *Conflict Resolution and the Lawyering Process: Materials for Clinical Teaching of Law* (1971).

BELLOW, Gary and Bea Moulton, *The Lawyering Process: Materials for Clinical Instruction in Advocacy* (Foundation Press, 1978).

BENNETT, W. Lance and Martha S. Feldman, *Reconstructing Reality in the Courtroom: Justice and Judgment in American Culture (New Brunswick: Rutgers University Press, 1981).*

BERLO, David, J.B. Lemert and R.J. Mertz, "Evaluating the Acceptability of Message Sources" (33 Pub.Op. Q. 563–567, 1970).

BIBLIOGRAPHY

BERMANT, Gordon, Charlan Nemeth and Neil Vidmar, ed., *Psychology and the Law* (Lexington: D.C. Heath and Co., 1976).

BIRDWHISTELL, Ray L., *Kinescis and Context: Essays on Body Motion Communication* (University of Pennsylvania Press, 1970).

BLACKMUN, "Thoughts About Ethics" (24 Emory L.J. 1, 1975).

BLAUSTEIN, Albert P. and Charles O. Porter, *The American Lawyer: A Summary of the Survey of the Legal Profession* (Westport: Greenwood Press, 1954).

BODIN, H. S., *Civil Litigation and Trial Techniques* (Practicing Law Institute, New York City, 1976).

BODINE, Larry, "The Case Against Guaranteed Verdict Agreements" (29 Defense L.J. 232, 1980).

BOND, James E., *Plea Bargaining and Guilty Pleas* (New York: Clark Boardman Co., 1978).

BRAND and PALMER, "Relevancy and Its Limits" (48 Mississippi L.J. 935, 1977).

BRANTON, James L., "Settlement Strategy, Evaluation, and Brochures" (12 St. Mary's Law Journal 407, 1980).

BRAZIL, Wayne D., "Civil Discovery: Lawyer's Views of Its Effectiveness, Its Principal Problems and Abuses" (American Bar Foundation Research Journal, No. 4, 1980:787).

BRIGHAM, E. F., *Financial Management Theory and Practice* 2d ed. (Hinsdale, Ill.: Dryden, 1979).

BROWN, "Some Applications of the Rules of Legal Ethics" (6 Minn.L.Rev. 427, 1922).

BROWN, Bert R., "The Effects of Need to Maintain Face in Interpersonal Bargaining" (4 Journal of Experimental Social Psychology, 1968).

BROWN, Steven R., *Political Subjectivity: Applications of Q Methodology in Political Science* (New Haven: Yale University Press, 1980).

BUECHNER, "Sliding Scale Agreements and the Good Faith Requirement of Settlement Negotiations" (12 Pacific L.J. 121, 1980).

BIBLIOGRAPHY

CARLIN, Jerome E., *Lawyers on Their Own: A Study of Individual Practitioners in Chicago* (New Brunswick: Rutgers University Press, 1962).

CARLIN, Jerome E., *Lawyers' Ethics: A Survey of the New York City Bar* (Russell Sage Foundation, 1966).

CHURCH, Thomas W., Jr., *The Pace of Litigation in Urban Trial Courts* (Williamsburg: National Center for State Courts, 1978).

Civil Trial Manual (R. M. Figg, R. C. McCollough II and J. L. Underwood reporters, updated through Jan. 1, 1976) (Joint Project of American College of Trial Lawyers and ALI–ABA Committee on Continuing Professional Education).

COCHRAN, W. Thad, "The Obligation to Settle Within Policy Limits" (41 Miss.L.J. 398, 1970).

COFFIN, Royce A., "The Negotiator: A Manual for Winners" (AMACOM, 1973).

COHEN, L. Jonathan, *The Probable and the Provable* (Oxford: Clarendon Press, 1977).

COHEN, Herb, *You Can Negotiate Anything: How To Get What You Want* (Secaucus, N.J.: Lyle Stuart, Inc., 1980).

COHN, Roy, *How to Stand Up For Your Rights and Win* (Simon and Schuster, 1981).

COLEMAN, Nancy A., "Teaching the Theory and Practice of Bargaining to Lawyers and Students" (30 Journal of Legal Education, 1980).

COMMENT, "Avoidance of Tort Releases" (13 West.Res.L.Rev. 768, 1962).

COMMENT, "Games Lawyers Play" (10 Trial Lawyer's Guide 5, Nov. 1966).

CONARD, Alfred F., James N. Morgan, Robert W. Pratt, Jr., Charles E. Voltz, and Robert L. Bombaugh, *Automobile Accident Costs and Payments: Studies in the Economics of Injury Reparation* (Ann Arbor: The University of Michigan Press, 1964).

COOK, Michael L. and Marcia L. Goldstein, "Settling with the Bankruptcy Trustee: More or Less Litigation?" (1978).

BIBLIOGRAPHY

COULSON, Robert, *How to Stay Out of Court* (New York: Crown Publishers, Inc., 1968).

CURTIS, "The Ethics of Advocacy" (4 Stanford L.Rev. 3, 1951).

DAVIS, Clifford, "Comparative Negligence, Comparative Contribution, and Equal Protection in the Trial and Settlement of Multiple Defendant Product Cases" (10 Indiana L.Rev. 831, 1977).

DEAUX, Kay, *The Behavior of Women and Men* (Belmont, Ca.: Wadsworth Publishing Co., 1976).

DEELEY, Edward L., "Denying Contribution Between Tortfeasors in Arizona: A Call for Change" (1977 Ariz.St.L.J. 673, 1977).

DEUTSCH, Morton, "Trust and Suspicion" (2 J. of Conflict Resolution 265–279, 1958).

DINWIDDY, *Elementary Mathematics for Economists* (Oxford, 1967).

DOBBS, Dan B., "Conclusiveness of Personal Injury Settlements: Basic Problems" (47 N.C.L.Rev. 665, 1963).

DOLE, "The Settlement of Class Actions for Damages" (71 Colum.L.Rev. 971, 1971).

DOUGLAS, A., *Industrial Peacemaking* (New York: Columbia University Press, 1962).

DOUGLASS, John Jay, ed., *Ethical Considerations in Prosecution* (Houston: The National College of District Attorneys, Inc., 1977).

DRINKER, H. S., *Legal Ethics* (New York: Columbia University Press, 1962).

DRUCKMAN, Daniel, "Prenegotiation Experience and Dyadic Conflict Resolution in a Bargaining Situation" (Journal of Experimental Social Psychology 4, 367–382, 1968).

DRUCKMAN, Daniel, *Negotiations: Social Psychological Perspectives* (Beverly Hills: Sage Publications, 1977).

DRUCKMAN, Daniel, "Boundary Role Conflict: Negotiation as Dual Responsiveness" (In Zartman, *The Negotiation Process*, 1978).

[*196*]

BIBLIOGRAPHY

DUPLACK, Ron, "Post-Accident Repairs and Offers of Compromise: Shaping Exclusionary Rules to Public Policy" (10 Loyola University Law Journal, 1979).

EDGAR, J. H., "Procedural Aspects of Settlement: An Overview of Texas Law" (12 St. Mary's L.J. 279, 1980).

EDWARDS, H. and J. White, *The Lawyer as a Negotiator* (West Publishing Co., 1977).

EISENBERG, Melvin Aron, "Private Ordering Through Negotiation: Dispute-Settlement and Rulemaking" (89 Harvard L.Rev. 4, Feb. 1976).

EISER, J. Richard, "Cooperation and Competition Between Individuals" in *Introducing Social Psychology*, (H. Tajfel & C. Fraser, eds., Penguin).

ERICKSON, William H., "New Directions in the Administration of Justice: Responses to the Pound Conference" (64 Am.L. Jour., Jan. 1978).

FARAGO, John M., "Intractable Cases: The Role of Uncertainty in the Concept of Law" (55 New York University L.Rev. 157, 1980).

FAST, J., *Body Language* (Simon & Schuster, 1970).

FAST, J., *The Body Language of Sex, Power, and Aggression* (1976, Hardback, $7.95).

FINKELSTEIN, Michael O., *Quantitative Methods in Law: Studies in the Application of Mathematical Probability and Statistics to Legal Problems* (New York: The Free Press, 1978).

FISHER, Roger and William Ury, *Getting To Yes: Negotiating Agreement Without Giving In* (Boston: Houghton Mifflin Co., 1981).

FISHER, Walter R. and Edward M. Sayles, *Perspectives on Argumentation* (Chicago: Scott, Foresman and Co., 1966).

FORDE, K., "Settlement of the Class Action" (5 Litigation 23, Fall, 1978).

FOSKETT, David, *The Law and Practice of Compromise* (London: Sweet & Maxwell, 1980).

[*197*]

FOTHERINGHAM, Wallace C., *Perspectives on Persuasion* (Boston: Allyn and Bacon Inc., 1966).

FOX, "Settlement: Helping the Lawyers to Fulfill Their Responsibility" (53 F.R.D. 129).

FRANKEL, Marvin E., "The Reform of the Adversary Process" (48 University of Chicago L.Rev. 478, Spring 1981).

FRANKLIN, Marc A., Robert H. Chanin and Irving Mark, "Accidents, Money, and the Law: A Study of the Economics of Personal Injury Litigation" (61 Col.L.Rev. 1, Jan. 1961).

FRICKE, Charles W., *Planning and Trying Cases* (West Publishing Co., 1957).

GAMSON, W. A., *Power and Discontent* (Homewood, Ill.: Dorsey Press, 1968).

GERGEN, K. J., *The Psychology of Behavior Exchange* (Reading, Mass.: Addison-Wesley, 1969).

GOLDSTEIN, Gersham, *Index to Federal Tax Articles* (Winter 1979–80 Supplement) (Boston: Warren, Gorham & Lamont, 1980).

GOSNEY, Cliff B., Jr., "How Insurance Companies Can Reduce Litigation Costs" (F.I.C. Quarterly, Spring 1981).

GOULDNER, Alvin W., "The Norm of Reciprocity: A Preliminary Statement" (25 American Sociological Review 2, 1960).

GRANELLI, James S., "Structuring the Settlement: Piecemeal Payments Gain in Popularity" (National Law Journal, Feb. 16, 1981).

GULLIVER, P. H., "Negotiations as a Mode of Dispute Settlement: Towards a General Model" (7 Law & Society Review 669–691, Summer 1973).

HALL, E., *Silent Language* (Anchor, 1973, Paperback, $1.95).

HARDINGHAM, "Setting Aside Agreements of Compromise" (8 Melb.U.L.Rev. 151, 1971).

HARNETT, D., L. Cummings and W. Hamner, "Personality, Bargaining Style and Payoff on Bilateral Monopoly Bargaining Among European Managers" (36 Sociometry 325–345, 1973).

BIBLIOGRAPHY

HARPER, Robert G., Arthur N. Weins and Joseph D. Matarazzo, *Nonverbal Communication: The State of the Art* (New York: John Wiley & Sons, 1978).

HAVIGHURST, Harold C., "Problems Concerning Settlement Agreements" (50 N.W.U.L.Rev. 599, 1958).

HAVIGHURST, Harold C., "The Effect upon Settlements of Mutual Mistake as to Injuries" (12 Defense L.J. 1, 1963).

HAVIGHURST, Harold C., "Principles of Construction and the Parol Evidence Rule Applied to Releases" (60 N.W.U.L.Rev. 599, 1965).

HENDERSON, Roger C., "Periodic Payments of Bodily Injury Awards" (66 American Bar Association Journal, June 1980).

HERMANN, Philip J., *Better Settlements Through Leverage* (Aqueduct Books, 1965).

HERRINGTON, "Compromise v. Contest in Legal Controversies" (16 A.B.A.J. 795, 1938).

HINDE, Robert A., ed., *Non-Verbal Communication* (Cambridge: Cambridge University Press, 1972).

HOLTOM, Robert B. *Restraints on Underwriting: Risk Selection, Discrimination and the Law* (Cincinnati: The National Underwriter Company, 1979).

HORNWOOD, Sanford, *Systematic Settlements* (The Lawyers Cooperative Publishing Co., Bancroft-Whitney Co., 1972).

IKLE, Fred Charles, *Every War Must End* (Columbia University Press: New York, 1971).

IKLE, Fred Charles, *How Nations Negotiate* (New York: Harper and Row, 1964).

ILICH, John, *The Art and Skill of Successful Negotiation* (Englewood Cliffs: Prentice-Hall, Inc., 1973).

JOHNSTONE, Quintin and Dan Hopson, Jr., *Lawyers and Their Work: An Analysis of the Legal Profession in the United States and England* (Indianapolis: The Bobbs-Merrill Co., 1967).

KAHN, A. and Kohls, J., "Determinants of Toughness in Dyadic Bargaining" (35 Sociometry 305–315, 1972).

KARRASS, Chester L., *Give & Take: The Complete Guide To Negotiating Strategies and Tactics* (Thomas Y. Crowell Company, 1974).

KARRASS, Chester L., *The Negotiating Game* (World Publishing Co., 1970).

KARRASS, Chester L., *A Study of the Relationship of Negotiator Skill and Power as Determinants of Negotiation Outcome* (Xerox University Microfilms, 1968).

KELNER, Milton, "What is Truth?" (24 Trial Law. Guide 264–268, Summer 1980).

KEMPF, Donald G., "Rule 68 Offers of Judgment: An Underused Tool" (7 Litigation 39(3), 1981).

KING & SEARS, "The Ethical Aspects of Compromise, Settlement and Arbitration" (25 Rocky Mountain L.Rev. 454, 1952).

KNIGHT, Frank H., *Risk, Uncertainty and Profit* (Chicago: University of Chicago Press, 1921).

KRASH, "Professional Responsibility to Clients and the Public Interest" (55 Chicago B.Rec. 31, 1974).

KRAUSE, Charles F., "Structured Settlements for Tort Victims" (American Bar Association Journal, Vol. 66, December 1980).

LANDSMAN, Stephan, "The Decline of the Adversary System: How the Rhetoric of Swift and Certain Justice has Affected Adjudication in American Courts," 29 Buffalo L.Rev. 487–530 (1980).

LAWLESS, William B., "Why Litigants Hate Lawyers" (Judges Journal, Vol. 17, No. 3, Summer 1978).

LEVIN, S., "Practical, Ethical, and Legal Considerations Involved in the Settlement of Cases in Which Statutory Attorney's Fees are Authorized", (Oct. 1980 Clearinghouse Review 515).

LINDSEY, Robert S., "Documentation of Settlements" (27 Ark. L.Rev. 27, 1973).

LINDSKOLD, Svenn, "Trust Development, the GRIT Proposal, and the Effects of Conciliatory Acts on Conflict and Cooperation" (85 Psychological Bulletin 4, 1978).

BIBLIOGRAPHY

LIVINGSTON, Ann C., "Settlements in Multiple Tortfeasor Controversies—Texas Law" (10 St. Mary's L.J. 75, 1978).

LONDON, Harvey and John E. Exner, Jr., eds., *Dimensions of Personality* (John Wiley & Sons, Inc., 1978).

LONGENECKER, R. R., *Some Hints on the Trial of a Lawsuit* (Rochester, New York: The Lawyer's Co-operative Publishing Company, 1927).

LYNCH, Eugene F., "Settlement of Civil Cases: A View from the Bench".

MACAULAY, Stewart and Elaine Walster, "Legal Structures and Restoring Equity" in *Law, Justice and the Individual in Society*, (Tapp, June Lovin and Levine, Felice J., ed., Holt, Rinehart and Winston: New York, 1977).

MACAULAY, Stewart, "Non-Contractual Relations in Business: A Preliminary Study" (28 Am.Soc.Rev. 55, 1963).

MACCOBY, Michael, *The Gamesman* (Simon and Schuster, Inc., 1977, 1978).

MACHIAVELLI, Niccolo, *The Prince and the Discourses* (Random House, Inc., 1950).

MACK, William C., "Settlement Procedures in the U.S. Court of Appeals: A Proposal" (1 Justice System Journal 17, March 1975).

MACNEIL, Ian, "A Primer on Contract Planning," 48 So.Cal.L. Rev. 627 (1975).

MALONE, Michael, *Psychetypes* (New York: Pocket Books, 1977).

MARU, Olavi, "Research on the Legal Profession: A Review of Work Done" (American Bar Foundation, Chicago, 1972).

MATHENY, Albert R., "Negotiation and Plea Bargaining Models: An Organizational Perspective" (Law & Policy Quarterly, Vol. 2, No. 3, July 1980).

MATHEWS, Robert E., "Negotiation: A Pedagogical Challenge" (6 J. Legal Ed. 93, 1953).

McCARTER, Charles C. and Beverly J. Greenley "Business Valuations" (Tulsa Law Journal, Vol. 16:1).

McCORMICK, Charles Tilford, *Evidence* (West Publishing Co., 2d ed. by E. W. Cleary, 1972).

McILVAINE, "The Value of an Effective Pretrial Conference" (28 F.R.D. 158).

McWHINNEY, Edward, *Conflict and Compromise: International Law and World Order in a Revolutionary Age* (New York: Holmes & Meier Publishers, Inc., 1981).

MELTSNER, M. & P. G. Schrag, *Public Interest Advocacy: Materials For Clinical Legal Education* (Boston: Little, Brown & Co., 1974).

MISHAN, E., *Economics For Social Decisions* (Praeger, 1972).

MOORE, Denton R. and Jerry Tomlinson, "The Use of Simulated Negotiation to Teach Substantive Law" (21 J. Legal Ed. 579, 1969).

MORLEY, Ian and Geoffrey Stephenson, *The Social Psychology of Bargaining* (George Allen & Unwin Publishers Ltd., 1977).

NAGEL, Stuart S., "Attorney Time Per Case: Finding an Optimum Level" (32 University of Florida Law Review 424, 1980).

NAGEL, Stuart S., "Introduction: The Legal Process and Decision Theory" (Law & Policy Quarterly, Vol. 2, No. 3, July 1980).

NEAL, Richard G., *Bargaining Tactics: A Reference Manual For Public Sector Labor Negotiations* (Richard Neal Associates, 1980).

NICOLSON, Sir Harold, *Diplomacy* (Oxford: Oxford University Press, 1963).

NIERENBERG, Gerard I., *The Art of Negotiating: Psychological Strategies For Gaining Advantageous Bargains* (New York: Cornerstone Library, 1968).

NIERENBERG, Gerard I., *Fundamentals of Negotiating* (Hawthorn Books, Inc., 1973).

NIERENBERG, Gerard I. and Henry H. Calero, *How To Read A Person Like A Book* (Cornerstone Libary Publications, 1971).

NOTE, "Rule 68: A 'New' Tool for Litigation" (1978 Duke L.J. 889).

BIBLIOGRAPHY

NOTE, "An Analysis of Settlement" (22 Stanford L.Rev. 67, 1969).

O'CONNELL, Jeffrey, "Harnessing the Liability Lottery: Elective First-Party No-Fault Insurance Financed by Third-Party Tort Claims" (Washington University Law Quarterly, Vol. 1978:693).

O'DEA, Dennis M., "The Lawyer-Client Relationship Reconsidered: Methods for Avoiding Conflicts of Interest, Malpractice Liability, and Disqualification" (George Washington Law Review, Vol. 48:693, 1980).

OSGOOD, C., *An Alternative to War or Surrender* (Urbana: University of Illinois Press, 1962).

PARKER, Douglas H., "Rhetoric, Ethics and Manipulation" in 5 Philosophy and Rhetoric 69 (University Park, Pa.: Pennsylvania State University Press).

PECK, Cornelius, *Cases and Materials on Negotiation (Unit Five of Labor Relations and Social Problems)* (Washington, D.C.: The Bureau of National Affairs, 1972).

PECK, Cornelius J. and Robert L. Fletcher, "A Course on the Subject of Negotiation" (21 J. Legal Ed. 196, 1968).

PERDUE, Jim M., "Is Your Case Worth Pursuing?" (Case & Comment, Nov.-Dec. 1980).

PLINER, Patricia, Lester Krames, and Thomas Alloway, eds., *Advances in the Study of Communication and Affect*, Vol. 2: *NonVerbal Communication of Aggression* (New York: Plenum Press, 1975).

POSNER, Richard A., *Economic Analysis of Law* (Little, Brown and Company, 1972).

PRICE, M. and H. Bitner, *Effective Legal Research* (Augustus M. Kelley, Publisher, 1969).

RADFORD, K. J., *Managerial Decision Making* (Reston Publishing Co., Reston, Va., Prentice-Hall of India Private Limited, 1975).

RAMBERG, Bennet, "Tactical Advantages of Opening Positioning Strategies" (In Zartman, *The Negotiation Process* 133–148, 1978).

[*203*]

BIBLIOGRAPHY

RENFREW, C. B., "Negotiations and Judicial Scrutiny in Civil and Criminal Antitrust Cases" (57 Chi.B.Rec. 130, 1975).

RIEKE, Richard D. and Malcolm O. Sillars, *Argumentation and The Decision Making Process* (New York: John Wiley & Sons, Inc., 1975).

RINGER, Robert J., *Winning Through Intimidation* (Fawcett Publications, Inc., 1974, Paperback, $1.95).

ROSENBERG, Maurice, *The Pretrial Conference and Effective Justice: A Controlled Test In Personal Injury Litigation* (New York: Columbia University Press, 1964).

ROSENTHAL, Douglas E., *Lawyer and Client: Who's In Charge* (New York: Russell Sage Foundation, 1974).

ROSETT, Arthur and Donald R. Cressey, *Justice By Consent: Plea Bargains in the American Courthouse* (Philadelphia: J. B. Lippincott Co., 1976).

ROSS, Laurence H., *Settled Out of Court: The Social Process of Insurance Claims Adjustment* (Chicago: Aldine Publishing Co., Rev. 2d ed., 1980).

ROSS, Raymond S., *Persuasion: Communication and Interpersonal Relations* (Prentice-Hall, Inc., 1974).

ROSSITER, Charles M., Jr. and W. Barnett Pearce, *Communicating Personally: A Theory of Interpersonal Communication and Human Relationships* (Indianapolis: The Bobbs-Merrill Co., Inc., 1975).

RUBIN, Jeffrey Z., and Bert R. Brown, *The Social Psychology of Bargaining and Negotiation* (Academic Press, Inc., 1975).

RUBIN, "A Causerie on Lawyers' Ethics in Negotiations" (35 La.L.Rev. 577, 1975).

RYCKMAN, Richard M., *Theories of Personality* (Litton Educational Publishing, Inc., 1978).

SAHAKIAN, William S., *Learning: Systems, Models and Theories* (Rand McNally College Publishing Co., 1970, 1976).

SALES, James B., "Contribution and Indemnity Between Negligent and Strictly Liable Tortfeasors" (12 St. Mary's L.J. 323, 1980).

BIBLIOGRAPHY

SCHATZKI, Michael, *Negotiation: The Art of Getting What You Want* (Bergenfield: The New American Library, Inc., 1981).

SCHELLING, Thomas C., *The Strategy of Conflict* (Cambridge: Harvard University Press, 1960, 1980).

SCOTT, L. Wayne, "Lawyers' Forum: Settlements—New Perspectives" (St. Mary's Law Journal, Vol. 12, No. 2, 1980).

SHARSWOOD, G., *Professional Ethics* (1854).

SHURE, Gerald H., Robert J. Meeker and Earle A. Hansford, "The Effectiveness of Pacifist Strategies in Bargaining Games" (Conflict Resolution, Vol. IX, No. 1, 1965).

SIEGEL, S. and L. Fouraker, *Bargaining and Group Decision Making* (New York: McGraw-Hill, 1960).

SIMMONS, Robert L., *Winning Before Trial: How To Prepare Cases for the Best Settlement or Trial Result* (Englewood Cliffs: Executive Reports Corporation, 1974) (2 vols.).

SMITH, Jeffrey M., *Preventing Legal Malpractice* (St. Paul: West Publishing Co., 1981).

SPIEGEL, Mark, "The New Model Rules of Professional Conduct: Lawyer-Client Decision Making and the Role of Rules in Structuring the Lawyer-Client Dialogue" (American Bar Foundation Research Journal, No. 4, 1980:921).

STEPHENSON, R. and JOHNSON, R., "Drafting Settlement Agreements" *(Negotiation and Settlement—Oregon State Bar 121, 1980)*.

STRAUSS, Anselm, *Negotiations: Varieties, Contexts, Processes, and Social Order* (San Francisco: Jossey-Bass Publishers, 1978).

SUMMERS, Robert S., " 'Good Faith' in General Contract Law and the Sales Provisions of the Uniform Commercial Code" (54 Va.L.Rev. 195, 1968).

SWINGLE, P., ed., *The Structure of Conflict* (New York: Academic Press, 1970).

THIELENS, Wagner, Jr., *The Socialization of Law Students: A Case Study in Three Parts* (New York: Arno Press, 1980).

BIBLIOGRAPHY

THURMAN, Phillips and Cheatham, *Cases and Material on the Legal Profession* (1970).

TRAYNOR, Michael, "Lawsuits: First Resort or Last" (Utah Law Review, No. 4, 1978:635).

Trial Manual 3 For the Defense of Criminal Cases (Amsterdam, Segal, and Miller reporters) (ALI–ABA, 1974).

VERBECK, Marvin E. and Stanley J. Michaels, "Structured Settlements and the Uniform Periodic Payments Act" (F.I.C. Quarterly, Fall 1978).

VOORHEES, Theodore, "Law Office Training: The Art of Negotiation" (60 Practical Lawyer 61, 1967).

WAAS, Darrell, "Expanding the Insurer's Duty to Attempt Settlement" (49 U. of Colo.L.Rev. 251, 1978).

WALD, Robert L., "FTC Settlement Procedures" (5 Litigation 8–11, Spring 1979).

Wall Street Journal, "More Law Firms Put Computers to Work to Find Cases, Print Filings, Bill Clients" (December 23, 1980).

WALSTER, Elaine, G. Williams Walster and Ellen Berscheid, *EQUITY: THEORY & RESEARCH* (Boston: Allyn and Bacon, Inc., 1978).

WALTON, R. and R. McKersie, *A Behavioral Theory of Labor Negotiations* (New York: McGraw-Hill, 1965).

WALTZ, J. R. and HUSTON, J. P., "The Rules of Evidence in Settlement" (5 Litigation 11, Fall 1981).

WARSCHAW, Tessa Albert, *Winning By Negotiation* (New York: Berkley Books, 1981).

WHITE, James J., "The Lawyer as a Negotiator: An Adventure in Understanding and Teaching the Art of Negotiation" (19 J. Legal Ed. 337, 1967).

WILL, Hubert L., Robert R. Merhige, Jr. and Alvin B. Rubin, *The Role of the Judge in the Settlement Process* (Federal Judicial Center, 1976).

WILLIAMS, England, Farmer and Blumenthal, *"Effectiveness in Legal Negotiation"* in Harry T. Edwards and James J. White, *The Lawyer as a Negotiator* 8–28 (West, 1977).

BIBLIOGRAPHY

WILLISTON, *Williston on Contracts*, (3d ed., W. Jaeger, 1970).

WISE, R. L., *Legal Ethics* (New York: Mathew Bender, 2d ed., 1970).

WRIGHT, C. and MILLER, A., *Federal Practice and Procedure* (1973).

WRIGHT, "The Pretrial Conference" (28 F.R.D. 141).

YOUNG, Oran R., *"Bargaining: Formal Theories of Negotiation"* (Chicago: University of Illinois Press, 1975).

ZARTMAN, I. William, *The 50% Solution: How to Bargain Successfully With Hijackers, Strikers, Bosses, Oil Magnates, Arabs, Russians, and Other Worthy Opponents in This Modern World* (Garden City: Anchor Press/Doubleday, 1976).

ZARTMAN, I. William, ed., *The Negotiation Process: Theories and Applications* (Beverly Hills: Sage Publications, 1978).

ZEMANS, Frances Kahn and Victor G. Rosenblum, *The Making of a Public Professional* (Chicago: American Bar Foundation, 1981).

†